Providing Support and Superv

D1036463

The focus of governments across Europe and the US in recent years has been on an agenda for social inclusion: the need to ensure that all members of society feel engaged and play an active part. This has special resonance with some young people in society, who for various reasons have become excluded, particularly from education, training and employment. This vital new guide to providing support in this changing world is ideal both for anyone working with young people and those who are charged with providing support and supervision to youth support workers themselves.

The book will help you to understand the underlying concepts behind support and supervision and to engage with the concepts, models and techniques that determine effective day-to-day practice. With contributors coming from both academic and practice-based backgrounds, the book highlights the complementary and conflicting ideas and concerns that shape the practice, and covers a range of diverse yet vitally important issues such as:

- What is support and supervision?
- How psychoanalytical ideas can inform supervision
- Outcome focused supervision
- Integrative approaches to supervision
- Multicultural issues
- Evaluation in supervision
- Ethical dilemmas, confidentiality and the law.

In addition, the book clarifies the benefits and limitations of support and super-vision by drawing on the knowledge and experience of those currently involved in the activity, providing insights into supervision from the supervisee, supervisor and organisational perspectives. The writers bring a breadth and depth of know-ledge and experience across the range of helping professionals to create a book that will help practitioners, their managers, the organisations for which they work, as well as those on a wide range of professional training courses.

Hazel L. Reid is programme director for an MA in Career Education, Development and Guidance and for the Qualification in Careers Guidance. She is also co-chair of the Research Committee for the Institute of Career Guidance, and teaches on a supervision course. Hazel is a member of the Higher Education Academy.

Jane Westergaard is programme director for the Personal Adviser Diploma and Understanding Connexions courses. In addition she teaches on a supervision course and is a qualified and practising counsellor. Jane is a member of the Higher Education Academy and is an accredited UKCP registered counsellor.

Providing Support and Supervision

An introduction for professionals working with young people

Edited by
Hazel L. Reid and
Jane Westergaard

Routledge
Taylor & Francis Group

LONDON AND NEW YORK

DISCARDED

BOWLING GREEN STATE
UNIVERSITY LIBRARY

First published 2006
by Routledge
2 Park Square, Milton Park, Abingdon, Oxon OX14 4RN

Simultaneously published in the USA and Canada
by Routledge
270 Madison Ave, New York, NY 10016

Routledge is an imprint of the Taylor & Francis Group

© 2006 Hazel L. Reid and Jane Westergaard

Typeset in Sabon by
Florence Production Ltd, Stoodleigh, Devon.
Printed and bound in Great Britain by
TJ International Ltd, Padstow, Cornwall

All rights reserved. No part of this book may be reprinted or
reproduced or utilised in any form or by any electronic, mechanical,
or other means, now known or hereafter invented, including photocopying
and recording, or in any information storage or retrieval system,
without permission in writing from the publishers.

British Library Cataloguing in Publication Data
A catalogue record for this book is available from the British Library

Library of Congress Cataloging in Publication Data
A catalog record for this book has been requested

ISBN 10: 0–415–37606–8 (hbk)
ISBN 10: 0–415–37607–6 (pbk)

ISBN 13: 978–0–415–37606–8 (hbk)
ISBN 13: 978–0–415–37607–5 (pbk)

BOWLING GREEN STATE
UNIVERSITY LIBRARY

Contents

Contributors

Dr Hazel Reid is principal lecturer in the Department of Career and Personal Development at Canterbury Christ Church University. She teaches in the area of career and guidance theory and career counselling skills, at both undergraduate and postgraduate level. She is co-chair of the Research Committee for the Institute of Career Guidance and a member of the International Association of Vocational Education and Guidance. She has published widely and presented papers at national and international conferences. Her recent research was concerned with the meanings given to the function of supervision within guidance and youth support work.

Jane Westergaard has been a lecturer in education for 11 years. She is also a qualified, UKCP registered, practising counsellor, working with young people in London. Jane's counselling approach is integrative, drawing from a range of perspectives including humanistic, psychodynamic and cognitive behavioural. As a requirement of counselling practice, Jane has received one-to-one, group and peer supervision. She has developed an accredited Certificate Course for supervisors of youth support workers. Her current academic research focuses on the role of youth support workers and the extent to which counselling could or should be fundamental to their role, and she has delivered papers on this subject at national and international conferences.

Helen Reynolds combines two careers. She is a senior lecturer in Education at Canterbury Christ Church University, where she teaches on teacher education programmes in the Department of Post-Compulsory Education. She is also a qualified psychoanalytical psychotherapist and manages her own practice. In the past she has worked as a primary care counsellor and, in an earlier period, as a careers adviser.

David Bucknell has worked as a new-town planner and as a research and development officer in a Social Services Department. He has worked as a social worker, social work manager and lecturer in social work. He is now a freelance trainer and lecturer, specializing in solution oriented practice, supervision and working with families. He is a consultant to social work teams and has been active in developing outcome focused practice in different settings, including the Connexions Service. He is currently engaged in a project to develop an effective outcome focused methodology for social work practice.

Dr Jenny Bimrose is a principal research fellow at the Institute for Employment Research at the University of Warwick. She has more than thirty years experience of professional practice, teaching at postgraduate level on career guidance and counselling courses, researching in higher education and project management. Most research projects on which she has worked have focused on different aspects of career counselling and guidance practice, including multiculturalism, both in the UK and Europe. She is a Fellow of the Institute of Career Guidance, co-chair of its Ethics and Standards Committee and a member of its Research Committee.

Miche Tetley is a Connexions personal adviser, working in the Borough of Haringey for North London Connexions Partnership Ltd. She sees a 'generic' caseload of young people, working with them on a variety of issues. Her work focuses particularly on promoting and teaching anger management skills on a one-to-one basis and raising young peoples' confidence and self-esteem. She is a trainee psychotherapist at the Spectrum Centre for Humanistic Psychology in Finsbury Park, London, where her interests lie in the somatic organization of experience and healthy living in the areas of love, intimacy and sexuality.

Stephen Harrison works as an associate tutor with the YMCA George Williams College and is a freelance supervisor and trainer. Having qualified as a Youth and Community Worker in 1993, and obtaining a degree in informal and community education in 1994, he has worked for the British Forces Youth Service in Hong Kong, community-based drug projects as an arrest referral worker and as a drugs education worker. From 1997 to 2004, Stephen was a full-time tutor with the YMCA George Williams College, where he was able to pursue his interest in the philosophy of education. In that post he held responsibility for professional practice and supervision.

Ros Garrod-Mason is a senior manager in a Connexions service. After gaining a degree in Sociology and International Relations, Ros went on to train as a Careers Adviser and worked in that role for around seven years. She then worked for Grimsby College, teaching students with special needs, where she also studied for a Certificate in Education. After gaining experience in a variety of roles, Ros went on to become the senior professional manager for the newly formed Connexions Humber. Her interest in supervision began after she undertook an evaluation of supervision in the Humber region and realised the potential that it has to support the work of practitioners within the Connexions Service. In her current role, developing supervision practice across this new profession remains an ongoing challenge.

Dr Mary McMahon is a lecturer in the School of Education at the University of Queensland, Australia. She has lectured and conducted training in supervision for many years. Mary has several publications in the field including a co-edited book, book chapters and refereed journal articles. Her particular interest is in the supervision of school counsellors and career counsellors, supervision training and the use of supervision as a form of lifelong learning. More recently her work has examined the application of email and online facilities for supervision and supervision training.

Revd Andrew Edwards is head of the Department of Career and Personal Development at Canterbury Christ Church University. His interests in supervision have emerged from teaching and from practice and relate to a range of professional contexts including work with young people and the Christian ministry.

Debbie Daniels is a qualified teacher, holds an MA in psychotherapy and counselling and is a UKCP registered psychotherapist. She began working as a counsellor in secondary schools in 1987 and has since been employed as a psychotherapist in schools in London, Bermuda and Kent. Debbie is the co-author of *Therapy with Children: Children's Rights, Confidentiality and the Law* (Daniels and Jenkins, Sage 2000). She has taught on the counselling diploma and the MSc in supervision at the University of Kent. She is now the director of a generic psychotherapy and counselling centre where she works mainly with adults.

Foreword

A.G. Watts

The OECD Career Guidance Policy Review indicated the growing policy attention that is being given in all OECD countries to early school-leavers who are drifting in and out of unemployment, labour-market inactivity and marginal unskilled work. From work done in many countries, it is widely recognised that successful strategies involve a highly individualised approach, in which attention is given to young people's personal and social needs as well as their educational and vocational guidance needs (OECD 2004: 49–51). This requires close collaboration between the various agencies and institutions working with such young people, and between the professionals that staff their services.

The establishment of the Connexions Service in England provided an opportunity for reviewing the support and supervision arrangements for such professionals. The aim of Connexions, as outlined in the Social Exclusion Unit report *Bridging the Gap*, included developing 'a network of personal advisers to provide a single point of contact and ensure that someone has an overview of each young person's ambitions and needs' (SEU 1999: 81). The notion was that these personal advisers would represent a 'new profession' that would 'end the current fragmentation of services' and 'take responsibility for ensuring all the needs of a young person are met in an integrated and coherent manner'. They would 'be drawn from a range of backgrounds including the Careers Service, Youth Service, Social Services, teachers and Youth Offending Teams, as well as from the voluntary and community sectors' (DfEE 2000: 35, 45).

The need for support and supervision for personal advisers has been widely recognised within Connexions, both at policy level and on the ground, and this is likely to continue in future partnership arrangements. Particularly in the case of those working with young people with acute personal and social problems, there is a risk that youth support workers will find themselves in complex and disturbing situations. Moreover, the boundaries within which they are working may be unclear. Many will be working within and across three systems: the setting within which they are operating (a school/college or agency); the formal structures of the partnership arrangement (e.g. Connexions); and the social systems of the young people with which they are engaging. Transactions across these systems can pose difficult issues about where the primary responsibility of the youth support worker lies, and where their role begins and ends. There is a risk that all three parties – the school/college/agency, the partnership, and the young people themselves – will make competing demands on the youth support worker, and that the strains of coping with these demands will result in conflicts, crises and premature burnout. Support and supervision can help youth support workers to avoid or resolve these difficulties.

Youth support workers from some backgrounds – social work or youth work, for example – are able to draw on a well-established tradition of support and supervision. This is not, however, true in the case of career guidance, where traditionally support and supervision provision have been more limited (Bimrose and Wilden 1994). This raises two issues. First, what can be learned from the different models in designing an appropriate cross-professional system of support and supervision for multi-disciplinary youth support services? And second, should such provision be confined in the main to those working with young people at risk, or should it be extended to all youth support workers – including those working primarily with 'mainstream' young people – as part of reflective practice and continuous professional development?

These and related issues are addressed in this book. It explores the different functions of support and supervision, and the different forms it can take. It also explores some of the professional and organisational issues that need to be addressed, including ethical and legal issues.

The book is particularly relevant to those working in youth support services in England, but it also has a wider relevance. Whatever the organisational structure within which services for young people are managed, there is a need to address the issues of support and supervision for those delivering the services. The cross-disciplinary nature of the structures adopted in England has reframed these issues in ways from which others will be able to learn and benefit.

Bibliography

Bimrose, J. and Wilden, S. (1994) 'Supervision in careers guidance: empowerment or control?' *British Journal of Guidance and Counselling*, 22(3): 373–383.

Department for Education and Employment (2000) *Connexions: the Best Start in Life for Every Young Person*, London: DfEE.

Organisation for Economic Co-operation and Development (2004) *Career Guidance and Public Policy: Bridging the Gap*, Paris: OECD.

Social Exclusion Unit (1999) *Bridging the Gap: New Opportunities for 16–18 Year Olds Not in Education, Employment or Training*, London: Stationery Office.

1 Introduction

Hazel L. Reid and Jane Westergaard

To begin

> I mean I had a shock . . . in school . . . a young man told me something that I'd rather he hadn't, and I was very upset for the remainder of the day, and I was very shocked at how what he'd said had upset me so much. I came back to the office in the afternoon and I hadn't really, it didn't sink in until quite later on in the day exactly how the depth of feeling . . . and I think I probably, possibly would like to talk it through with somebody even now.
>
> (Personal Adviser, A)

> I think I do have a fear that I'll do something wrong and muck their lives up! . . . I was worried that I could, I was really fearful that I could make her worse.
>
> (Personal Adviser, B)

> People need to be resilient in this job . . . you need to make sure they are coping with the demands placed on them by, so called, challenging clients. . . .
>
> (Personal Adviser, C)

The above quotes are taken from a recent qualitative study of views about the function of support and supervision (Reid 2005). Why are they included in this introductory chapter? They illustrate the need for support and supervision for professionals working with young people, where 'challenging' becomes a euphemism for 'dangerous and disturbing' (Newman 2001). They help to set the scene for the changing context within which guidance work, career counselling, youth work and youth support work take place.

Having set the scene, this introductory chapter will describe the policy background of support and supervision for personal advisers and youth support workers in the United Kingdom. The aim is to clarify the need for this book within the continuing development of holistic, helping services for young people. Interest in policies of inclusion and the development of integrated youth support services is not limited to the UK. It is expected that this book will be relevant to other countries where youth support services, either discrete or 'joined up', are developed or are developing. This chapter will also discuss the purpose of the book. Finally, it will give an overview of the chapters that follow, linking each to the function of, and context for, support and supervision for professionals working with young people.

A holistic youth service

The UK government's Social Exclusion Unit first outlined the role of 'the personal adviser' for the Connexions service in England in 1999. The intention was to draw personnel from a number of youth support services, for example the Careers Service, parts of the youth service and a range of other specialist agencies concerned with the welfare of young people, in order to provide an integrated service. As the service has developed, some personal advisers are working with small caseloads of young people who are facing multiple barriers in terms of access to learning or employment. Personal advisers and youth support workers working with the so-called 'harder-to-help', will not be addressing wider education and career guidance needs until the appropriate point in the relationship, once more pressing needs have been worked through. Practitioners working in this intensive way may already have a professional qualification, for example from career guidance, youth work, social work or teaching, or be working towards a relevant qualification. Those who have completed social work or youth work training may be familiar with the concept and practice of supervision, many of their colleagues, their trainers and their managers will not.

The need for support and supervision as a context within which to manage the work of personal advisers and youth support workers in the UK, has been highlighted in a number of papers (Hulbert 2000; Reid and Nix 2001; Hughes 2002; Reid 2002; Westergaard 2003). While the requirement for those working intensively may appear clear, other personal advisers (working with large caseloads in ways similar to previous career guidance work in schools) are also working in a pressurized environment where their need for support and supervision can be overlooked (Bimrose and Wilden 1994). It is, however, the focus on work with those young people who are excluded, or who risk exclusion, that has led to the development of support and supervision within Connexions, and for the growing number of youth support workers in other settings.

The advent of the Connexions service in England has been the impetus for this book; that said, the issues discussed are relevant to other youth support agencies in the UK and elsewhere. Although the other 'home' nations in the UK have not created a Connexions service, careers services and other youth support agencies (for example youth and social services, youth offending teams, health and counselling services) are working together in a similar way to develop services that meet an inclusion and lifelong learning agenda. The worry about those young people who exist on the fringes of 'mainstream' society and are viewed as excluded, is an area of concern for many national governments.

The situation in the UK continues to be dynamic. At the time of writing it seems inevitable that the Connexions service will be adapted further and become part of local Children Trusts (DfES 2004). The aim of such trusts will be to create 'more integrated service delivery and better outcomes for children and young people' (DfES 2004: 17). A UK government Green Paper on youth has been published (DfES 2005) that sets out the proposals for a new service for young people. It is unclear at the present time how separate helping professions will work together to support young people, but the role of the personal adviser or youth support worker will continue, regardless of the framework in which the role is organized. With increased emphasis on child protection and pastoral support in schools and other establishments, it seems that a growing number of professionals and paraprofessionals may require structured support and supervision for their work. With that in mind, the intention is that the book will be relevant for the current and future context of these practitioners.

There is a growing number of texts on supervision in the helping professions, although its meaning is still being developed. Texts that are well known draw from experience in the counselling and health field, but very little has been written that relates directly to supervision for youth support work, guidance and career counselling. The book's authors have different professional backgrounds, and represent diverse positions within the development of theory and practice for support and supervision: the editors think this makes the book a stimulating read. The authors have practical, academic and/or research experience and offer different perspectives on the themes that inform the growing interest in, and debates on, support and supervision in the helping professions. The approach to each chapter is academic and critical but also grounded in practice; using case study or research examples where appropriate.

What's in a name?

Before moving on to introduce the individual chapters it will be useful to clarify the nomenclature used in this book. Authors are influenced by their professional background and their experience of support and supervision, and will use terms accordingly. However, while the word 'supervision' is accepted within many professions, for practitioners new to supervision, it may be perceived as a negative term carrying overtones of surveillance, direction and control. As such, 'supervision' can sound like a threat to professional autonomy. For instance, in the study mentioned earlier (Reid 2005) it was found that personal advisers preferred the use of 'support and supervision'. Although distinctions can be made between 'support' and 'supervision', when combined the term will, generally, be used in the singular in this book. For personal advisers using both words highlighted the recuperative, alongside the monitoring aspects of the process. In a similar vein, the word 'structured' was preferred to 'formal' when considering the development of any models for their practice. The title of the book aims to reflect these views.

The book title also refers to 'professionals working with young people'. In part this is to indicate the wide and growing field of youth support work, but in addition to reflect the changing role, and often title, of many practitioners who work with young people. The latter point will resonate particularly with career advisers in England, whose job title and professional identity have been subject to change in recent years. The authors hope that the book will appeal to a wide range of professionals, their managers and trainers – all of whom have a sincere interest in working with, and caring for, young people. There is a cost to caring, and the practitioners involved need supervision, but they also deserve the kind of support discussed in this book. Whatever the level and experience of practitioners, in terms of their work and their understanding of support and supervision, there is much on offer here to sustain and enhance that work.

Content overview

The chapters in this book have been selected to address the key aspects of supervision in the context of youth support services, and fall into four distinct categories. These are:

- theoretical approaches to supervision;
- personal and organizational perspectives on supervision;
- supervision as a tool for ongoing career and personal development;
- underpinning themes – working professionally, ethically and within a legal framework.

The book has been ordered in this way to enable the reader to select a particular area of supervision practice that is relevant to them, be it a theoretical approach or a personal perspective, and so on. Of course, there is nothing to stop readers from starting at page one and reading through to the end.

Chapter 2, however, falls outside of these categories as it provides the reader with an overview of the purpose of support and supervision. In a book such as this, which focuses on a specific context (youth support work) for a generic activity (supervision), it is important to begin with a shared definition and understanding of support and supervision in the context of youth support work. In this chapter, Reid undertakes a review of the literature on support and supervision, drawn from the counselling, health, youth, social work and career counselling fields. She also refers to findings from a recent study undertaken with personal advisers, which provides some interesting and thought provoking material for anyone who is involved in either working with young people directly, or supporting practitioners who deliver the service.

Chapter 2 identifies both shared understanding and difference in understanding of the purpose of support and supervision. It does not, however, attempt to evaluate the effectiveness of any model in place (this comes later in the book). These understandings are not fixed, and arriving at a settled definition is difficult for those involved. This chapter, therefore, focuses on clarifying any differences rather than solving the problem of changing or unsettled definitions of purpose. In addition Reid asks pertinent questions about the range of discourses (ways of talking about support and supervision) in the field. She argues that there is potential for those with the greatest power (policy makers, employers) to determine the priorities for support and supervision, which may not be clear to, or shared by, youth support workers and those who are supervising them. Making sense of a shared definition of support and supervision is influenced, inevitably, by the context of the speaker: hence the importance of translating the meanings of the different discourses around support and supervision in order to increase effectiveness.

Theoretical approaches to support and supervision

In Chapters 3 to 6, the authors explore specific, but different theoretical approaches to support and supervision. These underpinning theoretical perspectives are:

- Chapter 3 – psychoanalytic
- Chapter 4 – outcome focused
- Chapter 5 – integrated
- Chapter 6 – multicultural.

In each case the author has set out to introduce the approach, explore its origins, its key features and its application to support and supervision. Each approach is grounded in a counselling tradition and is drawn from established, and (in the case of multicultural approaches), emerging counselling theory. This provides a clear link to the parallel process of supervision, whereby the feelings and the work within the supervision sessions may well reflect or 'parallel' the feelings inherent in the supervisee's client work. The parallel process is one of the key features of supervision and an understanding of the theoretical approach which underpins the work, be it psychoanalytic, outcome focused, integrated, multicultural (or others) will enrich and enhance the supervisory relationship.

Because of the growth in youth support services in recent years and the creation of a range of new youth support professions (personal advisers, teaching assistants, learning mentors, youth offending workers), there is a danger that those who are called upon to support these practitioners do not have the necessary training in, and understanding of, a theoretical basis from which to engage with the task. Our rationale then, for including chapters on particular theoretical approaches, is quite clear: we want to encourage interest, inspire curiosity and invite supervisors and practitioners to reflect on how their work can and should be informed by tried, tested and respected theoretical perspectives.

Clearly there are differences between the approaches. For example, the psychoanalytic approach is grounded in a belief that our judgements, motivations and actions are influenced by our experiences in conscious and unconscious ways. The concept of the power of the 'unconscious' is not one that is explored in depth in either integrative, outcome focused or multicultural approaches. Likewise, the impetus to focus on solutions for problems rather than to explore and understand their origins, is evident in outcome focused approaches but is not shared in either psychoanalytic, integrative or multicultural concepts. The drawing on a range of underpinning theoretical perspectives in integrative practice, including humanistic and cognitive behavioural approaches, may well be anathema to psychoanalytic and outcome focused practitioners. Neither is the attention to and significance of *difference* in the multicultural approach immediately evident in psychodynamic, outcome focused or integrative theory.

Having identified some of the philosophical differences between the approaches, it is important to note that there are similarities too. There are key features shared between psychoanalytic, outcome focused, integrative and multicultural theory; perhaps the most central of which is the need to establish an effective working alliance between supervisor and supervisee. The concept of the working alliance cuts across all counselling theory and is equally important in the effective establishment of the supervisory relationship. Without a relationship based on trust, openness, respect and non-judgemental attitudes, it is likely that, regardless of any specific theoretical persuasion, the relationship between supervisor and supervisee will not be an effective one.

Each chapter in this section acknowledges the significance of the working alliance. Reynolds (Chapter 3) focuses on the containment of the supervisee's anxiety, citing the importance of a 'facilitating environment'. This environment, she argues, is dependent on an effective working alliance where 'sometimes the experience, for the client, of working with someone else successfully is as helpful as any insights they might gain'. Bucknell, (Chapter 4), explains that in outcome focused supervision, the aim is to 'develop an open relationship in which language, expectations and ground rules are explored and made explicit and common understandings developed': the working alliance. In Chapter 5, Westergaard examines the part that the working alliance plays in integrative approaches. She explains that 'coming to supervision as a whole person, being open and self aware and feeling comfortable enough about who they are and what they feel and what they bring to the relationship' will impact upon the development of the supervisory relationship (or 'working alliance'). This will, in turn determine how effective the supervision sessions are in meeting the needs of the supervisee, the organization and, most importantly, the clients. Bimrose, in Chapter 6, also identifies the significance of the working alliance. She argues that supervisors need to become multiculturally competent, to increase their multicultural awareness and to understand and acknowledge the 'differences' present in the relationship. Only once this has happened, can a working alliance be formed, whereby skills used and strategies discussed may need to be 'adapted or changed to enhance their effectiveness'.

The differences as well as the similarities between the approaches are to be celebrated. This section does not set out to identify 'the right way' to 'do' supervision, or the 'best' theoretical approach to adopt. It would be irresponsible and unrealistic to attempt such a venture. What it does, is to provide ideas and options for those who will be undertaking supervision, either as supervisor or supervisee: ideas that they may wish to reflect on and explore further.

Personal and organizational perspectives on support and supervision

This section includes Chapters 7 to 9.

- Chapter 7 – the supervisee
- Chapter 8 – the supervisor
- Chapter 9 – the organization.

Each chapter in this section focuses on a specific perspective from those involved both in the supervision process, and in youth support work. This is important. Supervision is a generic activity, which is carried out in a range of contexts and is provided for those who undertake a helping or counselling role with clients, be they young people or adults. Although there are shared issues, approaches and concepts, regardless of the client group with which the supervisee works, we felt that as this book focuses on supervision for youth support workers, we wanted to provide a unique perspective from those who work in that sector. This, of all the sections in the book, provides the most personal insight into supervision, from the viewpoint of a youth support worker in receipt of supervision, a supervisor of youth support workers, and a youth support service which is setting up a system of supervision. The authors each have direct experience of supervision and draw on this experience for their writing, exploring the benefits and challenges that supervision can bring to all involved.

There is a shared view in this section that supervision is a 'good' thing. Tetley, from the supervisee's perspective, argues strongly for the need for supervision for youth support workers who are undertaking 'intensive' work with clients. Garrod-Mason and Westergaard, from the organizational perspective, also recognize the need for youth support services to provide adequate support for employees. They acknowledge that the process of supervision aims to ensure quality of service to clients, and also serves to protect and develop the workforce. Harrison and Westergaard recognize the need for supervision for those who are undertaking a youth support role, and they and Tetley provide dynamic examples from their own practice. These examples illustrate the significant role that the supervisory relationship plays in ensuring a quality service to young people.

Tetley (supervisee) and Harrison and Westergaard (supervisors) focus on their own experiences of the one-to-one relationship in supervision. They identify the key features of the relationship, focusing on what works, what is helpful and what barriers might exist between supervisor and supervisee that will need to be addressed and overcome. Tetley identifies her own need for different 'models' of supervision (with a range of supervisors), which fulfil different functions. Garrod-Mason and Westergaard, writing from the organizational perspective, explore models in more depth by analysing the features of line manager, experienced practitioner and external supervision.

All three chapters refer to the three key functions of supervision (Inskipp and Proctor 1993), noting the importance of using supervision to oversee the 'management' of the supervisee's work (normative function), the 'development' of the supervisee's practice (formative function) and the 'support' of the supervisee (restorative function). Garrod-Mason and Westergaard use material gathered in a pilot programme (whereby youth support workers experienced a range of different models of supervision within their organization and were asked for their responses), to inform their critique of different models of supervision, with direct reference to these functions. Harrison and Westergaard, and Tetley identify the importance of ensuring that supervision addresses each function. Tetley, in particular, stresses the importance of the supportive or 'restorative' function of supervision. As a supervisee, she values the opportunity to attend to her own psychological and emotional needs through supervision. Harrison and Westergaard analyse the challenge to the supervisor of ensuring that the supervisee's needs are fully addressed, while, at the same time, encouraging autonomy.

Again, this section of the book does not seek to provide a 'how to' guide for support and supervision from the supervisor, the supervisee or the organization's perspective. Rather, it invites the authors to draw on their own personal experiences, to ask questions, share thoughts and highlight challenges that are raised for those involved in support and supervision within youth support agencies. It is hoped that these insights will be of use to others who may find themselves in the position of setting up a system of supervision within an organization, undertaking the supervision of youth support workers themselves, or engaging with supervision as a supervisee.

Supervision as a tool for ongoing career and personal development

Chapters 10 and 11 focus on the ways in which supervision may be used as a tool for the development of the individual, which can and should continue throughout their working lives.

- Chapter 10 – supervision, a lifelong learning process
- Chapter 11 – supervision, a tool for evaluation.

This section seeks to broaden the debate about the purpose of supervision, to consider its application not only as a potential tool for evaluating practice, but also as a mechanism for reflecting on practice and developing skills, knowledge and approaches on an ongoing 'life-long' basis. Both authors identify the need for supervision as a means by which practitioners can engage with continuous professional development. Edwards argues for the need for supervision to be implemented to ensure effective evaluation of youth support practice, and McMahon goes further by arguing that supervision should extend throughout the working life of a youth support worker, through the concept of 'self-supervision'.

Both Edwards and McMahon provide us with new and original perspectives on supervision as a tool for evaluation and development. Both undertake a review of the existing literature from which they provide an analysis of evaluation, self-monitoring and continuing professional development. Both authors invite the reader to extend their understanding of the ways in which supervision can be used and the contribution that it can make, not only to clients and organizations, but in a more intrinsic way to the learning and development of the youth support worker. Edwards provides a new model for evaluation within supervision, drawing from his own experience of working with a group of supervisors in a large youth support agency. This model is based on the concept of a learning culture that McMahon acknowledges and takes further, referring to the significance of 'learner-driven' learning based on reflection.

The underlying theme of the book – the 'goodness' of supervision – continues and is developed in this section. McMahon writes 'lifelong learning positions individuals well to thrive and adapt in a world of rapid change'; she goes on to add, 'to conceptualise supervision as a lifelong learning mechanism locates it within a contemporary issue facing workers in the knowledge economy'.

Underpinning themes – working professionally ethically and within a legal framework

The two chapters in the final section focus on quite different, but related aspects of supervision; they are:

- Chapter 12 – ethics, confidentiality and the law
- Chapter 13 – a cautionary tale.

Both chapters address key issues of professional and ethical working for supervisors and supervisees who work with young clients. Daniels provides the reader with critical information about the legal context in relation to supervising those who work with young clients, and Reid shares some thought-provoking insights that at times contest the notion of supervision as a 'good thing'.

The rationale for including these two chapters is clear. In the case of Chapter 12, a book that focuses specifically on the supervision of those who undertake in-depth work with young people, would not be fulfilling its function if it did not address the very complex and crucial issue of operating within a legal framework. Both editors have had direct experience of working with youth support workers and supervisors of youth support workers. Both groups consistently cite the need for clear and detailed information on aspects of the law, particularly in relation to child protection issues. Questions often arise in supervision concerning child protection legislation and issues of confidentiality and disclosure. These questions can pose dilemmas for supervisor and supervisee alike. Daniels' chapter seeks to answer these questions. It sets out very clearly the key features of the law, about which youth support workers and their supervisors must be aware. She provides case study examples to highlight issues of confidentiality, demonstrating the importance of the relationship between youth support worker and client, and considering this relationship within a legal framework. Daniels draws on her knowledge of the Children Act (DoH 1989) and the Gillick ruling relating to England and Wales (Gillick v. West Norfolk AHA 1986), in order to clarify these points.

Chapter 13 also considers issues of professional and ethical working, but from a quite different perspective. Reid sets out (as the title suggests) to provide a 'cautionary note', and to some extent, challenge the central premise running throughout the book that supervision is a necessary and good thing for youth support workers. The chapter challenges the notion of power in a supervisory relationship and poses key questions about how supervision could and should be used, depending on how it is defined and understood by all involved in the process. Reid draws on the work of Feltham (2002) who suggests that supervision is not always understood, accepted or valued by all therapists. She argues that there is a need for those involved in supervision at all levels, to be aware of the criticism that the practice can add to the development of a low-trust, surveillance culture. Because of this, some practitioners may resist, or be anxious about engaging with supervision. Within a framework that makes use of discourse theory, issues related to the use, and potential abuse of power within supervision are discussed.

Like Daniels, Reid considers the need for ethical work within supervision, particularly in a relatively new profession, like youth support work, where there may be little shared understanding of the purpose of, and processes for, this area of practice. Reid encourages readers to explore a range of methods, within a negotiated and collaborative approach, for the ongoing development of support and supervision. Although opening Chapter 13 with a cautionary note, Reid concludes by re-emphasizing the need for support and supervision for those who work intensively in one-to-one relationships with young clients.

As editors, we feel confident that every chapter in this book brings valuable ideas and much needed clarity to the debate around support and supervision both for organizations, supervisors and youth support workers. We have sought to address the pertinent issues inherent in supervision in the context of youth support work, and have included contributions from authors who have approached the topic from a range of perspectives. We have enjoyed the process of putting this book together and have learnt much from our colleagues. We hope you will gain a similar level of both enjoyment and learning in the work that follows.

Bibliography

Bimrose, J. and Wilden, S. (1994) 'Supervision in careers guidance: empowerment or control?', *British Journal of Guidance and Counselling*, 22 (3): 373–383.

Department for Education and Skills (2004) *Every Child Matters: Next Steps*, Nottingham: DfES publications.

—— (2005) *Youth Matters; cm6629*, Norwich: HMSO.

Department of Health (1989) *Children Act*. S.1, S.22, S.47, London: HMSO.

Feltham, C. (2002) 'Supervision: a surveillance culture?', *Counselling and Psychotherapy Journal*, February 2002: 26–27.

Gillick v. West Norfolk AHA (1986) at 423, (1985) at 420, (1986) AC112, (1986) at 423.

Hughes, D. (2002) 'A new Connexions service: exploring the personal adviser role', in K. Roberts (ed.) *Constructing the Future: Social Inclusion, Policy and Practice*, Stourbridge: Institute of Career Guidance.

Hulbert, S. (2000) *Working with Socially Excluded and 'At Risk' Young People: Research into the Need for, and Appropriate Form of, Support and Supervision for Personal Advisers Working within the new Connexions Support Service*, Stourbridge: The Institute of Career Guidance.

Inskipp, F. and Proctor, B. (1993) *The Art, Craft and Tasks of Counselling Supervision, Part 1. Making the Most of Supervisors*, Twickenham: Cascade Publications.

Newman, S. (2001) 'A connexions service pilot: developing the personal adviser role and working with schools', *Careers Education and Guidance*, Spring: 8–11.

Reid, H.L. (2002) 'Shared meanings: visions of support', *Career Guidance Today*, vol.10 (5), Stourbridge: Institute of Career Guidance.

—— (2005) 'What advisers want from support and supervision: "pit-head time to wash off the dust of their labours"', *Career Guidance Today*, 13 (1), Stourbridge: Institute of Career Guidance.

—— and Nix, C. (2001) 'Support and supervision for guidance practitioners in a personal adviser role', in A. Edwards (ed.) *Supporting Personal Advisers in Connexions: Perspectives on Supervision and Mentoring from Allied Professions*, Occasional Papers Canterbury: Canterbury Christ Church University College.

Social Exclusion Unit (1999) *Bridging the Gap: New Opportunities for 16–18 Year Olds not in Education, Employment or Training*, London: Stationery Office.

Westergaard, J. (2003) 'Counselling and the PA role – are these connected?', *British Journal of Guidance and Counselling*, 31 (2): 241–250.

2 What is support and supervision?

Hazel L. Reid

Introduction

This chapter will provide a brief overview of relevant literature on support and supervision, drawing on texts from the counselling, health, youth and social work fields. It will also refer to the small but growing literature on support and supervision from the author's professional background of career guidance and counselling. The prime purpose of this chapter will be to investigate the function of support and supervision. It will make use of the findings from a recent research study that explored views about the purpose of support and supervision from the perspectives of the groups involved. This discussion on function will also outline the two main methodological approaches for supervision, i.e. one-to-one and group supervision. The chapter will conclude that for models of supervision to be effective, debates about purpose and meaning need to be placed in the foreground of initial and ongoing development of the practice.

The study

In the context of a holistic youth support service (the English Connexions Service) practice for many professional helpers has changed (DfEE 2000). Many are now given the generic title of 'personal adviser' although their professional backgrounds may vary. Personal advisers from a range of helping professions, working intensively with 'harder-to-help' young people appear to need support and supervision. For former careers advisers (at practitioner, manager and a professional institute level) this is a novel practice, and the meanings and perspectives on what it is, and what it can do, are not shared. The study explored these views using a qualitative approach with the intention of foregrounding differences and similarities. During 2002/3, thirty interviews took place with careers advisers working as personal advisers, line managers and representatives of the career guidance professional and training body. The first two groups worked in a large careers company in England, and the representatives of the career guidance professional and training body had a national and/or regional perspective. Analysis employed the techniques of a grounded, thematic approach that searched for the most important themes for each group.

Although there were many similar views about the purpose of support and supervision, there were differences in emphasis between the groups. For practitioners, the central purpose was to manage stress and avoid burn out: support and supervision was viewed as offering a 'restorative' space (Inskipp and Proctor 1993) within, at times, a stressful work environment.

While line managers and representatives of the career guidance professional and training body also talked about this restorative function, their views about purpose brought to the fore other aspects. Line managers viewed monitoring of performance as a central function of support and supervision. For the professional representatives, the purpose of support and supervision was to enhance professional development within a bigger picture of organizational change. Both groups made use of a professional discourse that placed the needs of the client at the centre of the purpose of support and supervision. They also viewed support and supervision through a lens that must consider accountability and use of the resources of time and personnel: for line managers this was the primary focus of their talk about support and supervision.

The central story for the practitioners, the need for a restorative space to manage stress and avoid burn out, was a discourse on purpose positioned above the function of benefiting work with clients. The study concluded that this discourse needed to be heard and not silenced by other more powerful 'managerial' views on the purpose of support and supervision for youth support workers.

Foregrounding meaning

The aim of the study was to foreground meaning, rather than to place it as something shared or fixed and in the background of other 'more important' issues related to methods or content (Edwards 1998). The meaning given to support and supervision will, of course, be influenced by the context of the speaker. For instance where public funding is involved, policy makers will want to ensure that the work of practitioners is evaluated against standards and targets; and will need to take into account competition across government departments for such funding. For managers of public services it remains a high priority to secure and account for government funded contracts to deliver policy.

Managers will have to consider the cost implications and other resource constraints when considering the purpose of, and processes for, support and supervision. Practitioners, although working within the same policy constraints, may have expectations of support and supervision based on a different set of priorities. Practitioners in the study appeared less concerned with the cost implications and more concerned with personal support for their work.

An imposed model of supervision may meet the needs of all parties, but there is potential for those with the greater power to determine the priorities for support and supervision. For example, the 'need' for support and supervision for guidance practitioners was not discussed widely or negotiated until the advent of Connexions. Bimrose and Wilden argued the need for support and supervision for career guidance practitioners in the UK in 1994, but it was not viewed as a management priority at the time. More recently, Prieto and Betsworth (1999) have called for a comprehensive model of clinical supervision for trainee career counsellors in the USA, but their work has had little apparent impact on guidance training in the UK. Bronson, writing about supervision in career counselling in the USA, notes, 'While the value of counselor supervision as well as the potential problems associated with supervision has been widely documented, the role of supervision in career counseling has been largely overlooked' (2001: 222).

Now, with the introduction of the role of personal adviser in England and role changes elsewhere in the UK, managers, practitioners and the professional body are forming a discourse on support and supervision for personal advisers. Support and supervision is no longer viewed as a luxury, but seen as fitting into wider organizational needs related to accountability (Reid and Nix 2001).

Defining support and supervision

Bradley and Kottler (2001: 21) stress the importance of supervision in the helping professions and view supervision as 'indispensable' and 'a key to accountability'. Writing about the helping professions in the USA, where there is a growing body of research into supervision, Bradley and Kottler state:

> Saying that counselor supervision can be one of the most instrumental factors affecting future development of the helping professions is not an exaggeration. Furthermore, counselor supervision can have a similarly facilitative effect on counselor-offered services in other disciplines.
>
> (2001: 21)

We do not use the term 'counselor-offered services' for Connexions and the work of the personal adviser is not described as counselling, although it is sited in the 'helping professions'. Counselling skills are needed in a range of youth support services and work with 'difficult' clients can be stressful. Several of the personal advisers in the study talked about how the work can actually, rather than metaphorically, 'keep you awake at night'.

All the participants in the study stated that there was a need for a structured process for support and supervision, although there was some discussion about terminology. To provide adequate support and supervision there is a need for statements that clarify process in terms of intent and direction (Scaife 2001). Within counselling, Bradley and Kottler (2001: 3) discuss purpose via the 'principles, process and practice' of supervision. They explain that the term supervision can be divided into two words 'super' and 'vision'. The implication is that an experienced person looks over, from above – 'super', the work of a less experienced person and has a view – 'vision', of the work of the other.

According to the British Association of Counselling (1988: 2) the primary purpose of supervision 'is to address the needs of the client'. Support and supervision has more than one function of course. Reynolds (2001: 34) defines supervision in terms of its three main functions:

- monitoring – control, standards, managerial;
- educational – theoretical and skills development; and
- supportive – development of personal understanding and processing the client's impact on the therapist.

She goes on to note that the weight given to each of these activities will depend on the context and the level of experience of the practitioner. Certainly for the experienced practitioners in the study it was the supportive role that was seen as the primary purpose, rather than other functions given greater emphasis in the literature. Again, within counselling, Inskipp and Proctor (1993) have described support and supervision as having *formative*, *normative* and also *restorative* qualities. Linked to the above definition formative would resonate with an educational function, normative would be related to the monitoring function and restorative would be similar to the supportive function. Kadushin (1976) offers a broadly similar definition, employing the terms *managerial*, *educative* and *supportive*.

Differences in emphasis about the purpose of support and supervision

All the groups viewed the supportive or restorative function as important, but there was a difference between the groups as to the central or prime purpose of support and supervision. Cottrell and Smith (2003) highlight the difference in emphasis as to function that occurs across different professional fields. They write that in the field of nursing supervision, greater emphasis is placed on the function of *support* and less emphasis is placed on the control function of *supervision*. They conclude that 'there seems to have been little emerging consensus of definition over the last decade' (2003: 4).

The British Association of Counselling (1988: 1) states in its code that 'the primary purpose of supervision is to ensure that the counsellor is addressing the needs of the client'. This 'prime' definition of purpose has been challenged, for example McMahon and Patton (2000) in a study of supervision for career counsellors in Australia, found that:

> Client welfare received little specific mention by participants, and was commented on by supervised guidance officers more than those from the other two groups . . . support was cited as the predominant benefit of supervision. Many of the participants spoke of support in terms of emotional well-being, the reduction of stress and the prevention of burnout.
>
> (2000: 348)

Copeland (1998: 378) emphasizes the need for a shared understanding of the meaning of supervision within organizational cultures and suggests that one of the first challenges to confront is the word 'supervision'. She suggests that in the context of counselling the connotation is one of 'collaborative working' whereas outside of a counselling context, meanings are more likely to be associated to hierarchical and managerial authority. Within the study the practitioners preferred the use of the term 'support *and* supervision'.

Factors affecting a difference in emphasis about the purpose of support and supervision

Work in the helping professions can be stressful. Personal advisers in the study did expect a certain amount of stress in the work but they also expect additional support from the organization. They all have informal networks that they use to 'de-stress' and many have what they describe as good working relationships with their line managers. Morrison (1993, in Scaife 2001) argues that practitioners in the helping professions expect to encounter some primary stress, but are 'far more distressed by the secondary stress arising from the organization's response to them when this happens' (Scaife 2001: 31). Support and supervision can provide a 'restorative' function for practitioners experiencing a sense of isolation and anxiety by offering a reflective 'space' in which to discuss these issues, so that they can be understood and ameliorated (Scaife 2001).

People who choose to work in the helping professions are typically those who care deeply about vulnerable people. They are anxious to make a difference. Morrissette (2002) notes that in the mental health professions, until recently, little research attention has been paid to the emotional welfare of such helpers. The concept of 'burnout' however, has been reviewed extensively in the literature. Burnout has been defined as a 'state of extreme dissatisfaction with one's work' (Morrissette 2002: 135). Morrissette goes on to describe the key characteristics of burnout as: excessive distancing from clients; impaired competence; low energy; increased irritability; depression and physical, emotional and mental exhaustion. If youth support workers operate without adequate support and supervision will they be resilient enough to manage the inherent stress of the work and avoid burnout?

Burnout, performance fatigue, too much informal support and not enough formal support, all taking place in a target-driven environment, will not enhance the development of lifelong learning or critical reflection (Bimrose and Wilden 1994: 382). Critical reflection is unlikely to take place if the practitioner's need for the restorative function is not given enough attention in supervision. Being affected emotionally by the work does not automatically lead to burnout. However, as Cooper notes (2003: 57), 'truly emotionally engaged practice *is* exhausting' and practitioners need to have an opportunity to process their experiences, so that they can stay engaged.

That said, in discussing the supervision of primary health care practitioners, Burton and Launer (2003) caution the desire for practitioners to be endlessly self-critical and to expose their feelings. Too much focus on feelings requires practitioners to sustain the emotional impact of the work. Taken too far this can lead to breaching the necessary psychological defences that practitioners develop in order to manage the work. Maintaining professional boundaries with clients is an ethical practice, and part of the defence structure needed for practitioner wellbeing.

In terms of boundaries, the literature supports the need for a negotiated contract for support and supervision (Scaife 2001; Bradley and Ladany 2001; Holloway and Carroll 1999). However, Shohet and Wilmot (1991) stress that it is *as* important to have a good relationship between the supervisor and supervisee. Without this they state any contract will not overcome an imbalanced power relationship between supervisor and supervisee, where the contract may conceal decisions about purpose that are not, in practice, either negotiated or shared.

In attempting to define what is meant by 'good' supervision, Weaks (2002: 36) concluded that the supervisory relationship was fundamental to perceptions of what counted as 'good'. It was also suggested that not only did supervisees seek different things from supervision, but also the characteristics that led to definitions of 'a good supervisor' were also contested. It seemed that what was described as good supervision varied according to individual need and individual perceptions of the purpose of support and supervision.

Having a good relationship and a negotiated contract, then, does not remove the possibility of conflict. A range of factors, such as anxiety, power, time constraints, social and professional backgrounds, can affect the development of the relationship. Shohet and Wilmot (1991: 93) do not view conflict in the supervisory relationship as entirely negative as it can help to challenge both supervisor and supervisee, but this needs to take place within 'a clear agreement about styles of working' developed at the initial contracting stage.

Differences in emphasis about the purpose of support and supervision can be discussed at the contracting stage, and this would also need to clarify intent or intended outcomes. Assessing the outcomes of supervision as it relates to work with clients is an area that is not well represented in the literature. The main focus of research studies is on defining purpose and process (Bambling 2000). With an increased focus on evidence-based practice in the helping professions, the link with outcomes could become more important. However, evaluating the effects of supervision from the client's perspective would have many ethical and practical difficulties.

Other issues related to a difference in emphasis can be linked to who gives supervision. 'Management' needs in supervision can lead to subterfuge in the supervisee, due to conflict over the meanings given to support and supervision (Dryden *et al.* 1995). This can in part be avoided by keeping supervision outside of line management. Dryden *et al.* also highlight the difficulties where supervisor and supervisee may have been trained using different theoretical models (which is a likely occurrence in cross-agency youth support work).

Although organizational goals can take priority, a study by Turner (2000) claimed that many social work practitioners expressed the view that scarce resources would ensure that the roles of line manager and supervisor were combined. Separation of the roles was viewed as ideal but unlikely in an over-stretched service (Turner 2000).

In a study of child protection supervision a lack of expertise of line managers, in some cases, meant that front-line workers 'were deprived of an authority figure they could rely on and instead had one they had to look after' (Rushton and Nathan 1996: 371). Hawkins and Shohet (1989) recommend that if line managers are giving supervision they should also have a client caseload, so that they have a clear understanding of the situations faced by practitioners, as well as the experience to guide supervisees appropriately.

That need for experience suggests a requirement for training for the role of supervisor, for example Holloway and Carroll (1999) advocate training for supervisors. However, we need to question the assumption that formality in the supervision process is always beneficial, and question whether training for supervisors provides a valuable safeguard or a professional constraint. If a supervisor can only supervise a practitioner working in the same professional area, employing the same theoretical approach, then this may limit the number of experienced staff able to supervise the range of professionals involved in integrated youth support work.

While recognizing a need for training, practitioners in the study also talked about the supervisor having the 'right personality and skills', to facilitate a space for collegiate dialogue rather than a teaching approach to supervision. This view is supported by Weaks (2002) and Wright (2004) where both conclude that it is the quality of the supervisory relationship that appears key. In considering the level of experience of a supervisor, Wright asserts, 'better a good non-specialist than a less-skilled specialist' (2004: 41).

Supervision, lifelong learning and individual motivation

In considering the skill level of the practitioner, McMahon and Patton (2000) state that beyond initial training, supervision should continue throughout practice. Writing about school counsellors in Australia, they claim that without ongoing supervision the skill level of practitioners was seen to decrease. They suggest that self-monitoring counsellors can be unaware of 'blind spots' in their work (2000). They view supervision as valuable for both support needs and learning needs, as a route to life-long learning: McMahon develops this theme in Chapter 11 in this book. Prieto and Betsworth (1999) suggest that very experienced counsellors within their study placed great value on supervision. Although achieving a higher degree of autonomy than less experienced counsellors, they were less defensive in supervision and had greater awareness of their strengths and limitations.

Support and supervision, in the context of lifelong learning, could be viewed as part of a process of continuous professional development for youth support workers. The individual motivation implicit in linking super-vision to lifelong learning can lead to a view that the individual must take responsibility for their own supervision needs. However, this view needs to be contested if a) it overlooks the time pressures that practitioners face when trying to fit support and supervision into busy practice, and b) it is not clear who 'pays' for this. It is also important not to assume that support and supervision will be seen as lifelong learning, and to recognize the resistance that some practitioners may feel towards 'formal' models of support and supervision. In the author's study practitioners were uncomfortable with the word 'formal' which suggested a challenge to their autonomy: the word 'structured' was preferred. This may be a semantic argument, but when discussing the need for a shared understanding of the purpose of support and supervision words are important.

Continuous professional development in the helping professions involves enhancing one's understanding of theoretical models, processes and skills, developing ethical watchfulness in relation to work with clients, and reflecting on the emotional impact of work in 'difficult' circumstances. As already discussed, within counselling support and supervision is seen to have these *formative*, *normative* and also *restorative* qualities (Inskipp and Proctor 1993). However, how practitioners achieve ethical watchfulness (Reid 2004) is an area of some confusion in the data.

Ethical practice as a function of support and supervision

In the study most practitioners viewed ethical behaviour as reliant on 'common sense' rather than a code of practice. Even within professions that have established practices of supervision built around ethical codes, there is evidence that common sense is perceived as central to ethical decision-making. Bradley *et al.*, commenting on common sense and decision-making, state, 'Such a decision-making process works well only if the so-called "common sense" is consistent with established professional and societal standards of conduct' (2001: 356).

Bond and Shea (1997) identify the problems that exist when working across professional boundaries in multi-agency work, and suggest that ethical codes cannot cope with this type of unstructured or unbounded work. West notes the desire for services to have clear answers to ethical issues and to write these up into codes of practice (2002). He suggests that responsible and reflective practice cannot be encapsulated merely by a set of rules about behaviour, and views the consideration of ethical issues as 'a matter to be regularly addressed in supervision' (2002: 267).

It should not be assumed that support and supervision can deal with all of the issues faced by practitioners in their work. Then again, when considering the need for ethical behaviour in any profession, support and supervision seems prudent. Acknowledging the boundaries of expertise is a key aspect of ethical practice. Where the professional boundaries are ambiguous there is a need for these boundaries to be a regular point of discussion. For example, Bronson's comments are of particular relevance for careers staff moving to the role of personal adviser, or for other youth support workers who are not trained counsellors:

> If and when a counselor does not possess the ability to counsel both career and mental health issues, appropriate referrals need to be available and supervision needs to attend to issues of how and when to refer. It is clearly unethical to practice outside of one's expertise.
> (Bronson 2001: 241)

When youth support workers, or other practitioners in the helping professions, are placed in the position where they are working at or beyond the limits of their expertise, many will question their own competence. Without an adequate support structure that helps to clarify boundaries, this anxiety can lead to work-role stress. This stress can be exacerbated further where time for reflection is a scarce resource.

Time and 'space' for support and supervision

Finding time *within* busy practice is a key issue that affects views about the purpose of support and supervision and what can be achieved.

Inskipp and Proctor (1993) use the analogy of negotiating 'pit head time'. Miners had to gain agreement from their managers to be allowed time within the working day to 'wash off the dust of their labours' (Scaife 2001: 73). It may require a change of ethos within some youth support services to sanction that this time can be used not just for managerial supervision (i.e. looking at meeting standards and personal development – the *normative* and *formative* functions (Inskipp and Proctor 1993)), but also for expressing feelings, doubts, insecurities and mistakes – the *restorative* function.

The restorative function requires comfort, safety and trust, and is dependent on a good working relationship between supervisor and supervisee. Time pressures cannot be ignored however, and Scaife notes (2001) that sessions that are high on the restorative function are far less structured than those that focus on normative and formative functions. In addition, the effectiveness in terms of measurable outcomes is likely to be less obvious. However, providing a restorative space within time allocated for support and supervision can help practitioners to deal with the strong emotions that they may need to express, and can avoid serious issues being hidden in supervision. They may struggle to express these emotions: the supervisor will need patience and good listening skills.

Time constraints and the effective use of time, was a recurrent concern for participants in the study. It appeared to limit the opportunities for practitioners to meet and share practice. When pressed to provide information for managers, or to complete other 'paper-based' tasks, support and supervision was often 'put on the back burner', even when time had been allowed for a group meeting to take place.

In a study of occupational stress and social work, Storey and Billingham noted the need to increase the range of support strategies for practitioners. However, they state, 'such strategies cost money, and without proof that they actually help reduce and prevent stress and are actually cost effective, organisations do not appear to implement them' (2001: 668).

Then again, time constraints are not a suitable reason for ignoring or paying insufficient attention to the support needs of workers in any of the helping professions. Sending practitioners on 'time management' or 'coping with stress' courses will not address the organizational responsibility to ensure health and safety at work. Such approaches make work-based stress an individual pathology rather than a collective responsibility.

As a term, 'busy practice' does not adequately express the effects of work-overload, initiative weariness and compassion fatigue. Stress is not always experienced as a negative force, but time – 'a space' – is required in busy practice to ensure that the high demands of stressful work are matched by adequate support and supervision (Storey and Billingham 2001).

It might be thought that one time-saving solution would be to offer more group, or peer, support and supervision opportunities. However, neither personal advisers nor line managers in the study viewed this as an effective use of time for practitioners' *support* needs. Webb and Wheeler (1998) in a large-scale quantitative study found that counsellors were more able to discuss sensitive issues in one-to-one supervision. Alongside this, practitioners may be concerned about 'the problem to claim space' and how they may present themselves to others in group supervision (Dryden and Thorne 1991: 139). However if one-to-one supervision is line-management led this can also send the practitioner 'into a state of hiding' (Dryden *et al.* 1995: 118) if monitoring performance is perceived to be the main function. The need to share understanding of purpose is again paramount here, particularly in any profession where the managerial role of supervision for trainees has dominated (Bimrose and Wilden 1994).

Conversely, Arkin *et al.* (1999) discuss the benefits of group supervision in social work, and in particular its ability to reduce the sense of isolation felt by many practitioners. They state that group supervision can reduce the often hierarchical supervisor/supervisee relationship and can lead to a clearer conceptualization of problems related to ethical working and expertise.

Before concluding this chapter on purpose, it may be useful to comment further on the benefits and limitations of the main models, i.e. one-to-one and group supervision, and to note that Chapter 13 considers alternative and creative ways of implementing support and supervision.

Purpose in practice: one-to-one and group supervision

This chapter has emphasized the view that support and supervision is a complex practice. Views about the 'best' method of implementing it are not straightforward and are difficult to summarize. What follows is therefore partial and not offered as an embracing synopsis of the discussion.

One-to-one supervision has the potential to ensure that the supervisee's agenda can be met. That said, confusion about roles and purpose will not be overcome without a negotiated contract that clarifies both roles and purpose. 'Under the spotlight' the lone supervisee may be reluctant to expose weaknesses if these are viewed as failures or where competence is an issue. In addition, unless external to the agency, the supervisor cannot remain 'outside' the needs of the organization or the service targets that constrain the work of both supervisors and practitioners. It is often thought that one-to-one supervision gives a greater degree of confidentiality than group supervision. Rules about confidentiality may differ in private practice, but where youth support workers are working in public services, complete confidentiality cannot be guaranteed. As discussed elsewhere in this book, any issue that involves 'harm to the client' will need to be addressed within the dictates of agency policy or the law.

Group supervision that is led by a specialist has the advantage of economies of scale in that more than one practitioner can be 'supervised'. This may result in a limited opportunity to discuss issues or cases of immediate or particular interest to the individual. In turn this may reduce the value and work against any stated outcomes for support and supervision. However, there is an opportunity to learn from the experience of a number of practitioners, although it may be the more talkative or extrovert practitioner that 'holds the floor'. The presence of an experienced supervisor who leads the session can help to offset this tendency. In groups a collaborative and supportive environment is essential for support and supervision to be effective.

Peer-group supervision without a specialist supervisor, facilitator or 'manager' can be viewed as less threatening, and opens up greater possibilities for the individual to engage in restorative supervision. There is a possibility for enrichment of the individual's practice via the learning that takes place in the discussion of the dilemmas faced by others. However, peer group supervision needs to be well organized to avoid this approach becoming too unstructured. The result of not enough structure can also be that the practice is not valued and is perceived as an ineffective use of time.

Conclusion: why it is important to discuss function or purpose

If the practice of support and supervision is to be effective it needs to be acknowledged that there are likely to be different views, across the groups involved, with regard to purpose. There also needs to be space for those involved in the process to negotiate a range of methods that they view as appropriate. Flexibility extends to the ongoing practice of support and supervision in order to recognize that needs and purpose will change over time. It would seem essential to ensure time for the restorative function of support and supervision and to avoid the narrow doorway to 'what works', or a 'one-size-fits-all' approach.

It seems important also to avoid a therapeutic approach that either 'pathologizes' or makes victims of practitioners. In enhancing the nature of a collaborative approach, clarity is needed about the aims and process for the practice. There needs to be a recognition that imposing support and supervision can be counter-productive in some cases, and can lead to participation without engagement. Managers, supervisors and supervisees will need to be sensitive to the ways in which power is used, abused or hidden in the practice and to the ways in which support and supervision can de-skill and 'infantilize' practitioners (Feltham 2002). It needs to be recognized that many will resist an approach that pushes them to expose feelings that may make them feel vulnerable, particularly if the purpose of support and supervision is not negotiated.

The key story for the practitioners in the study was the need for a restorative space to manage stress and avoid burnout. Although not the only concern, this discourse on the purpose of support and supervision was positioned above the function of benefiting work with clients. This 'meaning' needs to be heard and valued. Providing time for restorative conversations, alongside the formative and normative dialogue in supervision, may require a change in ethos where 'care of self' takes priority over other functions.

When discussing the process of any helping intervention the metaphor of the journey is often employed. Although useful this sounds rather linear, fixed and 'mapped out'. While planning a supervisory contract is important it is also essential to have a degree of elasticity about purpose. *Conversation* in Latin means 'wandering together with': the restorative space for wandering cannot be constrained by a rigid structure that is outcome focused. It requires an investment in time and a flexible attitude to content and methods to be meaningful, purposeful and restorative for those involved.

Bibliography

Arkin, N., Freund, A. and Saltman, I. (1999) 'A group supervision model for broadening multiple-method skills of social work students', *Social Work Education*, 18 (1): 49–58.

Bambling, M. (2000) 'The effect of clinical supervision on the development of counsellor competency', *Psychotherapy In Australia*, 6 (4): 58–63.

Bimrose, J. and Wilden, S. (1994) 'Supervision in careers guidance: empowerment or control?', *British Journal of Guidance and Counselling*, 22 (3): 373–383.

Bond, T. and Shea, C. (1997) 'Professional issues in counselling', in S. Palmer and G. McMahon (eds) *Handbook of Counselling*, London: Routledge.

Bradley, L.J. and Kottler, J.A. (2001) 'Overview of counselling supervision', in L.J. Bradley and N. Ladany (eds) *Counselor Supervision: principles, process and practice*, Philadelphia, PA: Brunner-Routledge.

—— and Ladany, N. (2001) *Counselor Supervision: principles, process and practice*, Philadelphia, PA: Brunner-Routledge.

——, Kottler, J.A. and Lehrman-Waterman, D. (2001) 'Ethical issues in supervision', in L.J. Bradley and N. Ladany (eds) *Counselor Supervision: principles, process and practice*, Philadelphia, PA: Brunner-Routledge.

British Association of Counselling (1988) *Code of Ethics and Practice for the Supervision of Counsellors*, Rugby: BAC.

Bronson, M.K. (2001) 'Supervision in career counseling', in L.J. Bradley and N. Ladany (eds) *Counselor Supervision: principles, process and practice*, Philadelphia, PA: Brunner-Routledge.

Burton, J. and Launer, J. (2003) 'The nature and purpose of supervision', in J. Burton and J. Launer (eds) *Supervision and Support in Primary Care*, Oxon: Radcliffe Medical Press Ltd.

Carroll, M. (1996) *Workplace Counselling*, London: Sage.

Cooper, A. (2003) 'Supervision in primary care: support or persecution', in J. Burton and J. Launer (eds) *Supervision and Support in Primary Care*, Oxon: Radcliffe Medical Press Ltd.

Copeland, S. (1998) 'Counselling supervision in organisational contexts: new challenges and perspectives', *British Journal of Guidance and Counselling*, 26 (3): 377–386.

Cottrell, S. and Smith, G. (2003) *The Development of Models of Nursing Supervision in the UK*, www.clinical-supervision.com/developmentofclinicalsupervision, (accessed 10 April 2003).

Department for Education and Employment (2000) *Connexions: the best start in life for every young person*, London: DfEE.

Dryden, W. and Thorne, B. (1991) *Training and Supervision for Counselling in Action*, London: Sage.

Dryden, W., Horton, I. and Mearns, D. (1995) *Issues in Professional Counsellor Training*, London: Cassell.

Edwards, R. (1998) 'Mapping, locating and translating: a discursive approach to professional development', *Studies in Continuing Education*, 20 (1): 23–38.

Feltham, C. (2002) 'Supervision: a surveillance culture?', *Counselling and Psychotherapy Journal*, February 2002: 26–27.

Hawkins, P. and Shohet, R. (1989) *Supervision in the Helping Professions*, Milton Keynes, Bucks: Open University Press.

Holloway, E. and Carroll, M. (1999) *Training Counselling Supervisors*, London: Sage.

Inskipp, F. and Proctor, B. (1993) *The Art, Craft and Tasks Of Counselling Supervision, Part 1. Making the Most of Supervisors*, Twickenham: Cascade Publications.

Kadushin, A. (1976) *Supervision in Social Work*, New York: Columbia University Press.

McMahon, M. and Patton, W. (2000) 'Conversations on clinical supervision: benefits perceived by school counsellors', *British Journal of Guidance and Counselling*, 28 (3): 339–351.

Morrison, T. (1993) *Self Supervision in Social Care*, Harlow: Longman.

Morrissette, P.J. (2002) *Self-Supervision: a Primer for Counselors and Helping Professionals*, New York: Brunner-Routledge.

Prieto, L.B. and Betsworth, D.G. (1999) 'Supervision of career counseling: current knowledge and new directions', *The Clinical Supervisor*, 18 (1): 173–189.

Reid, H.L. (2004) 'Jiminy Cricket on my shoulder: professional common sense and formal supervision as routes to ethical watchfulness for personal advisers', in H.L. Reid and J. Bimrose (eds) *Constructing the Future: reflection on practice*, Stourbridge: Institute of Career Guidance.

—— and Nix, C. (2001) 'Support and supervision for guidance practitioners in a personal adviser role', in A. Edwards (ed.) *Supporting Personal Advisers in Connexions: perspectives on supervision and mentoring from allied professions*, Occasional Papers Canterbury: Canterbury Christ Church University College.

Reynolds, H. (2001) 'Supervision in counselling and psychotherapy: a critical space', in A. Edwards (ed.) *Supporting Personal Advisers in Connexions: perspectives on supervision and mentoring from allied professions*, Occasional Papers Canterbury: Canterbury Christ Church University College.

Rushton, A. and Nathan, J. (1996) 'The supervision of child protection work', *British Journal of Social Work*, 26: 357–374.

Scaife, J. (2001) *Supervision in the Mental Health Professions*, Hove, East Sussex: Brunner-Routledge.

Shohet, R. and Wilmot, J. (1991) 'The key issue in the supervision of counsellors: the supervisory relationship', in W. Dryden and B. Thorne (eds) *Training and Supervision for Counselling in Action*, London: Sage.

Storey, J. and Billingham, J. (2001) 'Occupational stress and social work', *Social Work Education*, 20 (6): 659–670.

Turner, B. (2000) 'Supervision and mentoring in child and family social work: the role of the first-line manager in the implementation of the post-qualifying framework', *Social Work Education*, 19 (3): 231–240.

Weaks, D. (2002) 'Unlocking the secrets of "good supervision": a phenomenological exploration of experienced counsellors' perceptions of good supervision', *Counselling and Psychotherapy Research*, 2 (1): 33–39.

Webb, A. and Wheeler, S. (1998) 'How honest do counsellors dare to be in the supervisory relationship?: an exploratory study', *British Journal of Guidance and Counselling*, 26 (4): 509–524.

West, W. (2002) 'Some ethical dilemmas in counselling and counselling research', *British Journal of Guidance and Counselling*, 30 (3): 261–268.

Wright, M. (2004) 'Supervising school counsellors: a case for specialism?' *Counselling and Psychotherapy Journal*, February 2004: 40–41.

3   Beyond reason and anxiety

How psychoanalytical ideas can inform the practice of supervision

Helen Reynolds

Introduction

Supervision is a form of professional learning and learning can be painful and difficult (Coren 1997: 58; Emmanuel 2000: 62; Salzberger-Wittenberg *et al.* 1999: 54). I sometimes find that I feel tired and reluctant to see my supervisor about my clinical work. But when I am there, I am engrossed in the discussion and when I leave I feel very thoughtful, engaged with ideas and feelings about my work. I might want to read something, certainly to think more about what we have discussed. I feel very different, and not tired at all. Sometimes I have thought of a way forward with a client, sometimes I have felt encouraged; sometimes I have felt just more confident and assured in my therapeutic role and capability. I wonder why this is so, and if others working with clients in various contexts have similar feelings about discussions of their work with their supervisors.

This chapter will examine aspects of psychoanalytical theory in an attempt to answer part of this question and consider the role of supervision more broadly, initially from the perspective of experiences in psychotherapy and counselling. I would, however, argue that there is a strong case for considering such perspectives in a range of 'helping professions', which involve close personal interaction with clients, including working with young people. Such work requires a direct use of our ability to relate to others in a very demanding and creative way. The way we relate to our clients is affected by our own histories and the way we have learnt to relate, as well as the way we have learnt to deal with our own worries and anxieties. Psychoanalytical perspectives, I would suggest, can help us to think in a broader way about how we work with clients. Importantly, they can help us to look creatively, beyond the obvious, the overly rational approach and take into account our own feelings about the client, and ourselves, and the anxieties we may have: for example, about our capacity to do a good job, and to make the right decisions. While these ideas are important in terms of understanding our clients and ourselves, and greatly enrich the work, they are difficult to apply without the support and guidance of a colleague, in fact without supervision.

Psychoanalytic ideas have been applied in many professional contexts, such as child development, counselling, social work, and research. Here, however, looking at a range of youth support work, I would like to concentrate on how psychoanalytic concepts can provide a basis for creating and understanding relationships in the fullest sense of the word. Many of the key ideas are familiar. We sometimes describe someone as 'defensive' if they do not engage with us in an open manner. The terms 'regression' and 'the unconscious' are also embedded in our language. However, in this chapter I will look particularly at two aspects fundamental to psychoanalytic thinking about how we relate to each other. First, there is the idea that anxiety is an essential part of the human condition and, second, the proposition that aspects of communication are 'unconscious'. To those new to these ideas they may seem strange and discomforting, but in practice, I maintain, an appreciation of them makes professional support work a safer, more comprehensible experience for practitioners as well as a more positive experience for their clients.

Psychoanalytical ideas

The history of psychoanalytical ideas is long, complex and littered with debate. Essentially, psychoanalytical thinking is concerned with models and ways of relating and ways of understanding the nature of human development. While these ideas tend to be associated with therapy and pathology, they have, I believe, ubiquitous relevance and an explanatory power to help us understand what it is to be human, in all its dimensions.

It is important to view psychoanalytic ideas as constantly evolving and changing, and frequently located in particular times and cultures. Just as Freud's ideas changed over many years, so, too, did other theorists and practitioners propose radically different perspectives. I am going to refer to three perspectives which focus on the nature of the relationship between the child and the caregiver. These examine interpersonal, inter-subjective dimensions, which have distinctive resonance for the process of supervision. Melanie Klein (1882–1960) believed that interpersonal communication originated in infancy and took a view of human development that was inter-subjective. Wilfred Bion (1897–1979) considered how we develop the capacity to think in relationship with another (person) and developed the idea of containment. Donald Winnicott (1896–1971) stressed the importance of 'good enough' relationships and the need for a 'facilitating environment'.

These concepts link practice more closely with the two related notions of anxiety and unconscious communication, and have particular relevance for the process of supervision. Where supervisor and practitioner are able to acknowledge and understand feelings of anxiety about work with particular clients, the practitioner will be able to work more effectively with those clients. It is important, therefore, for both to recognize the roots of anxiety and how prevalent it is. This will enable both to articulate the rationale for, and validity of, supervision in a more complex way.

Anxiety

Anxiety is closely associated with notions of learning, and why it can be difficult, as well as ideas about what it means to be human. Anxiety is part of the human condition, not something to be rubbed out and avoided but used creatively. For a very accessible discussion of anxiety see Emmanuel (2000): he draws heavily on the work of Klein, Freud and Bion and defines anxiety as

> the response to some as yet unrecognised factor in the environment or in the self. The response may arise from conscious or unconscious sources. This definition captures uncertainty as a central factor in anxiety, and is close to the definition coined by Bion as a 'premonition of emotion', which highlights that anxiety is connected to an emotional experience that is likely to be experienced imminently, and emphasises the unknown nature of it.
>
> (Emmanuel 2000: 6)

Work with vulnerable and challenging young people can evoke all kinds of anxieties and uncertainties in the practitioner, as can the process of supervision itself – we do not know for certain what might emerge either with the client or with the supervisor. So, it is proposed, in order to deal with these anxieties, we try to protect ourselves from them and to control them. Hollway and Jefferson, researchers who use psychoanalytical ideas, explain that

> threats to the self create anxiety, and indeed this is a fundamental proposition in psychoanalytic theory, where anxiety is viewed as being inherent to the human condition. For psychoanalysis, anxiety precipitates defences against the threats it poses to the self and these operate at a largely unconscious level. The shared starting point of all the different schools of psychoanalytic thought is this idea of a dynamic unconscious which defends against anxiety and significantly influences people's actions, lives and relations.
>
> (2000: 19)

Essentially, we develop, usually unconsciously, a range of defensive strategies to deal with these anxieties, to minimise the helplessness we feel in relation to them and to re-establish a sense of control. These can include denial, (refusing to accept that something bothers us), projection (attributing feelings or attributes to somebody else) and repression (seeking to bury the anxiety as deeply as possible). We have to move beyond the commonplace notion that someone is 'defensive' to understand, initially in ourselves, what this might mean. We need to recognize and evaluate our defences if we are to work effectively and empathically with clients, and supervision provides the context. Sometimes clients' behaviours and expressions can be helpfully thought about in terms of their defences, not to alter them, but to appreciate what might lie behind them and what their function might be.

In terms of youth support work it is interesting to consider psychoanalytic ideas, on defences and stages, or rather *states* of development, particularly in relation to adolescence (Coren 1997). It is important to reflect on ideas about human growth and development as states and loops rather than linear stages. Transitions of many kinds, for example, can evoke 'adolescent' feelings, including a desire to hold on to what may be under threat, and a resistance to change, for fear of the alternative. A guidance worker in a recently reorganized workplace could well be experiencing similar feelings to those of some adolescent clients for example. Supervision would provide the appropriate place to understand this.

The past

These thoughts take us to further notions about personal history and development. The past has an impact on the present or, put the other way round, experiences in the present can evoke issues from the past. Many of the anxieties and defences we experience in adulthood are seen to have been derived in infancy, but can be evoked by changed circumstances. For example, one has only to think of the impact of the breakdown of a significant relationship to see how early (emotional and developmental) experiences of loss, despair and helplessness can be evoked. However, this issue of the relationship between the past and the present is sensitive and complex, partly because of the debate it engenders about the usefulness, or otherwise, of delving into the past as opposed to looking for positive future solutions. Both are important, but in psychoanalytic thinking the present needs to be located and understood in terms of the past in an appropriate way. And the past has a habit of emerging in the present. It can emerge in supervision and in work with clients. The phrase 'where did that come from?' is often highly pertinent.

Unconscious communication

If communication is at the heart of relating then we need to consider what this might mean in more detail. If we accept that some communication is 'unconscious', this means we are often only aware of part of what is being communicated and we are unlikely to consider the origin or meaning of a communication. We might not be aware of what we as practitioners bring to an encounter with a client for example, and how that affects the interaction. The idea of 'unconscious' processes, in terms of defences, has already been mentioned in the discussion of anxiety. It is often difficult to bring unconscious aspects 'into the light of day' without some discussion and this is where supervision plays a crucial part. It enables the practitioner to recognize more clearly what might be happening, to understand both themselves and their clients in a deeper way.

There are three main, interlinked, unconscious communication processes. These are transference (having feelings about someone/something which have been 'transferred' from someone/something else, this often happens to teachers and social workers for example); counter-transference (the practitioner's feelings towards the client); projection (locating one's unwanted feelings and anxieties into somebody else, and then often disliking them for apparently having those feelings/characteristics). These all have an impact on work with young people. For example, a client might attribute the youth support worker with the qualities of their parents (transference) and react to the guidance in a way that is informed by those, inappropriate, feelings. It is important that the practitioner can appreciate that both they and the young person have their own multi-layered version of reality.

Freud initially identified transference as a problem when he saw that patients were relating to him as though he were another significant person, for example, a parent, in their lives. He realized later, that this was therapeutically beneficial because it brought the patient's problems, literally, into the room. The feelings could be experienced and faced in the present, not simply discussed as a kind of academic review. This can be seen to operate in other forms of counselling, with the concept of immediacy. Counter-transference too has a chequered history, initially being seen as a hindrance to therapeutic work but now considered crucial for understanding the client. The practitioner examines their own feelings (the counter-transference) when they are with the client, why do they feel bored, annoyed or overwhelmed for example? Do the feelings originate in the practitioner or the client? It is easy to rationalize some of these feelings, such as anxiety or feeling overwhelmed, because working with clients is demanding. Thus the communication from the client is lost. Supervision enables the unconscious communication from the client to be understood and relieves the practitioner of the feelings. For example, if the practitioner feels quite useless and unable to help the client quickly enough in a particular session, it is worth considering if any of these feelings might reflect those experienced by the client. If so, how might the practitioner proceed? There is no formula for this so it is important to discuss such issues in supervision.

The idea of projection, that someone can, unconsciously and defensively, project their fears into someone else, may initially seem startling. It raises, in turn, the notion of inter-subjectivity, that we are not totally 'boundaried' as people, that sometimes we 'blur' one with another. Klein is considered the first person to explore this notion in detail. The theory is complex, but provides insights into initial communication, and the role of defences in human development and learning. Hollway and Jefferson use Klein's (1988a, 1988b) ideas

> about how the self is forged out of unconscious defences against anxiety. Her account starts at the very beginning of life. . . . early experience is dominated by anxiety in the face of the infant's state of complete dependency. Because the infant has no conception of time, it is incapable of anticipating the satisfaction of a feed when it is feeling the frustration of hunger. Thus it experiences polarised feelings of 'bad' when hungry and 'good' when fed. Gradually the infant becomes capable of recognising the breast, and the mother, as a whole object containing the capacity to fulfil and frustrate. However, the good and the bad will, when necessary, be kept mentally separate in order to protect the good from the bad.
>
> (Hollway and Jefferson 2000: 19)

Klein proposes that the infant splits their good feelings from their bad, frightening feelings and projects them into the parent. Here we see clear links with the notion of anxiety and how it is managed. If the parent can handle these feelings and remain undamaged by them, the infant perceives them to be safe and can deal with them. We can see possible parallels for the process of supervision here if we move on to look at two related concepts: the facilitating environment and the containment of anxiety.

Containing anxiety and the facilitating environment

The notions of containing anxiety, as described by Bion, and the provision of a facilitating environment, as envisaged by Winnicott (1990), are very important for the process of supervision. How can anxiety be managed in supervision? The supervisor can provide a 'facilitating environment', in which they give total and closely attuned attention to the practitioner, noting any reactions and states as they discuss their clients. The supervisor can contain the practitioner's account of a particular client. This enables the practitioner to see that the situation is manageable because it has not overwhelmed the supervisor. It also provides some respite, and a chance to view themselves once again as competent, as the client is thought about by, and with, the supervisor. This enables the practitioner to re-engage with the client because someone else has recognized and thought about their anxieties. Clearly, however, anxiety does inhibit clear thinking and there may be times when the supervisor does present the solution, particularly perhaps where there are child protection issues. However, supervision remains an active process just as the facilitating environment is envisaged as an active rather than a passive state. This promotes a model for supervision which supports and develops creative and effective practitioners. Coren describes the facilitating environment as

> where the infant is recognized without being intruded upon or colonized by another. For Winnicott this area becomes a form of play, through the interaction between self, other and the transitional space created by the two, curiosity is allowed to flourish as opposed to being prematurely foreclosed.... the conditions which encourage curiosity include an experience of feeling real and recognized as of, but not part of, another without excessive compliance and impingement. Thinking, learning and curiosity may be impossible without this facilitating environment.... In the process of exploration we risk having to unlearn what we may know, in the hope of attaining mastery over the as yet unknown.
>
> (1997: 69)

It would be interesting to take the practice outlined here and, allowing for the particular language, consider how our experiences of supervision do or do not reflect this. Could it be turned into a form of professional protocol? Supervision has the task of fostering an attitude of curiosity. There may be difficult issues with a client; the practitioner might be feeling tired and impatient, looking for clear unproblematic answers, but from the point of view of developing a true understanding, both supervisor and practitioner need to keep this attitude of curiosity in mind. Supervision is a place for creative thinking, and the practitioner must feel able to use it without feeling unduly cautious about revealing their perceived shortcomings. It is a delicate balance for the supervisor to support the practitioner without disempowering them. In addition, though we, as practitioners, might want the supervisor to tell us what to do about a particular client, and though there is a place in supervision for discussion of technique, procedures and protocol, it is crucial that both practitioner and supervisor remain thoughtful, open and curious, and are prepared to live with some discomfort as they look at client/practitioner interactions.

The following account of a psychoanalytically orientated teacher educator shows us someone remaining thoughtful, open and curious about what the real meaning of the feelings and events evinced could be, despite the discomfort. I have quoted quite extensively from the case study because it illustrates important communication processes and reminds us of the need to think, particularly when we are experiencing uncomfortable emotions in a professional situation. The 'speaker' waits for her understanding to emerge, even though that waiting was clearly very uncomfortable. She effectively, though with difficulty, contains the students' anxieties without retaliation. I suggest that this account may resonanate with the way practitioners experience some clients, as well as showing how unconscious communication works in practice.

Experiencing and processing unconscious communication

Salzberger-Wittenberg *et al.* (1999: 54–58) describes how a group of in-service teachers become frustrated on the third week of her course and ask for 'answers' on behaviour management problems with their classes. She describes how the group dynamic changes, how her feelings of discomfort and inadequacy increase, and how she wishes to transcend the experience and impress the group with her stunning ability. It is the same, I would suggest in our work with clients. She works through the discomfort, contains it, and realizes:

> I was being made to have some of the painful feelings that teachers experience in the course of their work ... the way they talked and acted, as well as the more unfathomable, threateningly-charged atmosphere, were ways of communicating with me, letting me know how difficult it is to hold onto one's knowledge and thinking capacity in the face of a group of pupils who are demanding, impatient and aggressive when faced with the uncertainty and frustration which are inherent in learning: how undermining it is to face criticism and derision, how demoralising to be met by boredom and rejection, how frightening to be threatened with chaos and violence. ... In this way my group of students was saying to me: 'this is what we have to put up with every day, let's see how you cope with a difficult class'.

She is at pains to point out that this is not deliberate, conscious action on the part of the teachers and emphasizes the need to face the anxieties and to continue to think:

> It was a test of my capacity to withstand such anxieties and go on thinking, rather than falling into despair, evading the task or reacting by adopting a rigid system of teaching and controlling the group. They were presenting both what they had to deal with as teachers and demonstrating their own difficulties in finding themselves in a learning situation on a course.

She seeks to explain and use the experience productively. Having thought about and 'processed' the feelings she starts to 'return' them, to use them by discussing what they have all learnt from the situation, and how difficult it is not to opt for quick solutions and to cope with feeling inadequate. These feelings may well be felt by practitioners and supervisors alike.

Finally, she considers how the teacher might react to such communications and the potential outcomes:

> We also saw that the pain experienced by the learner, when intolerable, is got rid of into the teacher. If he [*sic*] is receptive to this he becomes

the one who feels inadequate, frightened, stupid, helpless, confused, and he in turn may try to escape from this. . . . Real learning and discovery can only take place when a state of not knowing can be borne long enough to enable all the data gathered by the senses to be taken in and explored until some meaningful pattern emerges.

The working alliance

There is one last feature of psychoanalytic thinking to which I would like to refer; that is the working or therapeutic alliance. This is a common feature in most counselling and psychotherapies. It is concerned with the way the therapist and client work together, how they need to develop the sense of a joint project. Sometimes the experience, for the client, of working with someone else successfully is as helpful as any insights they might gain. This process, the joint working and thinking, the joint struggling with problems, perhaps sharing a sense of humour, actively fosters the client's sense of themselves as a person with agency and self-efficacy. Again there are pointers here for supervision, the development of a joint enterprise and perhaps a learning alliance.

Functions of supervision

There are many definitions and views of supervision, which are explored in detail elsewhere in this book. This section draws particularly on work completed elsewhere (Reynolds 2001; West and West 2003), and will focus on aspects where a psychoanalytical perspective can help with understanding and developing practice. Essentially it will relate to the earlier discussions of anxiety, the complexity of communication and the importance of an open and curious approach. Supervision, it is often suggested, has three main functions: to monitor practice, to encourage professional and personal learning and to support the practitioner in processing and managing work with clients. Different contexts, cultures and imperatives, as well as the experience of the practitioner and supervisor, will determine the importance attributed to each function. Therefore, in some contexts it may well be difficult to be open and honest, which is essential if we are to identify and work constructively with our defences, anxieties and prejudices.

The monitoring function

Monitoring is a case in point. It is a core function of supervision to ensure that ethical behaviour and procedures are being followed. But there are problems; for example, how open can one be if the supervisor has direct line-management responsibility? Learning from mistakes, or perhaps, misunderstandings, or incomplete understandings, is central to supervision. Monitoring, however, also has an accountancy and quality assurance dimension, how many people have we seen and what are the outcomes of the intervention? However, it does depend how successful outcomes are defined and by whom. Such issues need to be considered in order to involve the practitioner wholeheartedly in developing their practice. Additionally, for the practitioner, it can be deeply reassuring, particularly in the early days, to know that their work is being monitored, that they are not alone, there is someone who can contain their anxieties, and that their responsibilities are not without boundaries.

Monitoring is also important for supervisors and they have responsibility for checking their own standards. Gee (1998) for example, researched his practice as a supervisor by taping some interviews. He was surprised by some of the results, finding that he did not always do in practice what he thought, intellectually, was most important. Furthermore, he became more aware of the need to monitor his own feelings in relation to supervisees and to look beneath the surface of the supervisee's communication. He cites a useful example (1998: 18) of how he felt about one supervisee's account. He was initially very critical of the supervisee for being unclear in the telling of the story, until he realized that the way the story was told was linked to the patient's state. The example highlights how complex communication can be, as what was being conveyed was actually to do with the patient's fears rather than the supervisee's lack of skill:

> Had I not realized that my feelings were about the supervisee/patient relationship, I might have concluded that they had to do with defects in the supervisee, which in turn might have resulted in my giving a negative report on that individual's work.
>
> (Gee 1998: 18)

This is a very real consideration for practitioners and supervisors in other settings.

The learning function

Supervision must enable the practitioner to learn about theory, skills, attitudes, procedures and themselves, as well as about the client. They have to learn about the client through, at least in part, examining themselves. Learning in supervision can be dynamic because of this link between theory and lived, felt, experience:

> Supervision is probably the main place where real, vivid learning and discovery happens ... where theory and reality meet in the challenge of actual clients and the idiosyncratic demands they make on counsellors. The opportunity and the need to de-brief, discuss and reflect on and anticipate next steps in clinical work are usually keenly appreciated.
>
> (Lawton and Feltham 2000: 6)

Although this refers specifically to trainees I would suggest that supervision fosters a sense of learning and engagement in any practitioner. Of course, real learning can be a struggle and, as we saw in the Salzberger-Wittenberg story earlier, is a complex, emotional business for teacher and student alike. This is because of the uncertainty and frustration that is part of the process, the types of anxiety that the learner experiences and the pressure on the teacher to provide solutions. This situation translates to supervision with the supervisor in the teacher role and the practitioner in the student role. The supervisor must be able to contain anxieties and facilitate the practitioner's understanding.

In fact, as argued in West and West (2003), supervisor and practitioner practise a number of different but interrelated processes, under the banner of learning. They focus on the theory/practice dialectic, enabling theory to be informed by the experience of the client's story, as well as the other way round. Linked with this, the practitioner needs to learn to be flexible in relation to theory, to use different approaches with different clients, while also adhering to some core principles of practice, as discussed in Westergaard's chapter in this book.

The practitioner can begin to feel more confident in the quality of their work as they gain a more nuanced and flexible perspective on the client, using ideas and techniques to inform rather than dictate their practice. Most important of all, the practitioner learns how to remain human in the work rather than detaching themselves from clients by objectifying them, and giving them a convenient but ultimately reductive 'label'. Psycho-analytical concepts and approaches enable us to understand the richness and complexity of what it means to be human.

The supportive function

However, this kind of learning will not occur without supportive relationships. It is important to develop supportive supervision which can enable the practitioner to understand more deeply, and use constructively, their counter-transference to the client, identifying what the client is communicating and what they themselves have brought to the case. It is important, too, to note another dimension identified by Salzberger-Wittenberg *et al.* (1999: 60), 'The teacher's capacity to be reflective and thoughtful about data rather than producing ready answers enables the learner to internalise a thinking person.'

If the supervisor can pay close attention to the practitioner, at the same time as keeping a reasonable detachment, and can contain and process with the practitioner the distress and messiness that can arise in work with clients, then this will have important results. The practitioner will learn about their clients in a meaningful way and will develop their skills by experiencing a 'containing process', which they, in turn, can use with their clients. This joint processing of the client's story will, therefore, help the practitioner to both practise more effectively and to maintain their own emotional good health.

However, it is important to consider that counter-transference is not just about what the client communicates but covers the interaction between the client and the practitioner. Feelings evoked in the practitioner could relate to their own emotional and relational histories, as much as to those of their clients. For example, practitioners who have experienced an eating disorder may be uncomfortable working with clients with a similar problem. While a shared experience may help the practitioner to empathize, the important point is that:

> The therapist has to be able to acknowledge such feelings and think critically with the supervisor about them, which, in turn, can enable the therapist to regain a more empathic connection to the patient. Patients' disturbance, and needs, can only be met properly by a 'well-enough' functioning therapist who is aware, or capable of becoming aware, of his or her own vulnerabilities as well as strengths.
>
> (West and West 2003: 46)

So, supervision should emphasize the human, not superhuman, nature of therapeutic work. Where it can foster an attitude of 'curiosity' in all concerned (client, practitioner and supervisor), it will help the practitioner to move beyond their own blocks to understanding, such as irritation with the client for not making progress, or a sense of inadequacy in themselves. This attitude of curiosity, the standing back and being interested, with someone else, helps keep the work with clients alive and the practitioner motivated. This can be particularly important when working with apparently intransigent problems either with clients or when the work environment feels frustrating.

While supervision does not provide therapy for the practitioner, there are parallel features such as the development of a working alliance and the notion of a joint enterprise. Within this it is important to incorporate the psychoanalytic notion of the process as a struggle for understanding, meaning and personal responsibility, rather than thinking of it in more mechanistic terms.

Conclusion

Psychoanalytic ideas, predictably perhaps, make us examine communication at deeper levels, not just in the service of therapy, guidance and support but in terms of professional and personal understanding. They provide some principles which can, and should, underpin a range of practices related to the work. They help us to engage with the difficulty of personal thinking and learning to achieve greater understanding of ourselves and others. To return to my question at the beginning, I do not always feel like taking some of the challenges on, and, at an extreme level, to have my identity disturbed by learning more about my clients and myself. But the actual process is containing and stimulating, I feel I can learn because I am not being supervised in a judgemental way. My engagement with the issues reminds me of the complexity of the work, the many layers it contains and my curiosity is rekindled. Both anxiety and reason are harnessed to the task of understanding communications and relationships. I feel hopeful and positive about the work. I would not get so far on my own.

Bibliography

Coren, A. (1997) *A Psychodynamic Approach to Education*, London: Sheldon Press.

Emmanuel, R. (2000) *Ideas in Psychoanalysis, Anxiety*, Cambridge: Icon Books Ltd.

Gee, H. (1998) 'Developing insight through supervision: relating then defining' in P. Clarkson (1999) (ed.) *Supervision, Psychoanalytic and Jungian Perspectives*, London: Whurr Publishers Ltd.

Hollway, W. and Jefferson, T. (2000) *Doing Qualitative Research Differently, Free Association, Narrative and the Interview Method*, London: Sage.

Klein, M. (1988a) *Love, Guilt and Reparation and Other Works, 1921–1945*, London: Virago.

—— (1988b) *Envy and Gratitude and Other Works, 1946–1963*, London: Virago.

Lawton, B. and Feltham, C. (2000) *Taking Supervision Forward – Enquiries and Trends in Counselling and Psychotherapy*, London: Sage.

Reynolds, H. (2001) 'Supervision in counselling and psychotherapy: a critical space' in A. Edwards (ed.) *Supporting Personal Advisers in Connexions: Perspectives on Supervision and Mentoring from Allied Professions*, Occasional Paper Canterbury: Canterbury Christ Church University College.

Salzberger-Wittenberg, I., Williams, G. and Osborne, E. (1999) *The Emotional Experience of Learning and Teaching*, London: Karnac Books.

West, H. and West, L. (2003) 'Supervision in psychotherapy and counselling: a critical space for learning' in J. Burton and J. Launer (eds) *Supervision and Support in Primary Care*, Abingdon: Radcliffe Medical Press Ltd.

Winnicott, D.W. (1990) *The Maturational Processes and the Facilitating Environment*, London: The Institute of Psychoanalysis and Karnac Books.

4 Outcome focused supervision

David Bucknell

Introduction

This chapter develops a framework for supervision based on an outcome focused approach. It makes suggestions which, it is hoped, will help those involved in youth support professions to work together in supervision to achieve the best possible outcomes for young people.

Much of the interest in supervision stems from the desire to help those involved in complex work, often with limited experience and training, to make sense of their practice, and to be effective given restricted budgets and staff resources. Thus the chapter aims to make suggestions which will help promote effective work. These suggestions are not intended to provide a template or a blueprint for supervision. They are written from the perspective of what others, employed in similar contexts, have found 'useful' (Bucknell 2000).

The chapter considers the assumptions underpinning outcome focused supervision that are rooted in 'constructionist' ideas. It then focuses on solution oriented practice and the methods from this approach which are relevant to the process of supervision, with illustrations of how the 'dialogue' between supervisor and supervisee might look in practice. It is hoped that this will provide tools that supervisors will find useful and, in turn, will help to promote effective supervision.

Assumptions underpinning outcome focused supervision

Since the 1960s a group of approaches to therapy, social work, personal coaching and practice have evolved which may be said, for want of a better shorthand, to be rooted in the 'constructionist' tradition, (McNamee and Gergen 1992). These include *Strength Based Social Work* (Saleebey 1994), *Solution Focused Brief Therapy* (de Shazer 1985, 1988), *Possibility Therapy* (O'Hanlon and Beadle 1996), *Narrative Therapy* (White and Epston 1990), *Competency Based Approaches* (Durrant 1995), *Appreciative Inquiry* (Annis Hammond 2000), *The Art of Possibility* (Zander and Zander 2000), *Reteaming* (Ahola and Furman 1997), and so on. Outcome focused supervision is based in this constructionist tradition. It takes its ideas from this tradition, particularly solution focused practice, and applies them to the process of supervision.

The 'constructionist tradition' suggests that reality is not something that can be sensed 'out there'. We all view the world differently, depending on where we stand. Thus reality is constructed and invented through interactions between people, and this is particularly relevant to the process of supervision. The interactional process in supervision, and the co-constructions which are generated between supervisor and supervisee, form the essence of the supervisory process.

Constructionist approaches depart from the 'positivist' tradition in other ways. The positivist tradition endeavoured to parallel the natural sciences, whereby problems are classified and used to build theoretical explanations of causality. These provide the knowledge-base for problem solving, involving an 'expert' with knowledge of these theories, making an assessment and prescribing appropriate action, i.e. an intervention, to alleviate the problem. This is the basis of the medical model for problem solving on which many approaches to therapy are based. Therapy is aimed at removing or correcting a problem through alleviating or taking away its causes.

Practitioners in the solution-finding tradition do not assume it is necessary to explore problems in detail, or to analyse their causes in depth, in order to help people find ways forward. Solution focused work, for example, builds on inductive reasoning, i.e. paying attention to solution building and what is working in terms of achieving desired outcomes, rather than building on pre-conceived theories informing us about the nature of problems and their causality.

These solution focused approaches assume that change is inevitable and that the worker's role is to help people to notice, to take control and to shape change in ways that are helpful to them. The approach builds on people's strengths, and endeavours to develop motivation through enhancing a sense of what is possible. The practitioner's role in these approaches is akin to a helpful coach or consultant. They are not the all-knowing expert who prescribes appropriate action. They are 'expert' in the processes of change, and their role is to help the person make the changes to which they aspire.

Solution focused work builds on the core skills of establishing rapport and listening to the young person's 'story', however long it takes to tell. It is fundamental that the young person feels listened to and that their view is respected and validated. The approach stresses the need to go slowly, 'searching for detail', engaging with the interactional process between worker and service user (young person). The work will not dwell on 'problem saturated' stories and when the young person is ready, the worker will encourage the 'possibility' of change and a different future. Focusing on the future and where the individual would like to get to (the solution), gives the work a sense of direction and purpose.

A key assumption in solution focused approaches is that there will always be times when the problem is absent, or less of a problem, or different. Consideration of these 'exceptions', may help people to feel more optimistic about the possibility of change and to identify the things they need to do to bring about change. Envisaging and describing the 'desired future' can be used to help young people sense that change is possible, and from this to develop and articulate 'useful goals' which they can work towards.

In addition, solution focused work aims to build on the young person's strengths. By identifying existing skills and competencies, they can utilize resources to move towards the desired future. Similarly, the work sets out to build on what people are doing in the present (or past) that is helpful in relation to the future they envisage. It will highlight what has been tried and is seen to be helpful, or unhelpful, in achieving the young person's goals. The person is not the problem: the problem is simply something the person wishes to be without (de Shazer 1988).

Solution focused approaches emphasize the importance of language in exploring and building meaning. The relationship between the worker and young person is a source for the co-constructions of new and more helpful realities. Generalizations and labels will be deconstructed, for example 'my young person is apathetic' can be deconstructed through descriptions of what the young person does, and what they might choose to do differently.

Practitioners, working from this approach, have produced a series of open questions that are helpful in encouraging the young person to develop detailed descriptions of the futures they envisage, and the actions they need to take. These include future oriented questions such as the 'miracle question' and questions that invite the young person to imagine or pretend. For example, 'What will it look like when the solution is found?', 'What will you be doing?' and so on. Other questions help the young person to think about 'exceptions' to the problem, how they have 'coped', what they have learned or what they have 'noticed'. 'Scaling questions', which will be described later, are another useful tool in helping young people to explore perspectives and build solutions. Solution oriented practice utilizes difference, and asks questions that help people to notice the changes for better or for worse, and this approach can be used to help people to make choices. The questions are aimed at helping the young person to reflect on their own situation and to develop ways forward that suit them.

Figure 4.1 is a schematic illustration of the process. A line is 'drawn' around the problem, its exploration and analysis, and the client is invited to envisage a different future (1). They are then asked to come back into the present (2) and to indicate present progress on a scale of 1–10 (3). The client will be invited to consider what the next step might be to help them move forward (4). Throughout the conversation the practitioner will be seeking and highlighting strengths, competencies and identifying what the young person is doing already that is helpful. The actual session will have its own character and content, but it is likely that this framework will underpin practice.

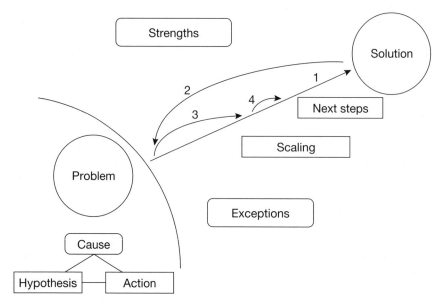

Figure 4.1 Problem to solution

Outcome focused supervision

Having considered solution focused work as an approach for helping young people, this section considers how these ideas can be applied to the process of supervision. It explores the (hoped for) outcomes of supervision and develops a framework and strategies for practical implementation.

The primary characteristic of outcome focused supervision is maintaining a focus on the intended results of the work, and to use this focus as a way of structuring supervision. Associated with the outcomes are activities that the supervisee, young person and others carry out as part of the plan. The outcomes are described in detail, and these descriptions form indicators that help the supervisor and supervisee review the progress of the work and 'keep on track'.

Core outcomes are likely to include the following:

- facilitating effective work, including promoting positive outcomes for young people;
- making sure the work is planned, that the objectives of the work are clear, and that activities are initiated to achieve these objectives;
- making sure that decisions are taken and the work does not drift;
- reviewing work and revising plans to keep it on track;
- utilizing scarce resources, including those of the supervisee;
- helping the supervisee to find solutions and resolve stuck issues;

- building the skills of the supervisee;
- supporting the supervisee and sustaining them as a resource in themselves;
- building motivation and a sense of possibility;
- coaching and developing new skills;
- staff development.

The primary outcome is that the supervisee should leave the supervision session with a sense of clarity about the direction of the work and the steps they are going to take. They should feel encouraged and energized by the process.

Building a collaborative relationship

Although the supervisor and supervisee have a different relationship to the work, they have a shared responsibility for its outcomes. Both will bring a range of viewpoints and resources to supervision and both will benefit if supervision is effective. Generally, the supervisor is not working directly with the young person and consequently engages with the work through the supervisee. Just as the young person is their own best 'expert' in what may work for them, so the supervisee, ultimately, has to find 'what works' in the context of their practice with the young person. The supervisee and the young person are central to the work: they are the experts. The supervisee has a unique style, character and individual strengths: these need to be harnessed and developed.

The interactional patterns between the supervisee and the supervisor are fundamental for achieving effective supervision. In the context of supervision, the approach builds on the process of dialogue and 'purposeful conversation' between supervisor and supervisee. The supervisor needs to use their skills in communication and in particular should listen to the supervisee with a 'constructive ear'; listening for the things the supervisee is doing that are helpful, building on what is going well, identifying strengths and capabilities. Rather than being the expert who analyses the data the supervisee provides, the supervisor adopts a position of 'not knowing' and 'curiosity' in helping the supervisee to reflect on their practice, within the context of the agreed outcomes for the work.

Supervisor and supervisee need to work towards a shared language; the language the supervisor uses and the questions they ask are important in prompting a process of reflection and in helping to develop effective practice. Developing constructive and purposeful language is important in creating a sense of confidence and possibility on the part of the supervisee.

In building the collaborative relationship, it is important to share perspectives, mutual hopes and aspirations for the work, and the process of supervision itself. For example, supervisors and supervisees can reflect, using questions such as, 'Why have we chosen this work?' 'What are our hopes for the process of the work?' 'Do we share an approach to practice?' 'Do we both value the process of supervision?' It will be helpful to listen to each other's 'stories' (experiences) of supervision, and one way of doing this is to take a 'supervision history'. 'What has been the supervisee's experience of supervision?' 'What have they found helpful?' 'What has been unhelpful and how can these experiences be built on?' 'What have they done previously?' 'How could these skills be useful to work effectively?'

Facilitating effective work

It has been suggested that effective work has a cyclical structure, i.e. outcomes, activities, indicators and review, as illustrated in Figure 4.2. It also has a process illustrated by the outcome focused cycle in Figure 4.3. This is likely to be mirrored in the supervisee's practice. In effective work, the worker will have 'joined' with the young person and listened to 'their story'. Hopefully, they will have managed to engage them in the process of development and change. They will have encouraged the young person to develop ideas about what they want to achieve and to establish their 'desired outcomes'. The work will have identified 'activities', which it is hoped will be helpful in achieving these outcomes, and 'indicators'. This will provide a basis for knowing when progress is being achieved, and the work will be continually reviewed to make sure it is on track.

These elements can provide a checklist or aide-memoire for the supervisor. They can ask themselves questions. For example, 'Does the work have a sense of direction?' 'Am I clear as a supervisor as to what the

Figure 4.2 Core elements for effective practice

practitioner is trying to achieve?' 'Do they have specific goals?' 'Have the young person's goals been acknowledged?' The supervisor asks questions aimed at prompting the supervisee to think about, and talk about, whatever it is that needs clarifying. In so doing they help the supervisee to review and develop their practice, and find solutions or ways forward when the work gets 'stuck'. As the supervisee reflects, so clarity emerges and ideas and plans are developed.

So, the process of supervision helps supervisor and supervisee to identify the desired outcomes for the work, and find ways of moving towards the outcomes and goals that have been identified. This is achieved by utilizing available resources and opportunities for change. In this way, the process described between the supervisor and the worker mirrors the process of the work in progress between the practitioner and the young person.

Future focus – clarifying desired outcomes

Outcome focused supervision adopts a future focus, developing clear descriptions of its desired outcomes and goals; it envisages the successful outcome of the work at the outset. Useful questions include, 'What are you trying to achieve?' 'What will it "look like" when the work is successful?' 'What will the young person be doing, what will you (the worker) be doing?' 'Who will be helping the young person?' The end of the work is thereby mapped out at the beginning. Detailed descriptions and 'evidence' of the 'end' are developed so that workers and young people know where they are heading, and when the end has been reached, i.e. 'What will it look like when we have come to the end of the work?'

Envisaging success may help to build a sense of 'possibility', and encourage the development of ideas for the actions, which are necessary to achieve the desired outcomes. Maintaining a focus on the desired outcomes is often more helpful than focusing on the causes of problems, as the latter can result in work getting 'stuck' in analysing current difficulties or obstacles (this is characterized as 'problem-saturated supervision'). Having a sense of a successful outcome can be helpful in maintaining the supervisee's optimism, motivation and energy. Maintaining a focus on the outcomes provides a basis for reviewing progress and keeping the work 'on track'. While the aim is to make the outcomes identifiable, they are not always immediately obvious, and the supervisor's role is to help the supervisee clarify the goals and the process of the work in order to achieve this. An illustration follows.

Dialogue one

Supervisor: What are you hoping to achieve?
Supervisee: Oh it is difficult. I can't get him to go to any appointments that I make. The problem is he has been out of school for so long he has lost confidence.

Supervisor: Is there anything he is good at, anything he likes?
Supervisee: Well he spends a lot of time playing pool.
Supervisor: Are you any good at pool?
Supervisee: No, I'm useless.
Supervisor: So could he teach you to play pool?
Supervisee: I'm sure he could.
Supervisor: Maybe this is something you could try. It would give you an opportunity to give him some positive feedback.
Supervisee: Yes, and maybe that would help build his confidence.

In the next session the supervisor can help the worker to review and develop the work: this is discussed later in this chapter. The desired outcomes can be refined, through discussion, into more 'helpful' goals that provide a specific focus for the actions of the supervisee. A number of qualities for 'helpful goals' have been developed by practitioners and, in the context of supervision, could include goals that:

- are relevant to the supervisee and young person;
- are positive – something the person *will* be doing rather than *not* doing;
- are tangible and concrete;
- involve small steps, i.e. 'What is the first thing you will do or notice?';
- are achievable for the supervisee within the context of the young person's life;
- are expressed in terms of the start of something and in terms of a direction of change;
- are described in interactional terms, who will be doing what, when, and with whom.

Of course, every worker has strengths, things they are good at, qualities and prior experience that they bring to the work. Outcome focused work endeavours to utilize and build on these strengths. Rather than highlighting the 'deficits' in the young person or the worker, outcome focused work pays attention to how strengths and capabilities can be utilized.

Enlisting support: working with other agencies

Along with the task of identifying and building on strengths, an important question is, 'Who else can help in the process of moving towards the desired outcomes?' The supervisee and the young person will have considered who can help, within a professional network and within the young person's family and social network. Part of the supervisory process will be to ensure that all those involved are clear about *how* they can support. They are enlisted because they can help to move towards the goals rather than because of the professional 'label' they wear.

Dialogue two

Supervisor:	So you and George have agreed to work on George being on time at College everyday?
Supervisee:	That's right.
Supervisor:	So who else could help?
Supervisee:	Well I suppose his landlady might help by giving him a call in the morning.
Supervisor:	Who else might be able to help?
Supervisee:	Perhaps his lecturer could make a special effort to congratulate him when he arrives on time.

Preparing for the work

The strategy of envisaging and imagining times when the work is successful can be used to rehearse the action the worker needs to take. This may involve dealing with unhelpful thoughts and language, in order to build a sense of possibility. It may also involve envisaging problems and obstacles beforehand and preparing to deal with them, if, and when, they arise.

Dialogue three

Supervisor:	So what are you hoping to achieve in the next interview?
Supervisee:	I hope to help him identify what he has achieved since we last met and not concentrate on all the things that have gone wrong.
Supervisor:	So what would I see you doing when you do this?
Supervisee:	Well I will probably start by asking what has gone well since we last met. But he may say 'nothing'.
Supervisor:	So what else will you do?
Supervisee:	I will probably ask him to take me through the week in detail, and then search for and pick out some little things that have gone well and build on these. This will help build his confidence and move towards his goal.
Supervisor:	That sounds good!

The emphasis will be on helping the supervisee to do what they are good at, and to build on this. This should assist them to try out new ideas and ways of working and to be creative in the context of the identified goals. It will also help the supervisee to consider and evaluate any suggestions that the supervisor might have. The emphasis will be on helping the supervisee to find pathways to the achievement of goals and for making progress. The supervisee needs to remain central to the process and will be the 'expert' in what works for them and the young person.

Providing constructive feedback, building on success and keeping on track

The supervisor needs to help the supervisee to focus on and summarize the work. They can do this by giving the supervisee constructive and positive feedback about what they have noticed that the supervisee is doing well, and the qualities they are bringing to the work. This should help to build the supervisee's confidence and to sustain them. It will also encourage the supervisee to do more of what is working well and help them to reflect on the progress of the work. Constructive feedback can be given during the session or as a summary at the end of the session. In the same way the supervisee can be asked to give their own summary of achievements made at the end of the session.

One way to start a 'follow up' session is to ask what has gone well since the last supervision session. Questions that the supervisor might use could include:

- So what's gone well since we last met?
- So what did you bring to the process?
- What did you learn from doing the work, which you could build on further?
- Is there anything you could have done differently?

The supervisor focuses the conversation on the goals that have been set and explores in detail what the supervisee has brought to the work. This helps to build a positive frame of mind, and encourages the supervisee to reflect on what they have contributed to the work and what they have learned.

One of the essential aspects of supervision will be to help the supervisee review progress and keep on track. Clear descriptions of goals can be used to generate 'indicators', and these help the supervisor and supervisee to review progress (or lack of it), and identify whether the activities need to be revised. The supervisor will focus on what is working and, if the work is 'stuck', they can focus on what has worked best or what needs to be different, by exploring alternative options.

Dialogue four

Supervisor: So how did you get on with the game of pool?
Supervisee: Oh he beat me really easily. But I gave him lots of compliments and he started to teach me how to pot the balls. He also started to tell me how nervous he got when he went to interviews, when he didn't understand the questions.
Supervisor: So do you think that helped build his confidence?
Supervisee: Yes I do.

Supervisor:	So on a scale 0–10, where ten is that he is super-confident and 0 is when he has no confidence, where do you think he is at?
Supervisee:	I would say about a four.
Supervisor:	So where do you think he would have to be at to get through an interview?
Supervisee:	At least a seven.
Supervisor:	So what would be the first sign he would be moving toward say a six.
Supervisee:	Well I suppose he might at least be looking at some brochures and choosing some options.
Supervisor:	So what might you do to help him get to a five?
Supervisee:	Well I could ask him about some of the things he would like to try and get the brochures for him to look at.

Future focus – use of the 'miracle' question

It is in the nature of the referral process that the young person is likely to be accompanied by negative descriptions that focus on their deficits or needs. When the supervisee meets the young person, their attitude may confirm the problems and difficulties. In these circumstances it is easy to label the young person as being unmotivated or resistant. Sometimes the supervisee may feel overwhelmed by the problems raised by the work. After acknowledging this, the supervisor can help build a sense of possibility and hopefulness by using a form of the 'miracle question' (de Shazer 1988). This draws a line around the problem and encourages the supervisee to envisage a successful outcome.

Dialogue five

Supervisor:	Suppose for a moment you had just had your first meeting. You have been away for a few days. Imagine, you come back to work and a 'miracle' happens before your next meeting and all the problems you describe had been resolved. Imagine when you meet him, what is the first thing you would notice (after the 'miracle' has happened)?
Supervisee:	Well the miracle would be that I would be taking him into college and he would be geared up to do a course. But that's not going to happen for a while. Maybe, realistically, all I could hope for would be that he was showing some interest in a course or at least some positive interest in anything.
Supervisor:	So what would you be doing if he was showing interest?
Supervisee:	Well I would be asking him about it. What he liked about it and what he enjoyed.
Supervisor:	So what would be the first sign of this beginning to happen?

Supervisee: Well, I think he would be engaging with me in the interview.

Supervisor: So is there anything he is doing now that gives you the feeling that this might be possible?

Supervisee: Well he is turning up and he does talk about his football sometimes.

Supervisor: So he is in a football team, that's good. How does he manage to keep in the football team?

Supervisee: I don't know but I could talk to him about it. He must show up for training, remember his kit and things like that. It shows he is motivated.

Supervisor: Is there anything else you would notice? (Looking for detailed description and small changes.)

Supervisee: He would be turning up on time for his appointments and beginning to talk.

This conversation enables the supervisee to identify several strengths in the young person: commitment to the team, discipline, showing up for training and games. The supervisee can feed this back to their young person in the next session and build on the strengths, linking them with the challenges the young person faces now.

Using scales to review progress

The scaling techniques used in dialogue four can also be used to review the supervisee's progress with a case in supervision. It can help to bring a sense of realism into discussions about what is achievable.

Dialogue six

Supervisor: So in relation to where you started the work where do you think you are now?

Supervisee: Oh, when I started things were pretty bad, say a two. I think we have made quite a lot of progress, say a five.

Supervisor: So where would you like to get to before you can close the case?

Supervisee: I'd like to get him into a job, say eight.

Supervisor: So do you know how you can get him to a six?

Supervisee: It's difficult because I am not sure he really wants to do more.

Supervisor: So how motivated are you to get him to an eight.

Supervisee: Oh, I still have a lot of energy, at least a nine.

Supervisor: So how motivated is he?

Supervisee: Oh, he probably isn't more than two?

Supervisor: So what ideas do you have for bridging the gap?

Supervisee: That's not going to be easy. Maybe realistically, when I think about it, I may have gone as far as I can go.

Facilitating a supervision session

The importance of building a good relationship in supervision is discussed elsewhere in this book. A critical task for the supervisor is to acknowledge and validate whatever the supervisee brings to the session. If the supervisee is feeling despondent, confused and overwhelmed, the supervisor needs to listen and acknowledge whatever the concerns are. They can then use the 'outcome focused cycle' (Figure 4.3) as a way of focusing the supervision and keeping on track. While this may be a sequential process, the supervisor can use the cycle to make sure the work is properly 'constructed'. This will help the supervisee to focus on aspects of the work that need to be strengthened, clarified or developed.

Reviewing supervision

The aim of supervision is to achieve good outcomes and at the same time support and sustain the worker. Consequently, it is important to review and evaluate the process of supervision itself and make sure it is 'on

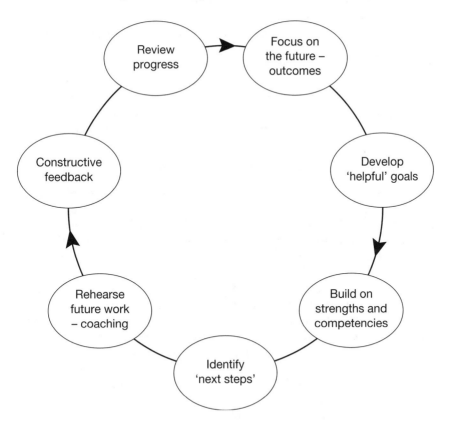

Figure 4.3 Outcome focused supervision

track'. A supervisor can establish the habit of reviewing supervision by asking, at the end of a session, how the session has been helpful. They can get the supervisee to give specific feedback by asking, for example, which sessions have been most useful, things they have found helpful and things they have not. This parallels the supportive and shared process that the supervisee is building with the young person.

The supervisor will have to assess whether the supervisee is confident to give honest feedback. The supervisor can use their own observations and judgements, but they might also ask, 'What would tell me that you are able to give honest feedback on the sessions? How would I know?'

One way of reviewing supervision might be to construct a post-session evaluation sheet. The supervisor and supervisee can devise the dimensions themselves, but they might include:

- I felt listened to and heard, 1–10.
- I left the session with a clear sense of direction and purpose, 1–10.
- I felt confident in the work I had to do, 1–10.
- I felt supported and encouraged, 1–10.
- We worked on the issues I felt were important, 1–10.
- I felt the agenda was shared between us and no one agenda dominated, 1–10.
- We didn't get interrupted, 1–10.

Supervisee and supervisor can score the dimensions from their own perspectives. This could lead to a discussion of differences and what each could contribute to improve the score and to develop the process.

Conclusion: benefits of outcome focused supervision

The framework outlined in this chapter should help supervisors keep 'on track' and work effectively, particularly where the temptation might be to try and solve complex problems which are likely to be insoluble. It should help the supervisor and supervisee keep focused in supervision and achieve effective practice. It should avoid the sessions becoming side-tracked or drifting without a direction or purpose. The suggested practice should maximize the resources and energy of supervisor and supervisee, and in turn, engage young people and others in their networks in an effective way. It should also provide a base for the supervisor to be creative and innovative, to build on their own strengths and resources.

A specific benefit of using this approach in supervision is that it parallels and models good practice in work with young people. The supervisee will begin to anticipate the questions and the process – they will begin to supervise themselves.

The cycle provides a way of planning the work and preparing the supervisee. It should help to build the youth support worker's confidence and should help them to feel supported. The framework should enable them to reflect on, and build, their skills and competence. It does this in an organic way as part of supervision practice, rather than breaking these processes down into their component parts. For example, supervisees often complain that their staff development reviews are tokenistic, 'one-off' events unrelated to the realities of their work. By comparison, in supervision, working through the 'cycle' provides ongoing support and development.

The approach is rooted in a philosophy that is based on effective practice. It has an internal consistency which can be used to tackle problems and issues, thus avoiding an unstructured or random approach to developing supervision. Outcome focused supervision draws from sophisticated ideas about communication, change and systemic work. It is an approach to practice, rather than a technique, and should not be regarded as a 'quick fix', only viewed as appropriate because of limited resources. Outcome research into outcome focused approaches (De Jong and Berg 2002) suggests that these methods are as effective, if not more so, than some of the traditional approaches to practice; indeed, with a positive focus on building solutions and moving forward, it seems they are more likely to engage young people.

Finally, it should be remembered that these ideas are intended as suggestions and not as a template. Although the questions can be used 'as they stand', in order to promote reflection, the process should not be experienced as mechanistic. It needs to be rooted in core values, such as respect and interest in the supervisee, and founded on key skills, such as rapport building and listening.

It is hoped that the reader will develop their own 'road map' and find out what works for them, given their unique style and their own situation. The ideas in this chapter provide a foundation to build on. By listening to feedback from supervisees, and the young people they work with, supervisors will learn what is helpful, what to do more of and what to change.

Bibliography

Ahola, T. and Furman, B. (1997) *Reteaming*, Helsinki: International Reteaming Institute.

Annis Hammond, S. (2000) *The Thin Book of Appreciative Inquiry*, London: BT Press.

Berg, I.K. (1994) *Family Based Services*, London: Norton.

Bucknell, D. (2000) 'Practice teaching: problem to solution', *Social Work Education*, 19 (2): 125–144.

De Jong, P. and Berg, I.K. (2002) *Interviewing for Solutions*, Canada: Brooks Cole.

de Shazer, S. (1985) *Keys to Solution in Brief Therapy*, New York: Norton.

—— (1988) *Clues: Investigating Solutions in Brief Therapy*, New York: Norton.

Durrant, M. (1995) *Creative Strategies for School Problems*, London: Norton.

McNamee, S. and Gergen, K.J. (eds) (1992) *Therapy as Social Construction*, London: Sage.

O'Hanlon, B. and Beadle, S. (1996) *A Field Guide to Possibility*, London: BT Press.

Saleebey, D. (ed.) (1994) *The Strengths Perspective in Social Work Practice*, 2nd edn, New York: Longman.

White, M. and Epston, D. (1990) *Narrative Means to Therapeutic Ends*, New York: Norton.

Zander, R.S. and Zander, B. (2000) *The Art of Possibility*, Boston, MA: HBS Press.

5 Getting the most from support and supervision

Attitudes and skills for supervisors and supervisees in an integrative approach to supervision

Jane Westergaard

Introduction

In order to engage effectively with, and make positive use of, support and supervision, both supervisors and supervisees will need to bring specific skills, attitudes and qualities to the process. Getting the most from support and supervision, as the title of this chapter suggests, requires more than simply setting time aside to sit together in a room and discuss aspects of the supervisee's practice. This 'working alliance between a supervisor and a counsellor' (Inskipp and Proctor 1993: 313) should represent a robust, open, supportive and challenging relationship between two professional practitioners. A commitment to the process and an understanding of what it sets out to achieve are vital to ensure that the supervisee, supervisor, and, most importantly, the client, benefit. At the very least, it demands an understanding by both parties regarding the function and purpose of supervision, the process of supervision, the principles of reflective practice, and the development of specific interpersonal skills to enable effective engagement and purposeful interactions to take place. No mean feat!

The supervision process has been central to a range of professionals working with young people, for some time. Counsellors, for example, are required to demonstrate a visible commitment to supervision. The British Association of Counselling recommends a minimum number of hours of supervision for every practising counsellor, which counselling agencies are required to adhere to (BAC 1987). The youth service and social work professions also identify the need for supervision as a requirement of professional practice, as does the mental health service. However, not all professionals who provide support to young people as a key function of their role, are themselves offered the kind of support and supervision so valued by their colleagues in other occupational settings. An obvious example of a group of practitioners who lack a structured programme of support, is the teaching profession. Teachers and teaching assistants often have no clearly defined opportunities for supervision, in spite of the fact that they may be encountering complex and challenging issues in their pastoral support function with individual pupils. There has been some attempt to address this need, particularly in the case of newly qualified teachers who are appointed an 'induction tutor' (or mentor). However, Field and Philpott are careful to point out that mentoring in schools can be complex and needs to be planned and well structured if it is to contribute to a process of supervision (Field and Philpott 2001).

The careers service has also been slow to acknowledge the need for a formal system of supervision for its staff, many of whom are working in demanding circumstances with young people. Bimrose and Wilden (1994) highlighted this issue and have made a strong case for the need to adequately support careers advisers.

Since the inception of the Connexions service (the youth support agency for all 13–19-year-olds in England), there has been a subtle, but visible shift towards the need for support and supervision for all those who are working at some psychological and emotional depth with young people. The draft Quality Standards for the Connexions Service stated 'All personnel are supervised to professional standards and receive the necessary training and support necessary to perform competently' (DfES 2001). The recognition of the need for supervision for youth support workers is to be applauded. However, my own experience from training those who will be undertaking the role of supervisor in the Connexions service, shows that there is a distinct lack of clarity about the purpose and practice of supervision in this context.

This chapter considers these issues by exploring the features of an integrative approach to support and supervision that is applicable across a range of professional backgrounds. It explores the key tenets of the approach, and focuses on the process of the supervisory relationship. In addition, it examines the skills and attitudes necessary for supervisory relationships to blossom and fulfil their function.

What is an integrative approach to support and supervision?

Integration has become a recognised approach in the field of counselling. A number of established academics and practitioners have contributed to the development of an argument for greater integration across theoretical orientations (Norcross 1986; Clarkson 1992; Dryden 1992). McLeod describes integration as referring to a process in which the counsellor brings together key elements from a range of different theories and models, and develops a new model for practice: 'To be an integrationist it is necessary not only to identify what is useful, but also to meld these pieces into a whole' (McLeod 1998: 208). An integrative approach is one in which the commonalities of established approaches are unified to create something new. Those who argue for integration identify the benefits of adopting a framework for practice that enables them to recognise and draw from existing established theoretical approaches (e.g. client centred, behavioural, constructivist) while focusing on an integrating concept (e.g. problem management, decision making, change). The case for integration is developed by O'Brien and Houston:

> No single theory or piece of psychological research fully explains what it is to be human. Each theory addresses some, but not all facets of human experience and behaviour. Acknowledgement of this makes for a more open minded and exploratory stance than is often the case in single-model approaches, supporting our plea for flexibility, which an integrative approach implies.
>
> (2000: 60–61)

Is it helpful then, or appropriate, to adopt an integrative way of working in the support of practitioners who are working with young clients? After all, supervision is not therapy. However, as we will explore later in this chapter, the notion of the 'parallel process' whereby the themes and issues raised in supervision (consciously or subconsciously) often correspond to, reflect or 'parallel' those which are apparent in client casework, is significant. This concept is central to supervision and it should come as no surprise that those who have researched into and written widely on the subject of supervision, have drawn, for the most part, from counselling and therapeutic literature.

The integrative approach may be particularly applicable for the supervision of youth support workers. These individual practitioners represent a range of professional backgrounds where different theoretical models will have been applied to their own client practice. An integrative model of supervision can recognise, acknowledge and actively embrace multiple strategies for practice as well as different phenomenological approaches. Grace (2004: 36) states 'even if supervisor and supervisee are both working integratively, that probably still means they are using different models'.

To explore the applicability of an integrative approach to supervision, it is necessary to focus on what the activity of supervision sets out to achieve. By understanding the purpose of supervision, we can consider how to work to achieve its aim. The functions of support and supervision, as identified by Inskipp and Proctor (1993) writing for the counselling field, focus on three areas. These are normative, formative and restorative. The normative function is concerned with the 'management' of the supervisee, ensuring that professional practice and standards are being adhered to. The formative function is concerned with developing the supervisee's skills and understanding of professional practice issues, and the restorative function focuses on the emotional and psychological wellbeing of the supervisee. Kadushin (1976) writing from a social work perspective, offers a similar definition, with his three 'functions' of supervision identified as administrative (managerial), educative and supportive.

Although both definitions are widely accepted by those involved in supervision across a range of disciplines, they do not, in themselves, provide a guide as to how these functions should be achieved in the context of one-to-one or group supervision. Indeed, there is room for tensions to emerge, and for supervisors to cleave to the function with which they feel they are most familiar, or which most closely reflects their working relationship with the supervisee.

In my experience of training new supervisors within the Connexions service (many of whom retain a line management function), the normative function may feel the most comfortable, safe and familiar, and in the early days of the training programme is often identified by participants as the 'key' function. By way of contrast, peers who have a supervisory role with colleagues may feel that they can fulfil the restorative/supportive functions, but are less comfortable with the normative/management aspects that the role demands. Supervisors who are external to the employing agency, and who do not therefore have direct line-management responsibility, may be at risk of focusing their work on the restorative and formative functions. The normative or 'management' function risks being neglected as a result. Integration then, may not only be concerned with the integration of a range of theories and concepts drawn from therapeutic disciplines, it may also be applied to the integration of functions, or even roles within the process. Hawkins and Shohet make this point clearly:

> The supervisor has to integrate the role of educator with that of being the provider of support to the worker and, in most cases, managerial oversight of the supervisee's clients. These three functions do not always sit comfortably together, and many supervisors can retreat from attempting this integration to just one of their roles.
>
> (2000: 4–5)

The integrative approach can provide supervisor and supervisee with a framework in which the functions of supervision can be fully addressed. It does not 'rule out' the use of any existing concepts or theories, but rather seeks to identify a common approach or model with which both supervisor and supervisee can engage, which has, at its heart, an integrating concept such as the management of problems. It is important to note that 'integration must never be hijacked into becoming just one more brand of therapy. There is no place for hard and fast rules about precisely what to integrate and just how to behave' (O'Brien and Houston 2000: 3).

A model for integrative supervision

A helpful starting point for those who are new to supervision, and are unclear about how to approach the interaction with supervisees, is to consider the approaches that those whom they are going to be supervising currently use in their one-to-one work with clients. The supervisees themselves (i.e. youth support workers) may be equally new to the process and expressing anxiety about what will happen, how it will happen and how it will impact on their work. Those who have some knowledge of supervision will be familiar with the term 'parallel process' mentioned earlier in this chapter. This parallel process, in very simple terms, refers to the commonalities evident in the relationship between supervisor/supervisee and practitioner/client. The explicit functions of supervision as identified by Inskipp and Proctor, might, it could be argued, equally be examined in the light of practitioner/client work. For example, most practitioners working with young people will be able to identify a normative function to their work with clients. They will be working alongside young people to help them to develop within an ethical and appropriate social framework. The current political emphasis on inclusion suggests that this social framework should address issues such as participation in education, employment and training. Watts identifies a possible tension between the ethos of a young-person-centred service and the need for youth support workers to carry out a 'control' function, with government imposed targets to be met (Watts 2002: 42).

The formative function will also be evident in work with young people. Clients will be encouraged to identify their own areas for development and practitioners will support them in this process, providing information and guidance as appropriate. Finally, youth support workers will undoubtedly be undertaking restorative work by offering emotional and practical support to their clients. However, there is a further dimension to the parallel process as discussed in some detail by Hawkins and Shohet:

> In the paralleling phenomenon the processes at work currently in the relationship between client and therapist are uncovered through how they are reflected in the relationship between therapist and supervisor. ... the job of the supervisor is tentatively to name the process and thereby make it available to conscious exploration and learning.
>
> (2000: 81)

Having established these links between the activity of client support and practitioner supervision, it is helpful to identify the approaches used currently by youth support workers to inform their practice with clients and then to reflect on the applicability of these to the supervision process.

Many professionals working with young people in a helping capacity, will, at some point in their training have been introduced to Egan and the three stage helping model for effective interactions (Egan 1994). This 'Skilled Helper' model is truly integrative, in that although it is a concept in its own right, it draws from a range of psychological and counselling perspectives including person centred, narrative and cognitive behavioural approaches. It has, however, an overarching integrating concept which is the management of problems. It is this management of problems or 'issues' that is particularly relevant to those working with young clients who often present with a number of difficulties, issues or problems in their lives. The three stages identified in the model, focus on a process that includes:

- helping clients to tell their stories;
- helping clients to set goals for the future;
- helping clients to plan actions for the achievement of those goals.

If the stages are worked through rigorously, but flexibly, Egan argues that clients will be helped to manage their problems. Jenkins explains this further:

> The goals of the skilled helper model are to assist clients to develop their understanding of key problems and to build the skills which will enable them to manage their situation in a more satisfactory and effective manner.
>
> For the counsellor therefore, the goals of therapy are:
>
> - to build an empathic and accepting relationship with the client
> - to assist the client in exploring key feelings, experiences and behaviours
> - to identify with the client future goals for change
> - to support the client in taking the practical steps which will achieve the goals of their own plan for action
> - to evaluate the change process together with the client, in order to realise the gains and learning which come out of this process.
>
> (Jenkins 2000: 168)

How applicable then, might Egan's Skilled Helper approach be to supervision? It is tempting to reflect on the bullet points identified above and contemplate substituting the word 'supervisee' for 'client' and evaluate the outcome. This, of course, would be a crude and very simplistic analysis of the applicability of this integrative approach to supervision. However, it is not without value as a first step in understanding how the model might be used in the supervisee context.

Telling the story (stage one of Egan's helping model) is as necessary in supervision as it is in work with clients. It sets out to accomplish two significant outcomes. First it encourages the client (or supervisee) to talk through their issues in depth. This will enable them to hear, and some-times even to discover for themselves their own story. Supervisees will value the opportunity to focus on aspects of their practice. Significant ideas, thoughts and feelings will emerge and often new perspectives on a situation will be gained, which could lead to the acceptance, or even resolution of difficult issues. This does not necessarily mean simply talking about problems and concerns. Supervisees should be encouraged to focus on positive stories as well as to consider aspects of their work that are proving challenging. By talking about their practice, supervisees will have the opportunity to reflect on and conceptualise their work. Second, the helper (supervisor) will hear a detailed and very personal account from which they can begin to gain an insight into their supervisee and the issues they are working with. The role of the supervisor in this early stage is to encourage the storytelling and to provide new perspectives, to enable greater insight into the work that the supervisee is undertaking. This emphasis on storytelling provides an integrative link to narrative approaches in therapy discussed by Bruner (1990). He argues that self-knowledge, understanding, and our ability to make sense of the world, is formed by telling stories.

Often, when working with younger clients, the stories told in supervision will be messy and complex. Supervisors may need to contain or 'hold' their supervisees throughout the process and should be particularly mindful of the need to actively listen, with all of their senses to the stories their supervisees are bringing. Of course, if this stage of the process is rushed there is a danger that the restorative function is unlikely to be addressed. Stage one of the process acts as the agenda setting or 'contract' stage for the remainder of the interaction, with both parties being clear as to the issues which will form the basis of their discussion.

In stage two, both supervisor and supervisee are beginning to focus on the aspects of the supervisee's work that need to be developed. Egan stresses the responsibility on the 'client' to identify goals and strategies (drawing from humanistic beliefs that the individual is best placed to make decisions about their own lives), and it is the role of the supervisor to support and draw out ideas from the supervisee, as well as to input possible strategies for the supervisee to consider. As the relationship between supervisor and supervisee develops, the parallel process will begin to play a more significant role. The meaning of the parallel process goes much further than simply a suggestion that the activities of client support and practitioner supervision mirror each other. 'The supervisor focuses on the relationship in the supervision session in order to explore how it might be unconsciously playing out or paralleling the hidden dynamics of the therapy session' (Hawkins and Shohet 2000: 70).

The supervisor will be alert to their feelings about the work with their supervisee (issues around transference and counter-transference are discussed in Chapter 3 of this book) and will encourage the supervisee to reflect on what is happening within the process of supervision itself, and relate it to the focus of their own work with clients. For instance, it could be that if a supervision session feels 'stuck' and lacking in purpose, the client work may be in the same place. Reflecting on this in supervision will enable supervisees to begin to explore ways forward in their work with clients. Youth support workers often experience feelings of 'stuckness' or even helplessness in their client work. Challenges that clients are experiencing in their lives may feel all-consuming and insurmountable, and this will often lead to workers (consciously or unconsciously) absorbing these feelings. Skilled supervisors will take time to acknowledge and reflect on these feelings in the session, thus enabling the supervisee to achieve greater understanding and clarity about the clients with whom they are working.

Stage three of Egan's helping model focuses on the need to plan action. 'Action' in terms of supervision could include a range of specific points which will relate to the 'stories' told in stage one and the 'goals' or strategies identified in stage two. Youth support workers will be familiar with this stage of the process. Many youth support agencies require their workers to identify and record action points with their clients, thereby formalising this aspect of the work. The benefits then, of identifying appropriate action points will already be known to supervisees, who should leave the supervision session with some ideas about how they can begin to focus on a specific area of their practice or develop strategies to work with a particular client.

Attitudes for effective integrative supervision

The three core conditions (or attitudes) of empathy, congruence and unconditional positive regard, a central tenet of the client (or person) centred approach to counselling, espoused by Carl Rogers (1951), have clearly been integrated into Egan's model. Rogers argued that in a therapeutic relationship, empathy + (the ability to focus on and understand the client's world), congruence + (the need to be genuine and real within the relationship), and unconditional positive regard + (the importance of ensuring that personal values and beliefs do not obstruct the counsellor's view of the client and their world), should be demonstrated by the therapist in order to encourage client 'growth'. Egan expresses these core conditions as attitudes required by the helper, which are integral to the helping process.

When applied to supervision, adherence to these core conditions requires supervisors to *empathise* with their supervisees, working hard to understand the issues they are facing in their work and to make sense of the feelings that are being invoked. *Congruence* in the supervisory process is all about the need for the supervisor to be genuine and real within the relationship. In other words coming to supervision as a whole person, being open and self-aware and feeling comfortable enough to be honest about who they are, what they feel and what they bring to the relationship. Finally, *unconditional positive regard* encourages supervisors to demonstrate a non-judgemental approach to their supervisees. This demands high levels of self-awareness and constant reflection on the part of the supervisor.

Mearns (1991) writing about the process of supervision identifies four conditions for supervisors. These are:

- commitment – a need to be fully involved in the relationship;
- valuing – a non-judgemental response;
- congruence – a transparent and genuine approach;
- empathy – grasping the supervisees frame of reference.

Again it could be argued that supervision is not, in itself, a therapeutic relationship, and therefore the application of these conditions to the work may not be appropriate. However, if the restorative/supportive function of supervision is to be viewed as a crucial aspect of the supervisory process, then the therapeutic nature of that relationship should be acknowledged and valued. Hawkins and Shohet make the point that 'A good working alliance is not built on a list of agreements or rules, but on growing trust, respect and goodwill between both parties' (2000: 56).

Applying these core conditions to supervision can be extremely challenging. The relationship between supervisee and supervisor may already be established in another context remote from the supervision process. The supervisor, for example, may already have a line-management function, which could include assessment, appraisal and discipline of the practitioner whom they are going to be supervising. Alternatively, they may have worked together for many years and have established a friendship outside their working lives, or, possibly, the supervisee is a considerably more experienced practitioner in the field than the supervisor. Each of these scenarios could provide a barrier to a supervisor adopting the core conditions. These barriers would need to be recognised, actively addressed and worked through as part of the supervision process, to enable the core conditions to be applied. Webb makes this point succinctly, 'The experience of supervision and relationships with supervisors invoke emotional reactions in counsellors. Supervisors may be perceived as incompetent, critical, demanding or even sexually attractive and supervision as unhelpful or positively harmful' (2001: 25).

It is interesting to note that a recent research study undertaken by Reid (2005) with careers practitioners working as personal advisers, has found that they identify the restorative function of supervision as the area that is most helpful to their own wellbeing and to their practice with clients. Ironically, it is also the function that is in danger of being least likely to be addressed, particularly if the supervisor holds a line-management as well as a supervision role. It is the area of the work which is often most feared by those Connexions supervisors with whom I have worked on training courses. They express feelings of anxiety and apprehension at working in some psychological depth with their colleagues. All the more reason then, for supervisors to adhere to an approach that, over time, will build trust between themselves and their supervisees.

The appeal of adopting Egan's integrative helping model to supervision is that, although it enables supervisees to tell their stories and encourages an empathic, real and accepting atmosphere within the session, it goes much further than simply providing a forum for a cosy chat. In this respect, the model encourages the supervisor to integrate behavioural and even solution focused approaches and techniques (as discussed in Chapter 4 of this book) by focusing on future goals and strategies for achieving them. Stage one of the approach sets out to form a contract by helping supervisees to 'tell their story' and to extract the key issues and features of their work which they would like to explore in more detail. Stages two and three, by contrast, aim to move the supervisee forward, to consider how their practice might develop, what changes they might want to make, what goals can realistically be set and what actions and strategies are then required to assist in the achievement of these goals (i.e. the formative or educative function of supervision).

Integrating alternative theory and approaches

It is important to note that Egan's helping model complements other theories and approaches to supervision. This, after all, is what integration is all about. There are clear links, for instance, between the skilled helper approach to supervision and the developmental model conceptualised by Stoltenberg and Delworth (1987), and the process, or Seven Eyed model devised by Hawkins and Shohet (2000).

For example, the developmental model identifies four distinct chronological levels of supervisee development. Knowledge of the characteristics of each level enables a better understanding of the dynamic at each stage within the supervisory relationship. Supervisors are helped to gauge 'where the supervisee is at' in their development within supervision. Supervisors who are working integratively will be mindful of their supervisee's development as the process of supervision continues over time.

Likewise, the process or Seven Eyed model developed by Hawkins and Shohet (2000) can be considered in relation to an integrative approach. Seven facets of supervision are identified and Hawkins and Shohet argue that each of these elements should be present for supervision to be deemed effective. However, the facets do not, in themselves provide a guide as to what should happen within the session, rather they identify and explore the underlying features of supervision of which both supervisee and supervisor should be aware. They can (and should) be used to inform and develop the supervisor's understanding of the process of supervision and can be integrated, as appropriate, within Egan's three stage helping model.

It is important to note that Egan's model is neither prescriptive nor inflexible. The model is fluid and should be used flexibly to meet the needs of the supervisee. It may be that all three stages are not addressed in every supervision session (in many cases, they will not be). Alternatively, it is possible to move back and forth between all stages. Indeed, Egan expresses the model in a cyclical format whereby stage three (the action planning stage) may raise new issues which have not previously been explored, but, once acknowledged, will need to be discussed in detail.

Skills for effective, integrative supervision

Integrative counselling places distinct emphasis on the skills required by counsellors to ensure that they are able to engage effectively with their clients and work towards positive outcomes. Egan's choice of book title, *The Skilled Helper*, emphasises the importance he places on the need for the counsellor to have available a set of skills that they can put to use. These skills are often referred to as generic 'interpersonal' or 'communication' skills and include the use of helpful questioning, summarising, and reflecting back (Culley 1992; Egan 1994; Nelson-Jones 1997). In addition, counsellors need to develop specific skills such as the use of immediacy and challenge to enable their clients to overcome the blocks and barriers they may face and to identify strategies for change. Supervisors, like counsellors, will develop their skills to ensure that they can meet the needs of their supervisees and fulfil the normative, formative and restorative functions of supervision. The use of any skill is first and foremost to encourage the supervisee to reflect on their practice. Woods suggests that assisting professional helpers to operate as reflective practitioners is an overarching aim of supervision (Woods 2001).

Supervisors should encourage their supervisees to reflect on practice in a number of ways. Most importantly, supervisors need to listen. This may be stating the obvious, but actively listening to and focusing on the supervisee is not always easy to achieve. There are, however, factors that can block the listening process. For instance, there can be practical issues and difficulties to overcome. Where the supervision session is to take place is of paramount importance. Each party needs to feel comfortable, both physically and with their surrounding environment. It is important that both supervisee and supervisor are clear about the time they have together and that both understand that this 'space' will not be interrupted. It can be difficult to 'leave behind' pressing work issues and it is important that both parties are able to adopt an attitude which establishes the supervision process as a priority, not to be changed or cancelled as other 'more important' work-related issues occur. In addition to the practical difficulties, there may be other factors that get in the way of active listening. The relationship between both parties will impact on the ability of the supervisor to listen to, and empathise with the supervisee, particularly if the supervisor has established a different kind of role with the supervisee (e.g. friend, manager) outside the process of supervision (as noted earlier in this chapter). It will be increasingly difficult to establish a working alliance if the supervisor is unable to fully listen, and it is critical therefore, that supervisors are able to reflect on their own feelings within supervision and use immediacy where appropriate to ensure that the relationship is not blocked.

Another key skill that supervisors need to develop, to ensure that they can be a skilled helper to their supervisee, is the skill of challenge. Henderson notes that 'supervisory relationships based on equality, safety and challenge were deemed to be the best' (Henderson 2002: 27).

Challenge does not mean being aggressive or confrontational, rather it involves enabling the supervisee to reflect on issues they are working with, dilemmas they may be experiencing and emotions they may be holding. Challenge can come in the form of a summary; simply paraphrasing the supervisee's words will provide the supervisee with the space to hear what they have said, reflect on it, and challenge themselves as to its validity. Alternatively, supervisors may use the skill of hypothetical questioning to encourage the supervisee to consider an issue in a different way, shedding new light and encouraging a reframing of the issue at the heart of the challenge. In addition, the use of the skill of immediacy, which means dealing with an issue in the 'here and now', can provide an effective challenge. For example, the supervisor who says to their supervisee, 'I get the feeling that what I've just said has made you feel quite angry', may enable the supervisee to acknowledge and own their feelings, and engage with what this may mean in their work. The skill of challenge is often one that both supervisors in their work with supervisees, and practitioners in their work with clients (the parallel process again) struggle with. This is not surprising. Whereas the words 'empathy' and 'active listening' connote helpful and supportive activities, the word 'challenge' brings with it a more combative flavour. In any helping relationship though, with clients or with supervisees, challenge should be viewed as a positive and enabling response to an issue, rather than negative and critical.

Conclusion

The integrative approach discussed in this chapter does not set out to offer a perfect or complete model for supervisory practice – this would be contrary to the concept of integration. It does, however, provide both youth support workers and supervisors alike, with an approach to their work that takes into account and accommodates a range of theoretical perspectives. It values the contribution made by each, while at the same time providing its own useful framework for practice. It is particularly pertinent to the supervision of those working in youth support services, because many of these practitioners are likely to have encountered integrative models already in their professional training, and should feel a familiarity with the process. In addition integrative supervision recognises and values the development of key attitudes and skills. For all supervisors, but particularly for those new to the process, this is a helpful and enlightening starting point. Development of these attitudes and skills should provide supervisors with the tools they need to enable them to engage effectively with their supervisees and to ensure that the process of supervision is a positive and useful experience for all concerned.

Bibliography

Bimrose, J. and Wilden, S. (1994) 'Supervision in careers guidance: empowerment or control?' *British Journal of Guidance and Counselling*, 22 (3): 373–383.

British Association for Counselling (1987) *How Much Supervision Should You Have?* Rugby: BAC.

Bruner, J. (1990) *Acts of Meaning*, Cambridge, MA: Harvard University Press.

Clarkson, P. (1992) 'Systematic integrative psychotherapy training', in W. Dryden (ed.) *Integrative and Eclectic Therapy: a Handbook*, Buckingham: Open University Press.

Culley, S. (1992) 'Counselling skills: an integrative framework', in W. Dryden (ed.) *Integrative and Eclectic Therapy: a Handbook*, Buckingham: Open University Press.

Department for Education and Science (2001) *Draft Quality Standards for the Connexions Service*, London: DfES.

Dryden, W. (ed.) (1992) *Integrative and Eclectic Therapy: a Handbook*, Buckingham: Open University Press.

Egan, G. (1994) *The Skilled Helper: a Problem Management Approach to Helping*, 4th edn, Pacific Grove, CA: Brooks/Cole.

Field, K. and Philpott, C. (2001) 'Mentoring in schools: from support to development', in A. Edwards (ed.) *Supporting Personal Advisers in Connexions: Perspectives on Supervision and Mentoring from Allied Professions*, Occasional Papers Canterbury: Canterbury Christ Church University College.

Grace, C. (2004) 'Working with theoretical difference in supervision', *Counselling and Psychotherapy Journal*, 14 (4): 36–37.

Hawkins, P. and Shohet, R. (2000) *Supervision in the Helping Professions*, 2nd edn, Maidenhead: Open University Press.

Henderson, P. (2002) 'Mistakes in supervision', *Counselling and Psychotherapy Journal*, 13 (8): 26–27.

Inskipp, F. and Proctor, B. (1993) *The Art, Craft and Tasks of Counselling Supervision, Part 1. Making the Most of Supervisors*, Twickenham: Cascade Publications.

Jenkins, P. (2000) 'Gerard Egan's skilled helper model', in S. Palmer and R. Woolfe (eds) *Integrative and Eclectic Counselling and Psychotherapy*, London: Sage.

Kadushin, A. (1976) *Supervision in Social Work*, New York: Columbia University Press.

McLeod, J. (1998) *An Introduction to Counselling*, 2nd edn, Buckingham: Open University Press.

Mearns, D. (1991) 'On being a supervisor', in W. Dryden and B. Thorne (eds) *Training and Supervision for Counselling in Action*, London: Sage.

Nelson-Jones, R. (1997) *Practical Counselling and Helping Skills*, 4th edn, London: Cassell.

Norcross, J. (ed.) (1986) *Handbook of Eclectic Psychotherapy*, New York: Brunner/ Mazel.

O'Brien, M. and Houston, G. (2000) *Integrative Therapy – a Practitioner's Guide*, London: Sage.

Reid, H.L. (2005) 'What advisers want from support and supervision: "pit-head time to wash off the dust of their labours"', *Career Guidance Today*, 13 (1), Stourbridge: Institute of Career Guidance.

Rogers, C.R. (1951) *Client Centred Therapy*, Boston, MA: Houghton Mifflin.

Stoltenberg, C.D. and Delworth, U. (1987) *Supervising Counsellors and Therapists*, San Francisco, CA: Jossey Bass.

Watts, A.G. (2002) 'Focusing on exclusion in England Connexions: genesis, diagnosis, prognosis', in *Constructing the Future: Social Inclusion Policy and Practice*, Stourbridge: Institute of Career Guidance.

Weaks, D. (2002) 'Unlocking the secrets of "good supervision": a phenomenological exploration of experienced counsellors' perceptions of good supervision', *Counselling and Psychotherapy Research*, 2 (1): 33–39.

Webb, A. (2001) 'Honesty in supervision', *Counselling and Psychotherapy Journal*, 12 (5): 24–25.

Woods, J. (2001) 'Supervision from an informal education/youth work perspective', in A. Edwards (ed.) *Supporting Personal Advisers in Connexions: Perspectives on Supervision and Mentoring from Allied Professions*, Occasional Papers Canterbury: Canterbury Christ Church University College.

6 Multicultural issues in support and supervision

Jenny Bimrose

Introduction

Within any helping relationship, differences are variously represented. The gender of the client, together with their ethnic background, age, socio-economic status, sexual orientation and whether they have any type of disability, are examples of the dimensions along which differences can be measured. In addition to differences brought by each client to every interview, practitioners also bring their own multifaceted identities, together with associated values, attitudes and beliefs that often originate from, and are grounded in, social differences. The impact of deeply held practitioner values, attitudes and beliefs that are at odds with those of their clients (e.g. views relating generally to the role of women in society and/or more specifically to abortion) may potentially – though not inevitably – have a negative impact on the helping relationship. How can these issues be addressed constructively in support and supervision? This chapter explores what a multicultural approach offers to personal advisers, youth support workers and their supervisors. Specifically, it examines what the approach comprises, considers why it is necessary, how it can be developed and some criticisms that have been made about the approach.

What is a multicultural approach?

'Multicultural' is a term associated with policies and practices related to ethnic difference. For example, in the UK, 'multicultural education' often refers to attempts to make education both more relevant to those from minority ethnic groups and more inclusive. In its application to counselling practice, which is at the centre of support and supervision, the meaning of 'multicultural' has been expanded beyond ethnic diversity to include other dimensions of social disadvantage, such as gender, sexual orientation, disability, social class, age and so on. Pederson (1991), for example, argued that 'culture' in the context of multicultural counselling should be defined to include 'demographic variables (e.g. age, sex, geographical location), status variables (e.g. social, educational, economic), and affiliations (formal and informal), as well as ethnographic variables such as nationality, ethnicity, language, and religion' (7). Guidelines published over a decade later by the American Psychological Association (2002) endorse this all-inclusive approach and define multiculturalism as recognizing 'the broad scope of dimensions of race, ethnicity, language, sexual orientation, gender, age, disability, class status, education, religion/spiritual orientation, and other cultural dimensions' (10). This type of broad and inclusive defin-ition challenges the view that differences are unimportant by emphasizing ways in which we are different from, and similar to, others – with every-one having various identities that become relevant at different times and in different places. By extending the meaning of multicultural beyond ethnicity, its importance is emphasized for every helping relationship, including the support and supervisory relationship that is crucial for personal advisers and youth support workers in their one-to-one work with young people.

The origins of a multicultural approach to counselling have been traced back to the racial civil rights movement in the United States in the 1950s, 1960s and 1970s (Bimrose 1998). Since this movement was concerned with the equal and fair treatment of all citizens in every sphere of society, it stimulated research into the usage of counselling services by ethnic minority groups, among many other issues. Findings were disturbing. A literature review undertaken by Pine (1972), for example, revealed that minority groups reported counselling to be a 'waste of time' and that 'counsellors do not accept, respect, and understand cultural differences; that counsel-lors are arrogant and contemptuous; and that counsellors don't know how to deal with their own hangups' (35). Sue and Sue (1999) summarize find-ings from other research undertaken around the same time and found that not only was the usage of services by minority groups limited, but that minority clients were more likely than white clients to finish counselling and therapy early.

If, as such evidence suggested, clients from minority ethnic groups were less than enthusiastic about counselling services, what could be the explan-ation? The most compelling and widely accepted view is that counselling practice is an ethnocentric activity. Over four decades ago, Wrenn (1962) argued that mainstream counselling and psychotherapy approaches are white, middle-class activities that operate with many distinctive values and assumptions. They are, in summary, ethnocentric or 'culturally encapsul-ated', holding at their centre a notion of normality that is different from and irrelevant to many clients. Since then, many have supported this view (e.g. Andrea and Daniels 2001; Arredondo 1998; Ivey *et al.* 1993; Lago and Thompson 1996; Ridley 1995; Sue *et al.* 1996), while others have speculated how poor training has resulted in culturally biased practices and techniques, which may be responsible for some clients lack of engage-ment with the helping process (Andrea *et al.* 1992; Bimrose and Bayne 1995; Leong *et al.* 1995).

What began with a concern about the relevance of mainstream counselling to ethnic minorities has, over the past three decades or so, developed into a significant movement that encompasses a wide range of client difference affecting clients' 'worldview' and life chances as well as providing a range of counselling responses. Pedersen (1991) proposed that 'we are moving toward a generic theory of multiculturalism as a "fourth force" position, complementary to the other three forces of psychodynamic, behavioural and humanistic explanations of human behaviour' and claimed that 'a multicultural perspective has changed the way we look at counselling across fields and theories' (6). Similarly, Ivey *et al.* (1993) argued that 'many are asking for a new view of counselling and therapy that respects and builds on the past but focuses on building new frameworks for a multicultural, multinational approach to the helping process' (ix). So how is this relevant to support and supervision?

The need for a multicultural approach to support and supervision

In health and social welfare, practice that routinely challenges discrimination and oppression is central to 'good' practice and, as Thompson argues: 'practice which does not take account of oppression and discrimination cannot be seen as good practice, no matter how high its standards might be in other respects' (1993: 11). However, traditional approaches adopted by practitioners have taken little or no account of the consequences of social difference (Thompson 1995) and anti-discriminatory practice starts with the practitioner. Support and supervision provides the opportunity for them to monitor and explore their 'dumb spots' (things they don't know or can't do), their 'blind spots' (fears and prejudices) and their 'deaf spots' (repressed aspects of self) (Ekstein and Wallerstein 1972). Discussing counselling work specifically with minority clients, Bernard and Goodyear (1991) identify five common 'blind spots' for counsellors that are relevant to dimensions of difference other than ethnicity and generally attributable to lack of information, rather than to negative bias or hostility. These 'blind spots' include a tendency for the counsellor to avoid (by maintaining psychological distance from) the client because of their own aversions; failure to deal with differences that play a role in the client's conflicts because of their need to deny such differences; and the tendency for the counsellor to assume that they are not prejudiced.

Indeed, research evidence indicates that it is not uncommon for practitioners to feel a level of discomfort when dealing with clients representing different aspects of diversity. For example, Allison *et al.* (1994), present the findings of a postal survey from the US that examined levels of competence in providing services to thirteen categories of clients from ethnic and diverse groups. Of 292 respondents who had completed doctoral programmes in clinical, counselling and school psychology, 96 per cent reported high levels of competence when counselling European Americans compared with much lower numbers of respondents who indicated competence with most of the ethnic and diverse groups examined (for example, 37 per cent reported high levels of competence in counselling African Americans, 64 per cent with the economically disadvantaged and 35 per cent with gay men). In the UK, Bimrose and Bayne (1995) also conducted a postal survey of qualified and practising counsellors (not all of whom had been exposed to multicultural training). They similarly found high levels of discomfort reported by counsellors working with diverse client groups (for example, 57 per cent reported discomfort based on gender and 46 per cent reported discomfort based on ethnicity).

Adopting a multicultural approach to support and supervision for personal advisors and youth support workers can help address these 'deaf, dumb and blind spots', by supporting practice with diverse clients. However, because multicultural approaches to counselling are relatively new, their implications for practice are still being worked out and worked through. There are, for example, fundamentally differing views of just how practice needs to change. Bimrose (1993) identified two distinct schools of thought in the literature regarding the appropriate response to client difference within a helping relationship. One emphasizes the need to integrate understanding of society's response to difference, together with relevant strategies and techniques, within current counselling theory and practice. The other, in contrast, stresses the need for practitioners to concentrate less on one-to-one work with clients and more on the structures and systems (e.g. economic, political and social) that create the need for counselling, with more emphasis on advocating structural change (e.g. adopting more of an advocacy role with agencies and systems). Of these two approaches, the emerging consensus favours integration, by suggesting that multicultural counselling should strive to select and build on the best of current counselling practice. A framework that has been developed over the past twenty or so years to do just that will now be examined and its relevance to support and supervision for personal advisors and youth support workers highlighted.

A framework for multicultural support and supervision

Within support and supervision, difference is important at various levels. For example (and perhaps most obviously), it is important for the critical review of practice that is at the heart of this activity. At this level, a multicultural perspective can be powerful in illuminating and addressing 'deaf, dumb and blind spots' that may emerge during supervision. Additionally, it is relevant at the level of the multidimensional differences represented by both the supervisor and supervisee within their support and supervisory relationship. Here, both parties may need to work on their relationship from a multicultural perspective. This may be particularly relevant where the personal characteristics of the supervisor reflect those associated with social advantage (e.g. male, white, middle-class, able-bodied, heterosexual), while the personal characteristics of the supervisee reflect those associated more with social disadvantage. Where there is already a power and status differential within the organizational context (that is, where the supervisor is in a position that is senior to their supervisee), an additional dimension will be present in the supervisory relationship (Bimrose and Wilden 1994). The reverse is also, of course, true. A few years ago, for example, a young woman who described herself as 'Black British' discussed with me problems she was experiencing with an older, white male supervisee who was not, she felt, taking her seriously.

So how can both supervisors and their supervisees become multiculturally competent? A review of the literature reveals a wealth of material – some of which is underpinned by research and some that is not – now available for this purpose. It is, however, largely left to the individual to make selections that suit their particular needs, circumstance and philosophical beliefs. A well-known and established competency framework from North America can help guide this selection. Originally, it was developed by Sue *et al.* (1982) and subsequently refined specifically for counselling (Sue *et al.* 1995). Recently, it has been adapted by the American Psychological Association (APA) as generic guidelines for multicultural education, training, research, practice and organizational change (2002). These guidelines focus on the need to address awareness and understanding of difference and stress how multicultural competence will enhance ethical practice. It is, however, the competency framework developed by Sue *et al.* (1995) for counselling that will be outlined briefly here, together with some methods of addressing multicultural development needs that are relevant both to supervisors and supervisees. Although originally developed for ethnic diversity and counselling, the framework nevertheless provides a useful tool for identifying and guiding self-development work on all aspects of diversity within helping relationships and so has particular currency for personal advisers, youth support workers and their supervisors.

This multicultural competency framework comprises a three by three matrix (Sue *et al.* 1995). Specifically, three main areas for personal development are identified: the need to increase *self-awareness* (of assumptions, values, and biases); the need to develop specialist *understanding* (of the worldview of the client); and the need to acquire a range of appropriate *interventions*. Within each of these three key areas, a further three sub-areas are identified: beliefs and attitudes; knowledge; and skills. In total, therefore, nine discrete competency areas for multicultural competence are identified. The following example illustrates how this framework can be used to identify multicultural self-development needs by providing examples of competencies from each of the sub-categories of beliefs and attitudes, knowledge and skill within each of the three major categories of awareness, understanding and interventions. This framework can be applied in supervision.

Focusing first on the need to increase self-awareness; an individual may need to appreciate how their own cultural background and experiences, attitudes, values and biases influence their practice (beliefs and attitudes). They may also need to address any lack of understanding (e.g. about different communication styles and how their own style may clash or facilitate the counselling process with, for example, minority clients). And they may need to develop relevant strategies and techniques (e.g. those required for non-racist and non-sexist practice). Moving on to understanding; individuals may need to develop their awareness of stereotypes and prejudices that they may hold (beliefs and attitudes). For example, stereotypical views about arranged marriages, or deeply held beliefs about homosexuality. Additionally, they may need to acquire a detailed understanding of, for example, sociopolitical systems and how they impact on the lives of various members of society (e.g. how many live on, or below, the poverty line and with what social consequences; the extent and nature of labour market discrimination suffered by members of minority ethnic groups and women). And they may also need to develop competence in a range of interventions to use this enhanced understanding as a positive force for change. Finally, focusing on the interventions required for effective multicultural practice, individuals may, for example, need to be aware of, and able to, work within minority community networks (beliefs and attitudes). They may also need to understand the potential cultural bias and impact of assessment instruments (understanding). Lastly, they may need to develop competence across a wide range of verbal and non-verbal responses (skills).

Methods for becoming multiculturally competent

While this provides a framework for identifying self-development needs, the question remains – how can these particular competencies be developed for practice? A theme in the multicultural literature is the need for change in practitioners in order that they become 'multiculturally skilled' and so transcend differences. Such change implicates training and continuing professional development, including support and supervision. Whatever the type of support and supervision that is available to personal advisors and youth support workers, it provides an ideal opportunity to develop multicultural competence. Particular dimensions of differences that may be giving rise to concern or presenting particular practical challenges can be identified and methods that may address these issues identified and agreed. D'Ardenne and Daniels (1991) identify four developmental stages for multicultural competence relevant to the support and supervisory relationship. These are:

- the 'culturally entrenched' stage, where little discussion related to the needs of minority groups is encouraged and core conditions of counselling such as genuineness, empathy and respect are regarded as sufficient to allow practitioners to transcend differences;
- the 'cross-cultural awakening' stage where cultural differences are acknowledged, but where the focus is (implicitly or explicitly) on between-group similarities and emphasis is given to developing empathy and positive regard;
- the 'cultural integrity' stage where various types of self-development activities are fully integrated into provision; and finally
- the 'infusion' stage where multicultural counselling goals are embedded into all elements of support and supervision. Where this stage is reached, multicultural issues would assume a prime focus, with, for example, resources to support relevant training needs automatically available.

The ideal is to shift the support and supervisory relationship along this continuum towards the 'infusion' stage.

The following three sections highlight one method for each of self-awareness, understanding and interventions, which should assist with this process.

Self-awareness

Many writers have stressed the need to embark on a continual process of multicultural self-awareness. A three-staged approach that focuses first on the individual, then second, shifts the focus from the individual to society, and then third, beyond the individual and society to 'worldview' values, is one way of addressing this development need. The approach both increases an individual's awareness of the extent to which personal value systems reflect the dominant system of societal values and their awareness of alternative value systems. The first task is to think about yourself; the second to identify the values of the dominant culture in which you practise counselling or communication; and the third task is to examine alternative value orientations. Various exercises and schema have been developed to assist with this type of critical self-examination (Bimrose 1998). One example of a practical exercise designed to help with the first stage of the process, (that is, an individual's exploration of cultural, broadly defined, origins and values), is provided by Locke (1992). He suggests that individuals work through the following questions:

- What is my cultural heritage? What was the culture of my parents and my grandparents? With what cultural group(s) do I identify?
- What is the cultural relevance of my name?

- What values, beliefs, opinions and attitudes do I hold that are consistent with the dominant culture? Which are inconsistent? How did I learn these?
- How did I decide to become a counsellor? What cultural standards were involved in the process? What do I understand to be the relationship between culture and counselling?
- What unique abilities, aspirations, expectations, and limitations do I have that might influence my relations with culturally diverse individuals?

(2)

If you are then able to compare your answers to some or all of these questions with others, then the effectiveness of the learning process is likely to be increased. All the questions have value, though in training I have found the second question to have most impact, perhaps because it highlights the extent to which the cultural conventions surrounding the naming system of the dominant society tend to be taken for granted by acculturated members of that society. It illustrates the ways in which naming systems differ, and how, for example, they can define and reinforce gender hierarchies.

Understanding

Increased multicultural awareness needs to be complemented by more in-depth understanding of client difference. Various methods can be used and various exercises have been designed to help with this (Flores and Heppner 2002; Pederson 1994; Ponterotto *et al.* 1995). Pederson (1994), for example, identifies some practical methods for developing understanding of difference, as follows:

- *Volunteering*: for work in an agency dealing with persons culturally (broadly defined) different from yourself. Select an agency or organization with which you are unfamiliar. Keep a journal on your observations.
- *Resource person*: invite people from populations generally unfamiliar to you (and your group) to join you as a 'resource person'. There should be one 'resource person' for about every five participants. Meet with this person in small groups to discuss the meaning and function of 'counselling' as seen in that person's setting.
- *Review publications*: refer to relevant counselling and professional practice issues in specialist journals and examine the description of research samples in empirical articles. Record the extent to which the sample's culture has been reported and what difference it might make to the research's conclusions if 'difference' had been accounted for more comprehensively.

- *Daily journal*: keep a written daily journal identifying insights regarding your own identity, assumptions, and culturally influenced behaviours. Look for patterns in your own behaviour that relate to culturally learned expectations and values. Try to identify where you learned those cultural expectations and values.

Interventions

In addition to working towards a greater cultural self-awareness and developing understanding of different aspects of diversity, personal advisers and youth support workers wishing to become multiculturally competent need to think about the way in which their skills and strategies need to be adapted or changed to enhance their effectiveness. And, once again, this is transferable to supervision practice. Nonverbal communication represents one useful focus, since it has been suggested that culturally appropriate nonverbal behaviour is crucial to successful counselling outcomes (Ivey 1994, Ivey *et al.* 1997, Singelis and Pederson 1997). Singelis adopts the definition of nonverbal communication as 'communication without words' (1994: 274). He cites research that suggests that up to 93 per cent of the social meaning of a message is carried via nonverbal channels. This includes how we look, how we move, how we sound and how we smell. Touching, eye contact and the use of space and time are also facets of nonverbal communication. Although words themselves are not a part of nonverbal communication, the other aspects of speaking such as tone, loudness and speed are an important part. Even doing nothing can carry meaning when interpreted by another person. Similarly, Ivey (1994) advocates that all practitioners: 'begin a lifetime of study of nonverbal communication patterns and their variations' (75). Various categories of nonverbal behaviour are identified and some cultural implications for each category are discussed:

- *Eye contact*: cultural differences abound regarding the use of eye contact during communication. For example, direct eye contact is considered a sign of interest in European/North American middle-class cultures. Some cultural groups, however, (e.g. American Indian, Inuit or Aboriginal Australian groups) generally avoid eye contact, especially when talking about serious subjects.
- *Body Language*: a comfortable conversational distance for the British and North Americans is approximately an arm's length, but many Hispanic people often prefer half that distance and those from the Middle East prefer to stand even closer.
- *Time*: while Europeans and North Americans have a highly structured, linear view of time, various South American and African countries operate on a more casual view of time.

(Ivey 1994: 29)

One way of demonstrating the importance of developing a comprehensive repertoire of nonverbal skills is by using a short and simple roleplay with a friend or trusted colleague. Select various combinations of the dimensions of nonverbal communication outlined above. Try to demonstrate effective listening without using the nonverbal behaviour that you would normally use in your counselling or communication. For example, if you normally try to sustain eye contact, you could communicate with someone without eye contact. Or you could sit either closer or farther away from someone with whom you are communicating than is your custom. Try doing both. How did this make you feel? Ask the other person how they felt. Is it possible to adopt different styles of nonverbal communication and still listen effectively?

So, where sexual preference, for example, had emerged as a central issue in the relationship between a practitioner and their client, the multicultural competency framework could be used within the support and supervision relationship to focus on this issue. Specifically, it could be used to: identify appropriate self-awareness training that would help achieve a more accurate and/or detailed understanding of sexual preference; acquire background knowledge of relevant legislation together with research evidence relating to the consequences of this dimension of inequality (e.g. bullying, employment discrimination); and develop strategies and techniques that might enhance practice with this client group.

Critiques of multicultural competence

Although multicultural counselling now has a strong following, it is not without its critics. For example, Ridley *et al.* (1994) question whether increased multicultural awareness will automatically improve the quality of counselling. They argue that there is no clear definition of the concept and that measurement techniques are underdeveloped. Their contention is that 'these flaws are fatal because they hamper application of the construct, destroying its usefulness for multicultural counselling, training and research' (125).

Other critiques relate to the potentially diluting effect of multiculturalism as an approach that embraces too many social differences. For example, Helms (1994: 162) argues that

> whereas multiculturalism may be a useful construct for encouraging discussion about matters of culture in society in general, it is virtually useless as a scientific construct. In particular, the lack of specificity about which aspects of individual diversity are appropriately subsumed under the rubric of multiculturalism has contributed to considerable confusion in theory, research, and practice.

If this dilution is to be halted, more rigour must be applied in the use of cultural – in particular racial – constructs.

Another weakness relates to the neglect of the client perspective. Pope-Davis *et al.* (2001) argue that a preoccupation with the need for counsellors to become culturally competent within the research literature has resulted in scant attention being paid to clients' views. They identify the importance of examining and integrating the clients' preferences and expectations as well as criticizing the adequacy of current evidence underpinning multicultural competence.

It is not, therefore, appropriate for personal advisers and youth support workers to embrace – uncritically – a multicultural approach to support and supervision, though a thoughtful, considered and structured approach to diversity within this relationship could only be regarded as a positive development.

Conclusion

Within helping relationships, it had been generally accepted that practitioners selected the theoretical approach with which they felt most comfortable (e.g. humanistic, behavioural, psychodynamic) to guide their practice, and that this approach was then applicable to all their clients. The development of a multicultural approach to practice has challenged this conventional wisdom by emphasizing how everyone exists within a social, political, economic and historical context and how this impacts on individuals differently. The adoption of a multicultural approach to support and supervision for personal advisers and youth support workers requires that the (often negative) impacts of diversity on clients are confronted and dealt with. An ongoing commitment to personal and professional development is required as well as the need for multicultural competence to be defined as integral to ethical practice. This applies both to the supervisor and supervisee relationship, and to the client and practitioner relationship. The need for practitioners to commit to long-term personal and professional development in this area, highlights the need for supervisors to model good practice by developing and maintaining an awareness of their own cultural identities, their understanding of the consequences of these identities, together with the ability to use relevant skills and strategies creatively. This has the potential not only to enhance the quality of the process of support and supervision for personal advisers and youth support workers, but also to improve the quality of helping services to young people offered by their organization.

Bibliography

Allison, K.W., Crawford, I., Echemendia, R., Robinson, L. and Knepp, D. (1994) 'Human diversity and professional competence: training in clinical and counselling psychology revisited', *American Psychologist*, 49 (9): 792–796.
American Psychological Association (2002) 'Guidelines on multicultural education, training, research, practice, and organizational change for psychologists',

American Psychological Association (online). Available: www.apa.org/pi/multiculturalguidelines.pdf (accessed 27 October 2004).

Andrea, M. and Daniels, J. (2001) *Respectful Counselling*, Pacific Grove, CA: Brooks/Cole.

Andrea, M., Daniels, J. and Heck, R. (1992) 'Evaluating the impact of multi-cultural counselling training', *Journal of Counseling and Development*, 70: 143–150.

Arredondo, P. (1998) 'Integrating multicultural counselling competencies and universal helping conditions in culture-specific contexts', *Counselling Psychologist*, 26: 592–601.

Bernard, J.M. and Goodyear, R.K. (1991) *The Fundamentals of Clinical Supervision*, New York: Allyn and Bacon.

Bimrose, J. (1993) 'Counselling and social context', in R. Bayne and P. Nicolson (eds) *Counselling and Psychology for Health Professionals*, London: Chapman and Hall.

—— (1998) 'Increasing multicultural competence', in R. Bayne, P. Nicolson, and I. Horton (eds) *Counselling and Communication Skills for Medical and Health Practitioners*, Leicester: BPS.

—— and Wilden, S. (1994) 'Supervision in careers guidance: empowerment or control'? *British Journal of Guidance and Counselling*, 22 (3): 373–383.

—— Bimrose, J. and Bayne, R. (1995) 'The multicultural framework in counsellor training', *British Journal of Guidance and Counselling*, 23, (2): 259–265.

d'Ardenne, M. and Daniels, J. (1991) 'Exploring the different levels of multi-cultural counselling training in counsellor education', *Journal of Counselling and Development,* 70, Sept./Oct.: 78–85.

Ekstein, R. and Wallerstein, R.W. (1972) *The Teaching and Learning of Psychotherapy*, New York: International Universities Press.

Flores, L.Y. and Heppner, M.J. (2002) 'Multicultural career counseling: ten essentials for training', *Journal of Career Development*, 28 (3): 181–202.

Helms, J.E. (1994) 'How multiculturalism obscures racial factors in the therapy process: comment on Ridley *et al.* (1994), Sodowsky *et al.* (1994), Ottavi *et al.* (1994), and Thompson *et al.* (1994)', *Journal of Counselling Psychology*, 41, (2): 162–165.

Ivey, A.E. (1994) *Intentional Interviewing and Counseling: Facilitating Client Development in a Multicultural Society*, 3rd edn, California: Brooks Cole Publishing.

—— Ivey, M.B. and Simek-Morgan, L. (1993) *Counseling and Psychotherapy: a Multicultural Perspective*, 3rd edn, Boston, MA: Allyn and Bacon.

——, —— and —— (1997) *Counseling and Psychotherapy: A Multicultural Perspective*, 4th edn, Boston, MA: Allyn and Bacon.

Lago, C. and Thompson, J. (1996) *Race, Culture and Counselling*, Buckingham: Open University Press.

Leong, F.T.L., Wagner, N.S. and Tata, S.P. (1995) 'Racial and ethnic variations in help-seeking attitudes', in J.G. Ponterotto, J.M. Casas, L.A. Suzuki and C.M. Alexander (eds) *Handbook of Multicultural Counseling*, Thousand Oaks, CA: Sage.

Locke, D.C. (1992) *Increasing Multicultural Understanding: a Comprehensive Model*, Newbury Park, CA: Sage.

Pedersen, P.B. (1991) 'Multiculturalism as a generic approach to counselling', *Journal of Counselling and Development*, 70 (1): 6–12.

—— (1994) 'Multicultural Counseling', in R.W. Brislin and T. Yoshida (eds) *Improving Intercultural Interactions: Modules for Cross-cultural Training Programs,* Thousand Oaks, CA: Sage.

Pine, G.J. (1972) 'Counselling minority groups: a review of the literature', *Counselling and Values*, 17: 35–44.

Ponterotto, J.G., Casas, J.M., Suzuki, L.A. and Alexander, C.M. (1995) (eds) *Handbook of Multicultural Counseling,* Thousand Oaks, CA: Sage.

Pope-Davis, D., Liu, W.M., Toporek, R.L. and Britain-Powell, C.S. (2001) 'What's missing from multicultural competency research: review, introspection and recommendations', *Cultural Diversity and Ethnic Minority Psychology*, 7 (2): 121–138.

Ridley, C.R. (1995) *Overcoming Unintentional Racism in Counseling and Therapy: a Practitioner's Guide to Intentional Intervention,* Thousand Oaks, CA: Sage.

——, Mendoza, D.W., Kanitz, B.E., Angermeiier, L. and Zenk, R. (1994) 'Cultural sensitivity in multicultural counselling: a perceptual schema model, *Journal of Counseling Psychology* 41, 2: 125–135.

Singelis, R. (1994) 'Nonverbal communication in intercultural interactions', in R.W. Brislin and T. Yoshida (eds) *Improving Intercultural Interactions: Modules for Cross-Cultural Training Programs.* Thousand Oaks, CA: Sage.

Singelis, T.M. and Pedersen, P. (1997) 'Conflict and mediation across cultures', in K. Cushner and R.W. Brislin (eds) *Improving Intercultural Interactions: Modules for Cross-cultural Training Programs, Vol. 2,* Thousand Oaks, CA: Sage.

Sue, D.W. (1999) *Counselling the Culturally Different: Theory and Practice,* 3rd edn, New York: John Wiley & Sons.

—— and Sue, D. (1990) *Counselling the Culturally Different: Theory and Practice,* New York: Wiley.

——, Bernier, J., Durran, M., Feinbrerg, L., Pederson, P., Smith, E. and Vasquez-Nuttall, E. (1982) Position paper: 'Cross-cultural counselling competencies', *Counseling Psychologist*, 10: 45–52.

——, Arrendondon, P. and McDavis, R.J. (1995) 'Multicultural counseling competencies and standards: a call to the profession', in J.G. Ponterotto, J.M. Casas, L.A. Suzuki and C.M. Alexander (eds) *Handbook of Multicultural Counseling,* Thousand Oaks, CA: Sage.

——, Ivey, A.I. and Pederson, P.B. (1996) *A Theory of Multicultural Counseling and Therapy,* Pacific Grove, CA: Brooks/Cole.

Thompson, N. (1993) *Anti-Discriminatory Practice,* London: Macmillan.

—— (1995) *Theory and Practice in Health and Social Welfare,* Buckingham: Open University Press.

Wrenn, C.G. (1962) 'The culturally-encapsulated counsellor', *Harvard Educational Review*, 32: 444–449.

—— (1985) 'The culturally encapsulated counsellor revisited', in P. Pedersen (ed.) *Handbook of Cross-cultural Counselling and Therapy,* Westport, CT: Greenwood.

7   The intensive support worker

Bringing a range of difficult issues to supervision

Miche Tetley

Introduction

The professional life of an intensive support worker working with young people is never dull. Every young person is unique and brings with them their own set of issues, demands and dramas, which we, as their workers, take on board and respond to as best we can. For a practitioner, this can be enormously exciting and rewarding when the hard work pays off and a young person makes some kind of personal breakthrough. The flipside, of course, is that the work can be challenging, demanding and often frustrating, causing personal stress for the worker and, in extreme cases, leading to burnout.

This chapter is written from a personal perspective and I will make the case that supervision is a key component of a healthy, integrated, professional practice, that it is 'a necessity and not a luxury' (Reid and Nix 2001: 40). I will suggest that it should be integrated thoughtfully into the structure of every organization that seeks to provide intensive support to young people.

Why is good supervision essential for the intensive support worker?

In January 2003, I started work for an inner-city Connexions partnership, as a Connexions Personal Adviser (the background to the Connexions service is examined in Chapter 1). I came to Connexions, having completed part of a training programme in humanistic and integrative psychotherapy, looking to employ the skills I had already learned, while working in my spare time to complete the training.

The literature (CSNU 2002: 53–55) describes Connexions as a 'young person-centred approach', where the service is designed to meet individual need by keeping young people at the heart of any process of change involving them. It seemed to me that the key to achieving success with this approach was to develop relationships with young people that are based on trust. In this, I could see a direct correlation between the ethos of Connexions and the Rogerian person-centred approach (Rogers 1951), which formed the basis of my counselling training. This is what attracted me initially to the Connexions service.

Coming from the world of counselling and psychotherapy, I have taken it for granted that supervision will be an integral part of my professional life. The British Association of Counselling and Psychotherapy states in its criteria for accreditation that a counsellor or psychotherapist must have:

> An agreed formal arrangement for counselling supervision, as understood by BACP, of a minimum of one and a half hours monthly on the applicant's work, and a commitment to continue this for the period of the accreditation.
>
> (BACP 2005)

In other words, having regular supervision is regarded as essential if you wish to achieve accreditation as a practising counsellor or therapist.

Over and above our professional roles, we are, of course, human beings influenced by our own social context. As practitioners, we must accept that we have beliefs, attitudes, expectations and patterns of behaviour, which will impact on our therapeutic relationships and practices. If we are to maintain a good standard of practice as professionals, we must have space to look at and deal with our own issues as they pertain to our work. Having another experienced practitioner to discuss these issues with, to offer another perspective and to support us emotionally, is an invaluable asset in maintaining professional standards in practice.

The advice and guidance work I do now is different in certain respects from counselling and psychotherapy, but also seems to share some fundamental similarities. For example, in describing the relationships personal advisers strive to make with young people, Westergaard says:

> These relationships are open, genuine and non-judgemental.... Personal Advisers are describing, and adhering to, the core Rogerian conditions which form the basis of person-centred counselling relationships (Rogers 1951). The activity of counselling *does* underpin the work.
>
> (2003: 245)

Within my practice as an intensive support worker, although I am not working as a counsellor, I am using therapeutic techniques such as cognitive behavioural methods, Gestalt roleplay work and others when it is appropriate. Because of the open and non-judgemental nature of the relationship between support worker and young person, clients will sometimes divulge extremely distressing information, which we, as workers, have to hold and deal with appropriately in the moment of disclosure and then address accordingly on a practical level.

It is essential that intensive support workers maintain a level of professionalism in this environment. Thus, it follows that they also have a responsibility to address their own issues, as a counsellor would, in order to ensure they are practising in an ethical and responsible manner. Supervision, in youth support work, as in counselling and psychotherapy, must be seen as essential.

And intensive support work *is* intense! Supervision is an opportunity to step back from the frontline and evaluate ourselves and our actions from a different perspective. Evidence from a survey suggests that professionals are over three times less likely to take time off because of stress if they are receiving regular support and supervision (Hulbert 2000). It is reasonable to expect that if workers are satisfied and supported, then clients will receive a better service and organizations are ultimately more likely to meet their targets. Thinking in these terms suggests that incorporating supervision into the managerial structure of an organization will ultimately lead to that agency functioning in a more efficient and productive manner.

Those of us who are employed within agencies and organizations, know that the work with our clients comprises only a part of our actual workload. The added demands and stresses of paperwork, targets, service inspections, inter-agency working, training, poor resources, lack of funding and bureaucracy cannot be underestimated. From my perspective, much of my day-to-day struggle is how to balance the responsibilities towards my clients, with the demands of the organizations I work for and with. As professionals we work continuously to address the requirements of our clients. But from the humanistic perspective, all people have needs, and that includes professionals themselves. It is difficult therefore, for an intensive support worker to successfully meet the demands of their clients if, within their own professional lives, their own needs are not being met.

According to Maslow's (1970) hierarchy of needs, in order for a person to proceed to higher forms of learning and development, it is necessary that their more basic requirements are met. Physiological demands must be attended to first, followed by the need to feel secure and safe, then to have a sense of belonging, before progressing to the desire for self-expression and eventually self-fulfilment. This is as true for the professional as it is for the client. I will discuss this further in the chapter, with reference to the necessity of dealing in supervision with issues to do with lone working and health and safety, among others.

So, I've argued that supervision should be an integral part of the professional life of an intensive support worker. But what form of supervision do I receive personally and just how does that supervision support, enable and protect me as a professional working with young people?

In terms of the functions of supervision, most researchers describe a tripartite approach. For example, Inskipp and Proctor, in describing counselling supervision, identify the three main tasks as:

- The *normative* task – the shared responsibility of supervisor and counsellor for monitoring the standards and ethical practice of the counsellor.
- The *formative* task – shared responsibility for the counsellor's development in skill, knowledge and understanding.
- The *restorative* task – the provision of space, or the chance to explore opportunities elsewhere, for discharging held emotions and recharging energies, ideals and creativity.

(1993: 6)

In the rest of this chapter, making reference to the above definition, I intend to discuss the different forms of support I receive; namely managerial supervision, caseload supervision and informal peer networking, and also my choice to continue in ongoing psychotherapy. I will evaluate these modes of support and their usefulness to my working practice by discussing specific issues that I have processed in each arena, thus providing a working example of supervision-in-action.

Managerial supervision

In terms of Inskipp and Proctor's definition (1993), my managerial supervision fulfils mainly the 'normative' task, although it has elements of the other functions. I see my line manager every four to six weeks for a two-hour session during which we discuss the progress of my work within the Connexions context, any management directives which affect my working practice, management information issues, organisational strategy and issues to do with my placement in a host agency.

This type of supervision has a 'management control' (Woods 2001: 27) function and is necessary from an organizational point of view, to ensure that each youth support worker is working within clearly delineated boundaries, thus providing consistency and continuity of service delivery. It also has a particular function for the worker. From a personal perspective, managerial supervision is an important vehicle through which I can raise awareness of my own needs within the work context. In accordance with Maslow's theory (1970), if our physical working conditions are poor, if we feel unsafe in the place we work or feel isolated as a lone worker, this may interfere with our professional capabilities, and therefore these issues must be addressed for us to feel empowered to perform the more cerebral aspects of our work.

One of the first issues I took to my managerial supervision, soon after being engaged by the partnership, was that my host agency was not providing me with caseload supervision. Being inexperienced in my role and with a growing caseload, I was beginning to feel insecure and indecisive and, although my managerial supervision was addressing one level of need for me, I felt I needed a different kind of focused support to complement this. Woods suggests that, 'If the worker is feeling "tentative and inadequate" they may be reluctant to make themselves more "vulnerable" to the line manager' (2001: 29). This was certainly my experience, especially as I was in a six months probationary period and wanted to prove myself to be a competent and capable worker.

After much debate, it was agreed that I would see another, more experienced intensive support worker every two to three weeks for caseload supervision. This arrangement has proved to be very successful, as I will describe later, and has now been adopted by the Connexions partnership as their preferred mode of delivery of caseload supervision, through the creation of 'team leader' posts. For my part, I have gone from feeling unsafe and afraid of my inexperience, to feeling secure, nurtured and appropriately supported and have found that my confidence in my own practice has grown as a result.

Although I am not suggesting that this kind of arrangement will suit all intensive support workers, there are definite advantages in having two different, but sometimes overlapping forms of supervision. The most obvious, of course, is the opportunity to discuss my relationship with the other supervisor if need be. On the one hand it is helpful to be able to utilize the power and authority of the line manager in effecting certain types of change, while, on the other hand, it feels safe to discuss mistakes and express vulnerability with someone who is a fellow practitioner. Keeping the two separate allows each relationship to be utilized to its full potential, reducing the possibility of a conflict of interest.

That said, what constitutes 'good supervision' is often contested. Weaks (2002) identifies three 'core conditions' for the establishment of an effective supervisory relationship: equality, safety and challenge. One of the features of good supervision should be that it takes into account the unique needs of each practitioner. This relates to the assertion of McNeill and Worthen (1996) who suggest that having 'a sense of being validated and affirmed' is a crucial aspect of the supervisory relationship for the supervisee.

A recurring theme through my own working life has been how to manage my work in the face of recurring migraine headaches, which can significantly interfere with my capacity to carry out tasks effectively. Earlier this year, I took a number of days off due to migraines. During supervision, my manager asked me about the cause of the headaches. She wanted to check whether they were in some way work-related. After some consideration, I saw a pattern I had not considered before: the glare and flicker from computer VDUs and strip lighting are often triggers for my migraine attacks. Added to this, I had been allocated a desk next to the door between the office and the youth club and had to endure the door bumping into my chair and, sometimes, my back, as people passed through it while the youth club was in session. The door was often left open behind me, letting in all the noises of the youth club. I was finding it hard to concentrate on paperwork and to make crucial and sometimes sensitive phone calls. I felt stressed by my working environment and this was increasing the frequency of my migraines.

After discussion with my manager, action was subsequently taken to fix the door and provide me with suitable glasses that reduced the glare. My stress levels have since decreased, as have the number of migraines. Without the process of supervision, this situation might not have been resolved and, potentially, may have resulted in 'burnout' due to physiological stress.

We can see from these working examples, managerial supervision can provide the intensive support worker with much needed back-up and support on a range of issues. It overlaps with caseload supervision in some respects, but also provides a qualitatively different type of support due to the power and authority of the manager. If used appropriately, this authority can be useful in child protection situations, resolving conflicts with colleagues, challenging non-delivery of service to young people from partner agencies, communicating frontline information back up the management chain and highlighting gaps in provision to be dealt with at a strategic level.

Ultimately, with this kind of support, I feel valued and empowered as a worker, which in turn enables me to value and empower young people. I am also able to ensure that my practice is up-to-date in terms of the Connexions strategy and requirements, and that I continue to work within organizational and ethical boundaries.

Caseload supervision

Caseload supervision is essential to, and inseparable from, my practice as an intensive support worker. For example, in my first job after university, as an assistant psychologist working with people with learning disabilities, we were coached to become acutely aware of our stress levels and their impact on our practice. The rationale was that chronic stress can cause normally ethical, caring and responsible practitioners to become neglectful, insensitive and sometimes abusive to those in their care, despite all good intentions to the contrary. With this awareness and with the current focus on improving practice around Child Protection, organizations cannot afford to have their workers practising in isolation, without recourse to appropriate mechanisms to deal with the stresses and strains inherent in intensive support work.

I would assert that without appropriate caseload supervision, I could not be confident with the integrity of my practice and my ability to uphold clear, ethical standards on a day-to-day basis. If I did not have access to caseload supervision, I simply would not continue in this type of work.

Happily, however, I am satisfied with the level of caseload support I receive in my present post. This constitutes two hours of supervision every three weeks from a more experienced intensive support worker, the content of which focuses mainly on issues to do with giving advice, guidance and information, caseload management, allocation of referrals, dissemination of work-related techniques and skills, emotional support and prioritization of workload. We discuss each of my cases individually, reviewing what progress has been made and addressing any issues arising in terms of my practice.

Thus, my caseload supervision relates mostly to the 'formative' and 'restorative' tasks (Inskipp and Proctor 1993): 'formative' in the sense that, over time, I have learned new skills, techniques and methods which inform my work with young people, allowing me to feel more experienced and confident as a practitioner, and 'restorative' in that I have someone to 'offload' to, both on a day-to-day basis by phone if necessary, and face-to-face every three weeks.

What are the features of this relationship that make it work for me? As with my relationships with clients, the supervisory relationship also centres on the core Rogerian conditions of empathy, congruence and unconditional positive regard (Rogers 1951). These provide a strong foundation for our working relationship, engendering mutual respect for each other's experiences and perspectives, and facilitating a safe space in which to explore and challenge elements of my practice. We share an explicit appreciation of each other's commitment to integrity, ethical standards and clearly delineated boundaries and this, in turn, encourages an environment in which my mistakes can be explored. Within this relationship, I experience challenge as a positive intervention rather than a critical attack.

Most of all, despite the difference in our level of experience, I feel a sense of equality in the relationship, which allows me to feel secure: my supervisor and I share similar job roles and she can understand what my day-to-day working life is like. Knowing she is available prevents me from succumbing to the feelings of isolation commonly experienced by lone workers. This in turn fulfils the need for a sense of belonging, as postulated by Maslow (1970). Through her, I am connected to the ethos of the larger organization. I can then concentrate on developing my practice along lines that meet my professional need for self-expression and self-fulfilment.

But exactly how does her support and expertise enhance my own professionalism? The first priority in this line of work is to identify child protection issues and ensure that they are dealt with appropriately. This is often one of the hardest situations a professional will face. First, we must hear and hold the information the young person is divulging and then respond sensitively and clearly, within particular boundaries set out by child protection procedures. We may have to consider breaking confidentiality, which can jeopardize our relationship with the young person, and this is a decision that is not to be taken lightly. We may often have to make judgements based on partial or confusing information, in situations open to different interpretations. And in some cases, workers may face hostility from the young person, their friends or family. Having recourse to a second opinion makes a supervisor an invaluable asset in these circumstances.

Let's consider, for example, the case of 'Anna'. Anna was 16 and studying for exams when she referred herself to me. She was living at home with her mother and sister, 'Rachel', who was ten. Anna's mother worked full time and was putting Anna under pressure to take on many of the responsibilities within the house. Anna felt angry and resentful: she was struggling to manage competing responsibilities at home and school and to find time to have fun with her friends.

Anna's parents separated when Anna was seven. She remembered her father being aggressive towards her mother and has vivid memories of seeing him attacking her. She was furious with her father and also very scared of him, but was expected to visit him and his family every second weekend with her sister. She wanted to stop going, but felt protective of Rachel following an incident about a year ago when her father left Rachel at home on her own one evening, returning late with a friend who, allegedly, hit her. At the time, Anna's mother talked to her father about the incident and threatened to stop Rachel visiting. Although Rachel was also fearful of her father, she loved him too and was very upset by this threat.

Anna then disclosed the following: the previous weekend, Rachel had seen her father snorting white powder in the living room. His response had been to tell her to keep what happens on weekends 'secret'. Rachel had told Anna, but asked her not to tell their mother because she was scared the mother would stop her visiting. However, Anna said she decided to tell their mother secretly. Apparently, her response had been, 'It's his business what he does.' Anna felt unhappy about the situation but got agitated when I suggested I might have to act on the information in some way. She said, 'I don't want you to tell anyone because Dad will kill us.'

And so I found myself in a dilemma. Was this indeed a Child Protection issue? Should I break confidentiality, and if so, whom should I tell? Should I consider speaking to Anna's mother directly or involve Social Services? And would outside involvement increase the risk to Anna and her sister by provoking her father? I was aware that this was a difficult situation that required careful handling. I was also aware that, by breaking confidentiality, I could potentially destroy an excellent relationship that I had built up over time with Anna. And yet, what were my responsibilities within the boundaries of my role as an intensive support worker? As per the Connexions' child protection procedure, I called my supervisor.

First, it was a relief to have someone experienced with whom to discuss the situation and share the responsibility. It can be reassuring to take direction from a person in authority, not least because it gives the option in situations of conflict to say 'I am acting on the direction of my supervisor.'

She advised me that I did indeed have a duty to break confidentiality and pass on the information to Social Services, even if this meant a breakdown in my relationship with Anna. I voiced my concerns that this could seriously disrupt all of Anna's family. We discussed the concept of 'keeping secrets' within families, which can allow abuse to thrive and continue. As professionals, she reminded me, we have a duty to act on our professional judgement for the sake of children, even if that means disruption to the families involved. She also suggested that perhaps I should speak diplomatically with Anna's mother about the referral, so she would have an opportunity to voice her concerns.

I rang Anna and told her I would need to make a referral to Social Services. She was very upset and scared, but not angry with me. In fact, she felt very angry with her parents for the action they took in the situation. She passed the phone to her aunt, who was hostile towards me to begin with, but who calmed down somewhat when I explained that I was 'acting on the direction of my supervisor' and that I had Anna and her sisters' interests at heart. After some discussion, she admitted that she was relieved that there might be some changes made in the family way of life and that she had concerns but did not know how to voice them.

Following my supervisor's advice, I also spoke with Anna's mother before I faxed the referral to Social Services. She was very angry both with me and with Anna. She demanded a meeting between the three of us the next morning. Again I consulted my supervisor and discussed the possible ramifications of this. We agreed that it could be very productive, if handled appropriately and she gave me more advice on how to accomplish this.

The meeting was indeed productive. By then, Social Services had decided that they would rather discuss more suitable access arrangements and boundaries with Anna's mother, than intervene with her father. Without his address, they were unable to take it further and neither Anna's mother nor Anna were prepared to give them that information. During the meeting, my main role was to advocate for Anna in her decision to disclose. Her mother did eventually admit that Anna had been put in an incredibly difficult position. She agreed to renegotiate the access arrangements for Rachel, so that she could see her father safely.

I continued to work with Anna on issues to do with her self-esteem and confidence. When we conducted her assessment review six months later she reported that her situation at home had improved significantly and she was feeling much more safe and secure. She thanked me for breaking confidentiality and said she felt I had 'handled the situation great'. I could not have wished for more praise than that.

For my part, the support and advice of my supervisor was invaluable throughout the process. The advice she gave me, the boundaries she set for me, and her conviction that I had the skills to manage the issue, all combined to provide me with a firm basis from which to operate. Without that support, I still might have performed well, but her involvement sealed my conviction that I was operating ethically and professionally. This ultimately increased my confidence in securing an appropriate outcome for Anna and her family.

This is just one working example of how caseload supervision provides me with a sound foundation from which to approach difficult issues within my work. Every working day brings new situations to explore, new issues to untangle, fresh approaches to uncover. For example, I have explored how to work in sensitive and respectful ways with young people born and raised in Britain, whose parents were raised elsewhere, leaving the young people feeling torn between two, sometimes conflicting, cultural identities. I have learned a variety of engagement techniques in order to work with a young person whose family has a history of social and educational disengagement. Losing contact with a vulnerable, homeless client who was suffering with a seriously debilitating agoraphobia, I was able to process my distress and realize that I did the best I could for her. I have worked through these and many more issues within the arena of caseload supervision. In all of these situations, caseload supervision has provided me with a forum in which to scrutinize closely my methods, opinions and responses. Ultimately, because of caseload supervision, I consider myself to be a better practitioner.

Informal peer networking

I use the term 'informal peer networking' to describe, collectively, the opportunities to share practice with peers; I consider this an invaluable source of support for the intensive support worker. As I have already discussed, intensive support workers are often based as lone workers in host agencies and therefore do not work alongside other colleagues on a day-to-day basis. In this environment, it has become part of 'support worker culture' to seek each other out as often as we are able, to phone each other regularly and to meet up when possible. These opportunities arise at collective training events, union meetings, on courses and in formal meetings with the chief executive. In my team, we meet for an hour every two weeks before our full team meeting and then have lunch afterwards.

Although it is not directly akin to formal supervision in its structure, informal peer networking fulfils all three functions of supervision (Inskipp and Proctor 1993): 'normative' in that we are able to agree methods of working that conform to the Connexion's agenda and compare our experiences of putting strategies into practice; 'formative' in picking up tips and techniques from each other in terms of the way we work with young people or, for example, identifying common training needs in the team, and 'restorative' in providing empathic and emotional support at times of stress and the chance to share experiences in an appropriate forum.

From my experience, this is an invaluable source of support in my working life. On a fundamental level, it satisfies a kind of 'tribal' instinct in me – to be with others who are 'like me'. Reid (2004: 50) states that,

'A consequence of the fragmentation of discrete youth services is that professionals can feel isolated and de-skilled'. In citing Jordan (2001), Reid suggests

> the diversity of personnel involved can lead to an absence of collective identities, organisations and purpose. A structured system of support and supervision could help to enhance a sense of working proficiently, however small the achievements in terms of outcomes, when working with the 'harder-to-help'. Being reflective about learning, it also has the potential to restore a sense of professional identity.
>
> (2004: 50)

Ultimately, meeting with my co-workers brings me back to the 'roots' of my practice, my fundamental desire to improve the lives of individual young people. In other words, meeting with them is good for my morale.

Ongoing psychotherapy

It may seem strange that I would choose to include here a discussion on such a personal element of my life. I have found that the boundary between professional and personal experience can blur, and it is useful to have an arena in which I can discuss this boundary in more depth. For some practitioners, supervision can address these issues – indeed it is the 'restorative' function to do just that. In my case, neither my manager nor my caseload supervisor is trained in psychotherapy and, being aware of my own professional background, I choose to process certain issues with a professional trained in psychotherapeutic techniques. However, this is a personal choice, and we need to be clear that supervision is not counselling and, for some practitioners, counselling in addition to supervision may not be welcome.

The following case study will hopefully illustrate how personal psychotherapy has supported me to manage aspects of work in a more productive manner.

'Jensen' was 19-years-old and attended the youth project where I work. He was smoking a considerable amount of 'skunk weed' (very strong cannabis) every day and was in and out of trouble with the police, for minor driving infringements and confrontational behaviour. He would come to the youth project out of normal session hours and, when asked by staff to return later at the appropriate time, would become angry. After several incidents, he was banned from the club altogether.

I was concerned about my own behaviour towards him. I was aware that, if I was dealing with him in these confrontational moments, the situation would escalate much quicker than if another member of staff was involved. I felt that in some way, my behaviour was exacerbating his oppositional attitude instead of helping to diffuse confrontations. Taking the situation to therapy, I quickly became aware of what was happening: Jensen looked like and acted like someone from my past, a person who was also a heavy cannabis smoker and aggressive in his manner. I was transferring my residual fear and anger towards that person, into the present situation. In looking at my own behaviour, I realized I was being aggressive and confrontational towards Jensen, to hide this fear.

Once I was aware of this transference, I was able to work with a therapist on the underlying unresolved issues, derived from my past experience. I looked at and developed more appropriate responses to Jensen, ones that would hopefully diffuse, rather than exacerbate the situation. Although Jensen's underlying issues did not change, my response to him did. I no longer felt as fearful and angry towards him and could engage with him in a level and diplomatic way. Consequently, he and I have had fewer disagreements.

As outlined above, I am not necessarily advocating psychotherapy for every intensive support worker – it has been a very personal decision for me. There is no doubt in my mind, however, that I have become significantly more effective as a practitioner because of the therapeutic input into my work life.

My Connexions partnership has now provided an 'employee assistance scheme', which is on offer to employees of the partnership through a contract arranged with an outside provider. Through this, intensive support workers can access one-to-one counselling sessions by telephone and arrange up to five face-to-face sessions, if required. This service promises to be a valuable additional source of personal and professional support. By using the employee assistance scheme to discharge and process difficult issues in a confidential and impartial environment, employees may be enabled to provide an enhanced quality of service to young people.

Conclusion

The scope of this chapter does not extend to include a variety of viewpoints on the benefits of supervision. However, in the course of my work, I do come into contact with a range of professionals who work with young people: youth workers, teachers, learning mentors and counsellors. In my experience, those who do not receive adequate supervision describe feelings of fear, inadequacy, confusion and often anger. They report feeling unappreciated by their parent organization and are often concerned about their ability to perform their duties in a safe and professional way. In contrast, those who feel well-supported, generally are happier and more secure and seem to struggle less with feelings of low morale within the work place.

Organizations that strive to deliver an excellent service to meet the needs of young people, cannot afford, ethically and financially, to ignore the support needs of their workers. To do so, would be to risk compromising the ability of those workers to provide that excellent service and could even lead to the worker harming, rather than helping, young people in their care, albeit unwittingly.

With the recent high-profile coverage in the press of child protection 'failures', intensive support workers are more aware than ever of their responsibilities towards young people. But we cannot do it alone. Simply put: if good supervision meets our needs and protects and supports us as workers, we are in a much better position to meet the needs of our young people and protect them effectively from significant harm.

Bibliography

British Association for Counselling and Psychotherapy (2005) *BACP Counsellor/ Psychotherapist Accreditation Scheme: Criteria for Application*, www.bacp.co.uk (accessed 2 January 2005).

Connexions Service National Unit (2002) *Understanding Connexions – Module Handbook, Part 2*, Sheffield: Connexions Service National Unit.

Hulbert, S. (2000) *Working with Socially Excluded and 'At Risk' Young People: Research into the Need for, and Appropriate Form of, Support and Supervision for Personal Advisers Working within the New Connexions Support Service*, Stourbridge: Institute of Career Guidance.

Inskipp, F. and Proctor, B. (1993) *Making the Most of Supervision (Part 1)*, Twickenham, Middlesex: Cascade Publications.

Jordan, B. (2001) 'Tough love: social work, social exclusion and the third way', *British Journal of Social Work*, 31: 527–546.

McNeill, B.W. and Worthen, V. (1996) 'A phenomenological investigation of "good" supervision events', *Journal of Counselling Psychology*, 43: 25–34.

Maslow, A.H. (1970) *Motivation and Personality*, 2nd edn, New York: Harper and Row.

Reid, H.L. (2004) 'Jiminy Cricket on my shoulder: professional common sense and formal supervision as routes to ethical watchfulness for personal advisers', in H.L. Reid and J. Bimrose (eds) *Constructing the Future: Reflection on Practice*, Stourbridge: Institute of Career Guidance.

Reid, H.L. and Nix, C. (2001) 'Support and supervision for guidance practitioners in a personal adviser role', in A. Edwards (ed.) *Supporting Personal Advisers in Connexions: Perspectives on Supervision and Mentoring from Allied Professions*, Occasional Papers Canterbury: Canterbury Christ Church University College.

Rogers, C. (1951) *Client-centred Therapy*, London: Constable.

Weaks, D. (2002) 'Unlocking the secrets of "good supervision": a phenomeno-logical exploration of experienced counsellors' perceptions of good supervision', *Counselling and Psychotherapy Research* 2 (1): 33–39.

Westergaard, J. (2003) 'Counselling and the PA role – are these connected?' *British Journal of Guidance and Counselling*, 31 (2): 241–250.

Woods, J. (2001) 'Supervision from an informal education/youth work perspective', in A. Edwards (ed.) *Supporting Personal Advisers in Connexions: Perspectives on Supervision and Mentoring from Allied Professions*, Occasional Papers Canterbury: Canterbury Christ Church University College.

8 Developing a meaningful relationship

A conversation about supervision from the supervisor's perspective

Stephen Harrison and Jane Westergaard

Introduction

The purpose of this chapter is to examine the activity of supervision from the supervisor's perspective. Initially it will explore how supervision can be understood in its widest sense, later focusing upon more specific concerns as the practice of supervision relates to the working context. Themes that are central to the chapter are the importance of developing a supervisory relationship, and the issues that are raised when attempting to establish an effective working alliance between supervisor and supervisee, Feaviour *et al.* (2002), Hawkins and Shohet (2000), Mearns (1991), Sawdon and Sawdon (1995), Stoltenberg and Delworth (1987). In addition, the chapter will investigate the role that the concept of 'care' plays as a guiding principle for supervisory practice, and the supervisory relationship, in the field of youth support work.

The chapter will also focus upon a range of issues underpinning effective supervision, and will attempt to illustrate some of the challenges faced by those with supervisory responsibilities, who are undertaking to build effective and supportive relationships with youth support workers. The perspective offered is one informed by the authors' experiences of providing supervision in both managerial and non-managerial contexts to youth support workers over the past decade. It is further informed by conversations with supervisors and trainee supervisors working across a spectrum of settings.

The chapter will examine the impact of the supervisor's understanding, disposition and abilities for realizing the potential for development present in supervision. It will emphasize the importance of establishing clarity of expectations about what supervision is, between supervisor and supervisee, and will seek to address some common areas of uncertainty or concern about supervision from the supervisor's perspective.

There exists within the literature a wide range of views on supervision from the viewpoint of the supervisor. Classic texts concerned with supervision in youth work include Tash (1967), who, in her study of the role of supervision in the initial training of youth and community workers, emphasized the importance it played in supporting the development of workers by enabling them to understand and meet their own needs. Christian and Kitto continued this theme stating; 'The supervisor's job is not to advise or to instruct, but to enable the worker to think better about his or her work, and therefore to work better' (1987: 2). A number of authors have contributed to this debate and they are discussed in other chapters in this book.

To facilitate an examination of supervision from the supervisor's viewpoint, various aspects of supervision will be explored in a 'dialogue'. This dialogue, or conversation, takes place between two supervisors – one who is an experienced supervisor and the other who is relatively new to the role. The conversation could also represent the internal dialogue of a supervisor engaged in a 'self-supervision' exercise. Extracts from the conversations will, it is hoped, provide a useful introduction and insight into some key issues in supervision viewed from a supervisor's perspective.

What do we mean by supervision?

Experienced Supervisor (ES):   What would you like to focus on today?
New Supervisor (NS):   I would like to start by thinking about what the
    activity of 'supervision' actually means to me.
ES: That's fine. A good start. Where would you like to begin?
NS: It's the term 'supervision' that I find problematic. I'm not sure what
    it actually means in the context of my work as a supervisor of youth
    support workers.
ES: This is often the case for those who are new to the role of super-
    visor. The word 'supervision' has a number of connotations ranging
    from the supportive to the punitive. It's important to establish exactly
    what is meant by supervision in the context of your work with youth
    support practitioners.

The term 'supervision' is difficult because it can have a wide application and interpretation according to the context in which it is used. An established means of defining a word such as 'supervision' is to look to the etymological roots of the word. This leads us to understand supervision in terms of 'super' – meaning 'above' – and 'vision' – meaning 'sight' or 'seeing' – hence the definition 'overseeing' applies (Woods 2001: 251). However, the process of attempting to define a term in its most literal sense may not always be helpful, as a stark definition rarely reflects the diversity of its application, or may identify specific, sometimes inappropriate, cultural connotations.

In reality, supervision is a term that can only be fully understood as it relates to broader social or organizational functions. Likewise supervisors do not occupy an isolated role; rather, the role of supervisor exists within a wider set of roles and responsibilities. Therefore to understand supervision in its broadest terms, we have to ask questions about the functions it is seeking to perform, the ends to which it is oriented and the values which underpin the methods deployed in achieving its goals, (as discussed in Chapter 2 of this book).

Supervision then, is a term that is loaded, depending upon the values ascribed to it by the user in any given context. The term supervision itself does not point to an activity that demonstrates inherent values. Supervision is a practice that can be deployed to serve a range of differing and competing ends. Furthermore the ends themselves can, in turn, have a bearing on the way supervision is practised. The term supervision appears to have concepts such as surveillance and control built into it. Surveillance and control are not necessarily bad things; however, questions have to be asked about what organizations are, and, in turn supervisors are surveying and seeking to control, and why. For example:

NS: I have found, in my early sessions with my supervisees, that I've had some difficulty in being clear with them about exactly what it is that our supervision sessions set out to achieve.

ES: Let me clarify what you are saying here. If I understand you correctly, you're implying that supervision cannot be clearly understood without reference to the context within which it is practised and the ends it sets out to achieve. Can you give me an example of the difficulty you're facing?

NS: Yes, sure. I'm a supervisor for a youth support worker who I also line-manage. It seems to me that the way I approach these sessions is different to my supervision sessions with colleagues for whom I don't have line-management responsibility. I guess that what this suggests to me is that the term 'supervision' can mean different things, depending on the context in which it is happening. Thinking about it, any existing relationship between the supervisor and supervisee will have an impact on the supervisory relationship too.

ES: Yes, this is a common concern for supervisors. It might be helpful then, to consider what any supervisory relationship, regardless of whether the supervisor is a line-manager or not, should set out to achieve.

Inskipp and Proctor (1993) view supervision as a confidential working relationship that works towards enhancing the competence of the supervisee in order to increase their ability to help clients. It could be argued that Inskipp and Proctor are identifying an aspiration rather than a definition (an aspiration with which all supervisors should concur, but one that nonetheless involves considerable work to achieve). Furthermore the translation of this aspiration into the reality of an effective supervisory relationship will be dependent on a number of factors, such as the skills the supervisor has to develop to engage with the work, any existing relationship with the supervisee, and the supervisor's knowledge and under-standing of supervisory frameworks. One of the most influential factors will be the supervisor's own previous experiences of being supervised.

Supervision as an aspect of daily life

What then are the expectations of those who are new to supervision likely to be based on? Supervision, in its broadest definition of being 'watched over', is an aspect of daily life from the cradle to the grave. The type and quality of supervision received will have a bearing on how new super-visory relationships are perceived and formed. Supervision as part of daily life performs a regulative function. Supervision in this sense can be related to two modes, 'watching over' and 'watching out for'.

Supervision as 'watching over', is characterized by constant surveillance and can be linked to a desire to regulate and control behaviour and actions. In the case of a small child who is learning to handle a sharp or pointed implement for the first time, close supervision is necessary and the supervisor would understandably be expected to watch over the process to ensure that the child comes to no harm. However, if this approach were to continue as the child developed and grew, their sense of judge-ment, competence and self-reliance would be stifled. At some point then, the supervisor exercises a judgement as to the competence of the child, and as trust is built, the supervisor retreats to a new position of 'watching out for'.

Within the 'watching out for' mode, the supervisor demonstrates an ongoing interest in, and care for, the child's development, without con-tinually imposing themselves or interfering in the situation. Their interest and care is demonstrated by enquiries into how things are proceeding at given points in time. This, of course, is not a universal experience of supervision in childhood activities. Some children receive limited, poor or no supervision, being left largely to their own devices and running the risk of being exposed to significant harm. Others are watched or fussed over constantly, with the result that exposure to any sort of risk is minimized at every turn, and the child does not have the opportunity to learn how to assess and manage difficult situations. It is this 'watching out for' mode that supervision in the context of youth support work most closely resembles.

Supervision performs a further function in our everyday lives as a process for checking that rules are being adhered to. A common scene on a housing estate some decades ago, would be the presence of a sign stating 'No Ball Games', usually placed upon walls that would provide ideal goal-mouth substitutes in the absence of adequate recreational facilities. The sign gazed down menacingly, containing the implicit threat of punishment should it be transgressed. Of course, it does not take long to learn that if there is nobody watching over the enforcement of the order, then would-be transgressors might happily continue to play ball games in these prohibited areas. Times have changed however, and now the 'CCTV cameras in operation' sign has become ubiquitous. No longer do the 'No Ball Games' warnings emit just a veiled threat. Now the gaze of the CCTV camera cannot be averted and transgressors take the risk of being caught and punished.

Supervision in this sense is about surveillance, and making and obeying rules. An understanding of the term supervision in this light, can have the effect of establishing a culture which implies 'do as you are told and you need not worry', and, if taken a step further, could suggest that if you have caught the attention of the 'supervisor', then you must have been doing something wrong. This culture can have an impact on the way in which people entering into supervision (either as supervisees or supervisors) may be disposed to it, irrespective of its intended purpose (Feltham 2002). It is therefore the responsibility of the supervisor to exercise care in the way in which they introduce and mediate the experience for their supervisees. For example:

NS: My feeling is that I would like my supervisory practice to be so much more than a means to oversee the work of my supervisees. However, I'm not really clear about what it does, or should involve, apart from monitoring their practice. If they are also coming with their own pre-conceived ideas about the control connotation of supervision, this can make building an effective supervisory relationship problematic.

ES: You're right. However, experienced supervisors from counselling and social work have attempted to define a broad set of functions of supervision, which include the monitoring of practice, but also identify other key areas to which an effective supervisor should attend. It's helpful for new supervisors to familiarize themselves with these functions. A good starting point is the work of Kadushin or Inskipp and Proctor.

Establishing a relationship in supervision

Kadushin (1992), in his study of supervision within social work in the USA, undertook an analysis of the activity, ascribing three main functions to the practice. He identified these as administrative (managerial), educational and supportive. Inskipp and Proctor (1993) use slightly different terminology to describe what are effectively the same three functions. They talk about the normative, formative and restorative functions of supervision. Leaving aside any critique of the functions themselves (this can be found in other chapters in this book), this chapter will now consider how these functions shape the supervisory experience.

When administrative (managerial) concerns underpin the purpose of supervision, other issues are less likely to be addressed, and the same will apply if supportive or educational functions dominate. Furthermore, the context and conditions within which supervision is taking place, and the assumptions about the competence of supervisor and supervisee, will have a bearing upon the prevailing purpose. In the main, within services for young people, supervision is likely to take place within a managerial context (the prevalence of non-managerial supervision or consultant supervision tends to be the exception rather than the rule).

NS: I can understand when my supervisees are not people whom I line-manage, that my role is to help them to develop and to support them emotionally. But with these supervisees, I'm less sure about my responsibility to the management function. Conversely, as I said earlier, my problem with the supervisees whom I line-manage, is that I pay too much attention to the management function and not enough to the other functions. I find it hard to get the balance right.

ES: You are not alone. It is almost as though you are identifying that there may be a dominant function which might be a reflection of a number of factors.

NS: Yes, and those factors could include the historical and current organizational context or my own thoughts, feelings and role, and those of my supervisee. All have an impact on the supervisory relationship.

ES: You are right, of course. But I would suggest that it is possible to establish a relationship with your supervisees that addresses all the key functions, regardless of whether you are a line manager or not. It is challenging. But it is possible.

If supervision is capable of performing a range of functions as Kadushin and others suggest, then the supervisor has to take time to reflect on any existing relationship they have with their supervisee (e.g. line manager), and should consider the ways in which they can establish their role in a different context (as a supervisor). Making explicit the nature of the supervisory relationship, determining the focus of supervision and ensuring that adequate opportunity is provided to cover a range of issues, are all challenges that every supervisor must face. How supervisors and supervisees are disposed to the task of supervision will have a key role to play, in terms of the culture that becomes established within the supervisory relationship.

In simple terms this applies to the supervisor's preferences in terms of their supervisory practice (i.e. how comfortable they feel in the role), taking into account the impact of other work roles they may have. More specifically though, attention must also be paid to their attitudes, values, and beliefs, their knowledge and skills, and how these come to bear upon the supervisory relationship. For example, in the case of a line-manager supervisor, it is likely that a certain degree of success may be achieved in supervision with respect to administrative and managerial tasks. Given that the primary concern of the manager is met, there may appear to be no real incentive for change, particularly in the absence of a strong challenge to the norms that have been established.

NS: What would you suggest I do to redress the balance of functions when I am both a supervisor and a line manager?

ES: It is important that the issue is raised and discussed with your supervisee and that the nature of the relationship is made explicit. If this does not happen it is likely that you will both make assumptions about your role, risking settling into familiar line-manager and worker territory.

Two main options present themselves to supervisors who may feel that they have administrative or managerial issues as their primary concern within supervision, and are struggling to find a way of establishing a supervisory relationship which allows for all functions to be addressed. The first option is to make provision for occasional non-managerial supervision through the use of consultant supervisors (someone external to the organization, or an experienced colleague who does not have line-management responsibility for the supervisee). This can be a straightforward and pragmatic way of dealing with the issue – funds allowing. However this option is not without its disadvantages. The line manager is then taken out of a very important loop in terms of exploring and examining practice alongside their workers. This will mean a missed opportunity to develop and support supervisees. The second option is to create the conditions for supervision to be a place where a balance can be struck between the needs of the organization, the manager, the supervisee and clients. Considering the intended outcomes of supervision can create these conditions. Bettelheim and Rosenfeld (1993), when referring to the client/therapist relationship suggested 'the end is in the beginning'. With regard to supervision, this suggests that the success of any relationship is determined from the outset. However, this does not simply 'happen' by chance. The supervisor will need to work hard to establish the relationship. Feaviour *et al.* (2002) have developed a model that tracks the course of the developing supervisory relationship. The model has five distinct stages:

- preparing for supervision;
- establishing the supervisory relationship;
- developing the supervisory relationship;
- the working alliance;
- ending the supervisory relationship.

Emphasis is given to the features of each stage, and the first three stages focus in depth on ensuring that the conditions are right for an effective working alliance between supervisor and supervisee, regardless of the role of the supervisor (i.e. line manager, non line manager).

Practicalities and boundaries in supervision

Moving on, the most important aspect in striking an appropriate balance of functions within supervision is dependent on the clarification of expectations. This is best achieved in an open manner in discussions between supervisor and supervisee. It should also be underwritten by a formal agreement supported by the organization. This process is often referred to as 'contracting'. Hawkins and Shohet have reviewed a number of approaches to contracting and have proposed five key areas that a contract should cover:

- practicalities;
- boundaries;
- working alliance;
- the session format;
- the organisational and professional context.

(2000: 54)

Back to our dialogue:

NS: OK, so the key to building a good, shared understanding of supervision is all about being transparent, and also about ensuring that both parties have 'bought in' to the process. That's helpful. Another thing that I struggle with is the practicalities of supervision. Where, for example should the sessions take place and how often should they happen?

ES: You are right to raise this, as the practical element is very important for the process of supervision.

Hawkins and Shohet explore the area of practicalities to a limited extent stating, 'it is necessary to be clear about the practical arrangements such as time, frequency and place, what might be allowed to interrupt or postpone the session' (2000: 54). However, it is important to investigate some practical issues here a little further, as they are linked to other areas of consideration such as professional boundaries and power. The environment for, and frequency of, supervision needs to be considered carefully. The setting chosen for supervision can reflect the value being placed upon it. Supervision undertaken within a busy open-plan office implicitly demonstrates a lack of care for confidentiality. The supervisory 'space' should be free from distraction and interruptions. It is important to note that the advance of communication technology may have an impact on the youth support worker's expectations about their supervisor's availability. The advent of the mobile phone has represented a paradigm shift in this area. However, just because supervisors are, in theory, contactable at any time, does not necessarily mean that they are available; in much the same way that the youth support worker is not always available to their clients. Therefore, consideration about practicalities also involves considerations of boundaries such as confidentiality, privacy and respect for the other and the process.

NS: So, is there an ideal setting for supervision?

ES: I do not want to suggest that there is an 'ideal' setting for supervision, as I am sure my ideal would not be practical or achievable because of a wide variety of circumstances. Rather, it is important to be attentive to the process of identifying an appropriate or adequate space where supervision can be undertaken; one that is conducive to the process of supervision and where the needs of the supervisor and supervisee are considered. So, for example, if you are a line manager as well as a supervisor, you should be aware of the importance of ensuring that the supervision sessions take place in a 'neutral' space, not in your office, in order to establish a more equal environment.

NS: And linked to the importance of getting the practicalities right early on, where does the issue of boundary setting arise? I'm aware, particularly in my dual role as line manager and supervisor, that I need to establish some boundaries in supervision.

ES: Of course. It's important to ensure that you are both clear about what the limits of your relationship are. However, this will be a familiar concept to youth support workers who have to ensure that they discuss issues of boundaries and confidentiality with their clients. This aspect of supervision is often referred to as the parallel process, where what happens within supervision mirrors, to a large extent, the relationship between youth support worker and client.

Inappropriate and heavy-handed boundary setting in the early stages of a relationship can result in a desperately rigid and prescriptive list of do's and don'ts. It is important to recognize that boundary setting is a process with two distinct stages. The first stage is about developing a sound foundation for the work to ensure a relationship characterized by mutual trust and respect. The second stage in boundary setting is an ongoing process of review and negotiation. It is no good establishing a whole set of boundaries that look good initially, but subsequently limit the potential for exploration of the work.

Focus of the work

NS: So, once the boundaries have been discussed and a contract agreed, what then? I'm not quite sure who sets the agenda for the session. Is it me, or my supervisee?

ES: Again, we can think about the parallel process between you and your supervisee and the youth support worker and their clients. Who sets the agenda in the client work?

In the early stages of the supervisory relationship it is important to discuss whose needs are to be met through supervision and how this might happen. When working with supervisors in training there is often a commonly held belief that the supervisee's needs or agenda are paramount within supervision. While this is, to some extent, an accurate perspective, it can mask the nature of competing demands and needs within supervision. To return to the functions of supervision, as part of the managerial or normative function, the supervisor may need to monitor work, check that best practice is being adhered to and ensure that targets are being met. This may not always appear to the supervisee as something that is meeting their needs in relation to the work that they are doing with clients: nevertheless, it is part of the function of supervision.

Within any supervisory relationship there will be different needs or agendas, relating to the supervisee, the organization, the supervisor and the client. Both supervisor and supervisee need to be aware of how these, at times competing, needs will be recognized and responded to and who will take responsibility for this. One of the main issues facing supervisors who provide supervision within a managerial context, is the extent to which supervision can be used to encompass too wide a range of managerial functions. Therefore if supervision is to realize its potential within a managerial context, clear boundaries as to the purpose of any given supervisory session need to be established, understood and respected. Having said this, the focus of most supervision sessions is likely to be determined, overall, by the supervisee. The supervisor will enable their supervisee to share any issues or concerns with their work (as well as any positive aspects of practice) and will encourage the supervisee to consider alternative strategies and approaches for working with clients. Only the supervisee will know what the key issues are in their work, and it is therefore imperative that the supervisor is skilled enough to enable the supervisee to bring to supervision what may, in some cases, be challenging and complex aspects of practice. Supervisors must be able to approach their supervisee 'holistically': this means attending to the whole person and every aspect of their communication. If this is done effectively, then the supportive and developmental functions of supervision will be met alongside the managerial.

Having all the answers

NS: I understand now the importance of keeping the focus on the supervisee and their needs, but what about if I don't feel that I have the 'answers' and can't make things right?

ES: Most supervisors would identify that not being able to 'make things right' is the hardest thing in supervision. Think about the parallel process again. Is it the role of youth support workers to have all the answers for their clients?

The purpose of supervision is, like the relationship between youth support worker and client, all about building a relationship of trust, and offering a supportive environment that is conducive to exploring issues and working towards strategies and solutions. Entering into a supervisory relationship can be difficult and this difficulty does not necessarily diminish with time. Within supervisory relationships, irrespective of their context or perceived function, it is essential to recognize that we are not simply acting upon objects but interacting with people. Therefore, one of the key virtues a supervisory relationship must have is the capability to demonstrate 'care'. Care can be understood as a principle that guides human action. While writers have discussed the potential supervision has for developing the worker, it is care for the work and for those that benefit from it, as well as those that carry it out, that underpins the humane dimension of the supervisory relationship.

Supervision presents the key opportunity to provide a space to attend to and care for the practitioner and their practice. Care is also linked to another guiding principle: respect. This is understood in terms of its attachments, or in relation to what is being respected, such as the worker's ownership of their practice and their capacities, and, in turn, the rights of the client. It is important to note that in the field of services to young people, supervision is a developing practice, unlike other areas of practice, such as counselling (BAC 1987), which has an established code for supervision. However, it is the responsibility of the supervisor to help supervisees to identify issues in their practice, to consider approaches to their work and to evaluate alternative strategies as appropriate. It is not the role of the supervisor to provide all the answers, in the same way as youth support workers do not take on this responsibility with their clients.

NS: It's helpful to know that I don't have to have all the answers! However, there will be times when my supervisee is looking for clear guidance around issues of child protection, for example.

ES: Yes, and this is an area about which you have a responsibility to give clear guidance.

Supervisors of youth support workers have a duty of care to clients as well as to their supervisees. This will involve them in taking responsibility for investigating key legal and ethical issues such as child protection and confidentiality (see Chapter 12 of this book). Supervisors may need to seek guidance from their organization (or from the organization to which the supervisee belongs, if different from their own) so that they can provide clear and accurate information and guidance in the case of legal or ethical issues. A supervisor who fails to familiarize themselves with the finer detail of the law and other key protocols such as information sharing, is not fulfilling a duty of care to their supervisee or to the young people with whom the supervisee is working.

Conclusion

NS: Our conversation has been useful in encouraging me to focus on some of the challenges I face as a supervisor. However, I still feel that I risk not being 'good enough' to undertake the work. Particularly with youth support workers who are bringing very challenging, and sometimes disturbing cases to supervision.

ES: Yes, but remember what I said earlier. Not being 'good enough' is a common anxiety for many supervisors – even those who are experienced. The challenge is to continue to support your supervisees through the difficulties they are facing, while at the same time acknowledging that their work is hard and that solutions aren't always easily found. If you have established a meaningful relationship with your supervisee, in which you are genuine, empathic and non-judgemental, you are providing the foundations for an effective relationship. Do not underestimate the power of being 'listened to'. Supervisees, like all of us, will value the fact that someone is taking time to listen to them and to understand the challenges they face in their work. I'm not suggesting that listening in itself is sufficient, but it will certainly go a long way to establishing a good working relationship.

It would be impossible to address every aspect of supervision from a supervisor's perspective and this chapter has certainly not attempted this task. What it has provided is the opportunity for the reader to be party to a dialogue around the key issues in supervision, which will face all supervisors. It has focused in particular on the establishment of an effective supervisory relationship, and the factors that will help or hinder this process. The development of this relationship and adhering to the core conditions of a person-centred approach (Rogers 1951), regardless of whether the supervisor is a line manager or not, is central to effective supervision. In addition, this chapter has addressed issues that are particularly pertinent to supervisors of youth support workers, such as the need to be familiar with legislation pertaining to children's rights.

As the development of a range of youth support roles, including personal advisers, learning mentors, teaching assistants and others, is relatively new, the need to identify individuals who can provide adequate support for these practitioners is key. Appropriate training for new supervisors is paramount, coupled with the need for a body of literature that sets out to support those who are undertaking this demanding role. Drawing on the experiences of those who are already undertaking the supervision of youth support workers, is another activity that is central to the promotion of effective supervisory practice. This chapter offers the opportunity for those who are new to the role (as well as more experienced practitioners), to draw on the knowledge of those who are already practising as supervisors in the field of youth support work.

Bibliography

Bettelheim, B. and Rosenfeld, A. (1993) *The Art of the Obvious*, London: Thames and Hudson.

British Association for Counselling (1987) *How Much Supervision Should You Have?* Rugby: BAC.

Christian, C. and Kitto, J. (1987) *The Theory and Practice of Supervision*, London: YMCA George Williams College.

Feaviour, K., Trelfa, J. and Watkins, K. (2002) *Connexions Training Materials, Supervision Course*, Moorfoot, Sheffield: DfES.

Feltham, C. (2002) 'Supervision: a surveillance culture?' *Counselling and Psychotherapy Journal*, February 2002: 26–27.

Hawkins, P. and Shohet, R. (2000) *Supervision in the Helping Professions*, 2nd edn, Milton Keynes: Open University Press.

Inskipp, F. and Proctor, B. (1993) *The Art, Crafts and Task of Counselling Supervision, Part 1. Making the Most of Supervisors*, Twickenham: Cascade Publications.

Kadushin, A. (1992) *Supervision in Social Work*, 3rd edn, New York: Columbia University Press.

Mearns, D. (1991) 'On being a supervisor', in W. Dryden and B. Thorne (eds) *Training and Supervision for Counselling in Action*, London: Sage.

Rogers, C. (1951) *Client Centred Therapy*, London: Constable.

Sawdon, C. and Sawdon, D. (1995) 'The supervision partnership: a whole greater than the sum of its parts', in J. Pritchard (ed.) *Good Practice in Supervision*, London: Jessica Kingsley.

Stoltenberg, C.D. and Delworth, U. (1987) *Supervising Counsellors and Therapists*, San Francisco, CA: Jossey Bass.

Tash, J. (1967) *Supervision in Youth Work*, London: YMCA George Williams College.

Woods, J. (2001) 'Using supervision for professional development', in L.D. Richardson and M. Wolfe (eds) *Principles and Practice of Informal Education*, London: RoutledgeFalmer.

9 The organizational perspective
Considering issues of providing support and supervision to practitioners working with young people

Ros Garrod-Mason and Jane Westergaard

Introduction

Engaging with young people and supporting them through the difficulties and challenges they face in their lives, can be demanding work. Those who embark on a career that involves 'actively engaging young people' by offering them in-depth support and guidance, will have received training to provide them with the necessary skills and knowledge to undertake this role effectively. As part of this training (whatever the specific specialism, be it youth work, social work or careers work) practitioners will have received ongoing support in various forms. Many trainees are assigned a 'supervisor' while undergoing professional training. This supervisor may be a course tutor, a peer or learning mentor, or a work-based supervisor within an organizational context. It is likely that the trainee is supported by a range of professionals who are able to contribute to the education, development and welfare of a colleague in training. It is widely recognized then, that there is a need to support individuals through their professional training and, perhaps, continue this formal support into a probationary work period. This chapter however, focuses on what happens once practitioners have completed their training. What are the issues that organizations need to consider to ensure that their employees continue to be supported in their role once initial training has ended?

In some professional contexts, the need for support and supervision as an integral part of ongoing practice has been recognized. Woods (2001: 27) writing from a youth work perspective argues succinctly for the case for continued support and supervision for youth workers, 'it is recognised that in order for professionals, working in these emotionally charged areas to function effectively, they need to have good support'.

Bucknall, commenting on supervision in social work, states:

> In contemporary social work there is an expectation that all social workers will be supervised. Successive child protection enquiries have

stressed the need for social workers to be supervised with a view to ensuring the quality of risk assessment and the associated decisions for children.

(Bucknall 2001: 8)

Counsellors too, as a requirement to practice, receive supervision as recommended by the British Association of Counselling (BAC 1987). However, there are significant numbers of youth support workers, once qualified, for whom supervision has not been recognized, understood or valued by employers. The Careers Service in the United Kingdom is a good example of an organization that, until recently, has not engaged in a formal process of supervision for staff beyond the period of initial training. Bimrose and Wilden (1994) have argued the case for continuous support and supervision for careers advisers. This argument was largely unheard and careers advisers, in the past, continued to undertake in-depth work with young people, often without receiving appropriate levels of support. Finally, it seems, the point has been made. The case for supervision for youth support workers with a specialism in careers guidance, has now been addressed. The Institute of Career Guidance has produced a positional statement on support and supervision for career guidance that states:

Practitioners and their managers should be encouraged to search for new perspectives, develop different professional responses, keep up to date with and contribute to research and reflect on various aspects of work continuously. Support and supervision are recognised mechanisms for achieving these goals.

(ICG 2004: 1)

Clearly, the task of setting up an appropriate mechanism for supporting staff can appear daunting to employers with little or no previous experience or understanding of supervision. If, as may be the case for any service or agency working with young people, there has been no acknowledged commitment to supervision, there is much to consider. For example, what is supervision? Who should receive supervision? Who should give supervision?

This chapter will explore these questions and will set out to offer some clarity (if not answers) on the organizational perspective when considering issues of providing support and supervision to practitioners working with young people.

The organizational context

When setting up supervision within a multi-agency organization (or indeed, within any organization for which supervision is a new concept), three key factors should be taken into account:

- the nature of the interagency partnership organizations, and the influence this will have on supervision structures;
- what is understood by supervision;
- what the organization wants to achieve through supervision.

A helpful example of an interagency organization that has considered these issues is the Connexions service in England. As the Connexions service was developed and a number of agencies offering support to young people (including the careers service, youth service, social services and the voluntary sector) were brought together, the issue of supervision of staff began to emerge. Some of these agencies had a strong tradition and commitment to supervision (the youth service, for example), while others did not (the careers service). In 2001 a Department for Education and Skills' (DfES) funded research project into support and supervision, was carried out by the newly formed Humber Connexions partnership (Garrod-Mason 2001). This set out to identify and evaluate a range of appropriate modes of delivery for the support and supervision of practitioners working in the Connexions service, or any other multi-agency group. The findings of this research project form the basis of this chapter.

Any organization made up of a partnership of different agencies working together, determined either through a contract or by a partnership agreement, will need to recognize the philosophy and values of the models of supervision already adopted by the partner organizations. Agreeing a definition for supervision and identifying what the organization would like it to achieve are the starting points for any multi-agency organization or, indeed, any employer who is considering setting up a system to support staff. The DfES, in their requirements and guidance for the Connexions service, advocate that 'all practitioners have both line management and effective supervision and support' (DfES 2003). However, the document does not provide a definition as to what this 'effective supervision and support' might mean. The first task for any organization planning to set up a system for supporting staff is to clarify what is understood by supervision.

What is supervision?

There are many definitions of supervision and, unfortunately, little agreement that actually captures the essence of what it encompasses. Hughes and Pengelly offer a helpful introduction:

> Staff supervision is a means of developing and controlling the quality of service, taking account of the needs and rights of users and the quality of staff performance. The needs and rights of staff must also be attended to, in order to get the best from them as the major resource of the organisation.
>
> (1997: 6)

In an early attempt at defining supervision through consultation with staff, Connexions Humber found that youth support workers and managers believed it to be a 'two-pronged process'. The aim of this process, it was felt, was to strike a balance between ensuring that youth support workers are enabled to provide a high quality and effective service to young people, and that the organization takes seriously its responsibilities to give appropriate support to those who undertake this work. Feaviour *et al.* confirm the importance of this two-pronged process in their working definition of supervision:

> A super-vision of practice is achieved through the alliance between the supervisor and the supervisee. The quality of this 'vision' is dependent on the willingness and ability to share and examine and develop the skills, capabilities and qualities as practitioners in order to promote and protect quality services.
>
> (2002: 7)

The strength of this definition is in its recognition of the quality of the relationship between the supervisor and the supervisee. From the employer's perspective, this may be determined by their relative roles within the organization, which leads to the question of where to position supervision within the organization and how far it should be independent of the management function. This issue will be explored later in the chapter.

The culture of the organization

In addition to considering who in the organization (or outside of it) is best placed to undertake the role of supervisor, employers should also reflect on the culture of the organization, in particular its approach and commitment to supporting staff. Hawkins and Shohet explore this in some detail:

> Supervision best flourishes in a learning development culture. Such a culture is built on a belief system that a great deal of the work in all helping professions is about creating the environment and relationships in which clients learn about themselves and their environment, in a way that leaves them with more options than they arrived with.
>
> (2000: 176)

It is necessary then for every organization to examine what they want to achieve in their work with young people, before they can decide how to support their staff in meeting these organizational aims. The Connexions service, for example, was charged with ensuring that young people would play an integrated part in the policy-making and design of its services.

While developing a Young People's Charter for Connexions Humber, the young people consulted were clear about what they wanted it to include. Written in to the document is the statement: 'allow young people a voice, listen, negotiate and actually share power, not just talk about it' (Youth Board of Connexions Humber 2002: 1). This implies that the organization should be willing to listen and learn from the views of the young people it is trying to serve, thereby establishing itself as a 'learning organization'. This concept was developed by Senge *et al.* (1994) who claim that managers alone are not responsible for 'fixing' problems. Instead all members of an organization should be involved in the decision-making process, thus encouraging the development of a learning organization.

Youth support workers, like the young people they are working to serve, have much to contribute to the design and development of good quality services within the organization. Their employers, therefore, need to have the means and will to listen to the voice of front line staff and to take into account their views when considering the most appropriate means of supervision to implement. If the organization believes that youth support workers and young people have valuable things to say, this will impact on the quality of the supervision process. Brown and Bourne argue the case that, 'both the supervisor and supervisee will be profoundly affected in how they interact with one another and what they discuss, by the policy and culture of their agency' (1996: 12).

Where does supervision fit within the culture and ethos of the organization? The rationale, values and principles behind any organization's supervision policy will reflect the values and principles of the organization itself. As a starting point for organizations it is crucial that there is a clear sense of striving to operate as a learning organization, taking account of and valuing the needs and views of clients and staff alike.

What do organizations want to achieve by supervision?

Brown and Bourne describe the aim of supervision thus, 'to enable the supervisee(s) to carry out their work, as stated in their job specification, as effectively as possible' (1996: 9).

One of the important functions of supervision is indeed for employers to ensure appropriate quality assurance. Inskipp and Proctor (1993) identify this as the normative function. Youth support workers work with, what Senge (1990) describes as, the 'messiness' of human interactions. This can involve dealing with difficult situations, managing the ethics and values inherent within these situations, being supportive to young people, challenging systems that are failing and working with supportive and unsupportive families. Workers need help to do this effectively, a place to reflect on what they did well, what they did less well and to consider how they would deal with similar situations when repeated in the future. The quality assurance aspect of supervision needs to be aligned with, and complementary to, the quality assurance systems already in place within the organization. Youth support workers need guidance and help on the principles and legalities of their practice, and their effectiveness as agents of the organization that they work for.

The supervision pilot project at Connexions Humber identified this 'normative' function as one which youth support workers valued. Key responses identified by supervisees in the evaluation of the project, were that supervision offered:

- a way of making sure you have explored all the answers;
- a time to be able to ask questions without being judged;
- a way of checking back that what you have done is okay, as we have a high degree of autonomy;
- a way of giving direction within the policy and procedures of the company.

Certainly these youth support workers were emphasizing the importance of 'time out' to focus on reflection and evaluation of the quality and consistency of their work. In addition, supervision offers the means by which supervisors (and, in turn, employers) can focus on standards of practice to ensure that young people are kept safe. This process aims to develop autonomous professionals, who are involved in the business of making judgements and decisions about their professional practice from an informed and supported position.

A further notable outcome of the supervision process is that the organization can begin to establish an evidence base for practice. By gathering evidence of 'what works' through discussions in supervision, youth support workers will be encouraged to reflect on the approaches and methods that they have adopted with their clients. Supervision should offer the opportunity to reflect on and build a repertoire of alternative strategies for practice. These strategies can be disseminated across the organization to enable other practitioners to develop their own work. The supervisors will also be building up a store of knowledge of effective approaches to practice across a range of issues that youth support workers face in their work. The best practice identified through supervision can be taken forward and shared at a higher level with partner agencies within the organization.

Effective supervision of youth support workers aims to ensure protection for the young people who they serve. It monitors the work of the youth support worker and evaluates their effectiveness. In addition it helps to prevent poor practice that is outside the ethical, moral, legal and theoretical frameworks adopted by the organization. At the same time it offers protection to staff. When youth support workers are unsure about guidelines or policy around a particular issue in their work, they can gain the support of their supervisor and their organization for any action that they are considering. Their administrative procedures can be audited, their stress levels monitored and unsafe practices discussed in supervision can be managed and curtailed.

However, organizations would be misguided in thinking that the function of supervision is solely focused on the management of a supervisee's practice. Supervision can and should also identify the professional development needs of staff. This 'formative' function (Inskipp and Proctor 1993) focuses on an analysis of strengths in professional knowledge and skills, and the identification of areas of practice requiring further development. Hawkins and Shohet explain further:

> Learning becomes an important value in its own right. Supervisors carry the attitude 'How can I help these supervisees to maximise their learning in this situation so that they can help the client too?', rather than the attitude 'How can I ensure that the supervisees make no mistakes and do it the way I think is right.
>
> (2000: 177)

This formative aspect of supervision should inform and feed into the staff development system of the organization. Employing organizations and interagency partnerships will need to attend to the ways in which they integrate the system of supervision with other staff development processes, such as review and appraisal. In addition to the management and development functions of supervision, organizations need to be mindful of the part that supervision plays in ensuring that the psychological wellbeing of staff is attended to. This 'restorative' function (Inskipp and Proctor 1993) is central to the effective supervision of youth support workers. Hughes and Pengelly state:

> Supervision is not counselling. However, supervisors should make it clear to supervisees that they will actively wish to know about the emotional impact of the work, and in this context would be interested and available to hear of any personal difficulties that might be affecting it.
>
> (1997: 37)

Reynolds goes further:

> Supervision must enable the therapist to use their feelings to understand and help the client. On occasion, when a therapist concentrates only on the client's problems, this can be a way of avoiding their own uncertainties, prejudices etc. It can be more comfortable to learn about the emotions of the client than those of the therapist.
>
> (2001: 36)

Who carries out supervision?

To ensure that the three key functions of supervision (normative, formative and restorative) are addressed, organizations are faced with challenges. Where is supervision to be positioned in an organization, so that it links in with other organizational procedures? How can organizations ensure that they recognize the importance of the complex balancing act of supporting youth support workers on the one hand, and ensuring quality of practice on the other?

In the 'Evaluation of the Models of Supervision', undertaken in 2001 by Connexions Humber (Garrod-Mason 2001), three key models of supervision were identified. These models were defined by the role of the person offering the supervision. They were:

- experienced practitioner supervision (with no line-management responsibility);
- management supervision (where the line manager acts as a supervisor);
- external supervision (where the supervisor is someone outside the employing organization).

Of course, this is not an exhaustive list of the possibilities for the provision of supervision. As part of the pilot project, youth support workers identified and valued other forms of support and informal supervision. One of the key recommendations of the pilot project was that employers should encourage a full range of additional support systems as well as a dedicated supervision process.

The experienced practitioner model

In the experienced practitioner model, the supervisor is an individual who has gained experience in the field, but who has no direct line-management responsibility for youth support workers. The experienced practitioner is likely to be a colleague in the supervisee's own organization, or a youth support worker based in another organization within the multi-agency partnership. This model originated in the Youth Service where there is a strong belief in the need for impartiality of supervisors. Woods argues that it may be impossible for supervisees to talk to their line managers about their supervisory relationship, thereby limiting the effectiveness of the process. An experienced practitioner supervisor, by contrast, should provide impartial and unconditional support (Woods 2001).

A further benefit of the experienced practitioner supervisor model is that the supervisor is familiar with the type of work that their supervisee is undertaking. They will be aware of some of the issues that may arise during discussions about individual clients, but would strive to avoid holding themselves up as an 'expert', rather they are someone with experience. In theory, this should allow for a more equal relationship between supervisor and supervisee. The supervisee in this model is the 'driver' of the content of each session, and they should feel encouraged and comfortable to bring their own cases and issues to supervision. Those who took part in the pilot viewed this model as 'independent monitoring'. Supervisees felt strongly that they would not be judged or criticized for asking questions. It was seen as an opportunity to explore issues and reflect on practice in a safe place, and was a chance to gain knowledge and expertise from an experienced practitioner. One of the most important aspects of this model was that it gave youth support workers an opportunity to receive praise and positive feedback. This affirmation is key to their wellbeing and is something which they felt could be neglected or overlooked by line managers. The result of this feedback was that they felt more positive about their work and more confident to try things out, thus leading to greater creativity in their practice.

However, the evaluation of this experienced practitioner model was not overwhelmingly positive. The managers who took part in the evaluation summarized the key weakness. They felt that where the supervision and management functions were separate, there would be a concern that they may not be made aware if a member of staff were not performing or were under stress (the normative function). To manage effectively, they also felt that they needed to be cognisant of the issues being raised in supervision, so that they could consider these in the light of the whole organization to ensure that they were learning from and supporting their staff.

For the experienced practitioner model to be effective, the relationship between the manager and the experienced practitioner supervisor would need to be clarified. Both parties should be aware of their roles and responsibilities and these should be clearly articulated to the supervisee. Where the functions of management and supervision overlap, there should be robust arrangements to manage this. For example, careful attention should be paid to the issue of confidentiality. The supervision sessions are considered to be confidential (although there are limits to this) and it must be set out clearly where confidentiality would need to be broken (for example in cases of child protection or gross misconduct). It would need to be made clear that if there was an issue about the competence of a particular supervisee, this would be communicated to the manager in order that appropriate support could be put in place and action be taken accordingly. The competence of youth support workers would then be addressed through the performance management system adopted by the organization.

The line-managerial supervision model

In the line-managerial supervision model, managers take on responsibility for supervision alongside their other managerial responsibilities. While this alleviates the weaknesses that managers identified in divorcing the two roles (described in the experienced practitioner model above, and implicit in the external supervisor model to be discussed), it can create a tension for supervisees. Nixon and Carroll argue against managers taking on a *counselling* role with staff within an organization. This argument could equally apply to managers undertaking supervision, 'it puts employees in an impossible situation, asking on the one hand that they share personal issues with their manager and on the other that they be ready for appraisal vis-à-vis their careers by the same manager' (Nixon and Carroll 1994: 31).

Although supervision is not the same as counselling, to attend to the personal and psychological support activity (restorative function), supervisors will need to employ counselling or 'interviewing' skills at all times. A great deal will depend on the skills and ability of the manager to form an effective working alliance with their supervisee. How they approach supervision may depend upon the culture and philosophy of the organization. In a hierarchical and procedurally based organization, the needs of the manager/supervisor may well override the needs of the supervisee. The manager may experience role conflict between managing the service and producing the required outcomes, and attending to the needs of the supervisee.

However, this tension may be reduced in an organization that places emphasis on a team approach. If the manager/supervisor is considered to be one member of a team who views the responsibility for organizational outcomes and support for practitioners as the team's collective responsibility, the risk of role conflict may be significantly reduced. Supervision in this context would involve identifying and supporting the team's strengths and working with them to address difficult situations and challenges. This line-managerial approach, it could be argued, would lend itself to a model of group supervision, whereby the team meet regularly with their line manager who takes on the role of group supervisor. Edwards (2001) makes the case for managerial supervision to be considered alongside other approaches, by stressing that line managers have a legitimate interest in work discussed in supervision and should be granted the opportunity to attend to issues that are raised.

The external supervision model

The third model piloted was the external supervision model. Here the supervisor is based outside of the supervisee's employing organization and should therefore be well placed to offer impartial and independent supervision. The supervisor will have an understanding of the work role of the supervisee, but will not necessarily have any direct personal experience of the work. The report from the pilot project is clear that the impartial nature of this form of supervision can lead to increased confidence, motivation and creativity among supervisees (Garrod-Mason 2001).

Carroll identifies the key strengths of this model, 'it is not part of the practice of the organisation and can challenge what is taken for granted within the company' (Carroll 1996: 33). That said, he also goes on to point out the major weakness. He argues that the supervisor may not understand the culture of the organization and will know very little about the work of the supervisee. Supervisees may experience frustration when their supervisor does not share their frame of reference, and is therefore unable to grasp the complexity of the issues they are facing in their work in sufficient detail. But, it could be argued that when the context of the work is not shared, time will need to be spent to explain and explore practice in depth, thus both supervisee and supervisor have the opportunity to enhance their learning and understanding.

In the external supervision model, the supervisor will provide the supervisee with a space to talk about their work, their relationships with clients, and to consider what issues their cases raise for them as individuals. Although the supervisor is external to the organization for which the supervisee works, there is no reason why the three functions of supervision (normative, formative and restorative) should not be fully addressed. For example, by ensuring that there are clear mechanisms for which issues and concerns can be 'fed back' to the employing organization, the normative function can be met. As with the experienced practitioner model, the relationship between the supervisor and the supervisee's line manager or employing organization needs to be made transparent. The supervisee will need to feel safe and confident that issues of practice are only fed back where appropriate. The supervisor should always seek the agreement of their supervisee when they feel that an issue to do with the supervisee's work needs to be disclosed to the line manager. However, unlike the experienced practitioner model where the supervisor is likely to be a colleague in the same organization as the supervisee, it may be less complex and problematic for an external supervisor to provide objective and impartial feedback to line managers. It is critical therefore, that within external supervision (as in the experienced practitioner model), there is a clear code with regard to confidentiality. This code should be explicit between supervisor, supervisee and the employing organization.

The formative or 'development' function of supervision can also be addressed in the external supervision model. Although the supervisor is external to the organization and may not undertake a similar professional role to the supervisee, they should have some understanding of the approaches that youth support workers use in practice. This will enable them to help their supervisees to conceptualize their work, to consider strategies to enhance their practice and to identify areas for their own professional development. External supervisors may suggest additional reading and information sources to support their supervisees. They can also help supervisees to identify specific training needs and to consider how these will be met. Of course, external supervisors will have no control over the practicalities of providing further training, whereas line-manager supervisors may have direct responsibility for providing training opportunities. They will not have the finances at their disposal to enrol their supervisee on a training programme, neither will they have the responsibility or power to effect change in their supervisee's work load. Their role, however, is to assist their supervisee in finding ways to manage and develop their practice. This may include, with their supervisee's permission, supporting agreed suggestions for further training.

Finally, the restorative function of supervision can be met with an external supervisor. Evaluation of the Humber project identified the value of giving supervisees a safe place to 'offload' and a chance to recharge their emotional and psychological 'batteries'. Some supervisees expressed feelings of safety and security with this form of supervision. It enabled them to be open about emotional issues that are difficult and frustrating to deal with. These issues may be problematic to discuss with an experienced practitioner supervisor (colleague), and may be even more difficult to raise with a line manager. Supervisees may not want to risk discussing areas of vulnerability with the person who will later be undertaking their annual appraisal. However, with a supervisor who is external to the organization, there are, perhaps, fewer barriers to achieving the restorative aspects of supervision.

From an organizational perspective, feedback of the external model of supervision showed that some managers felt divorced from the supervision process, and consequently were not fully aware of the issues raised. In addition, there are other practicalities to be considered: where, for example should supervision take place? What is the additional cost implication for the organization?

Conclusion

This chapter set out to explore a question which is critical to organizations that are considering the provision of supervision for youth support workers: that is, what are the issues that organizations need to consider to ensure that their employees continue to be supported in their role once training has ended?

First, it is clear that organizations need to have a thorough understanding of the purpose of supervision, with all its complexities. They need to be aware that undertaking supervision involves more than simply ensuring quality: it is also about developing confident and competent practitioners by attending to their psychological wellbeing. Supervision does not simply involve providing time and space on an ad hoc basis for two colleagues to get together to 'have a chat'. It is hard work, and requires trained and competent individuals who understand the purpose and functions of supervision in order to undertake the role. If these aspects are not understood at all levels, then the system implemented may fail. It therefore follows that organizations will need to consider training staff; not just those who may be carrying out a supervision function, but also those youth support workers who are going to be supervised. This will enable both supervisor and supervisee to feel clear and confident about engaging with the process.

Second, any organization that is considering developing a process of supervision will need to identify and understand its own culture and ethos. For example, it needs to model in supervision the approach that its employees (i.e. youth support workers) use with their clients. In other words, focusing on enabling and supporting individuals to identify solutions and work towards change. It will need to view itself as a learning organization where, at all levels, the emphasis is on listening, reflecting, developing and improving practice.

Third, organizations will need to ensure that they evaluate a range of models for supervision and select those that are appropriate for their working context. Decisions about the model selected should be underpinned by sound policies and supported by contracts and agreements between all parties. Organizations will need to access relevant literature, and should undertake research to inform their final choice. As this chapter has sought to demonstrate, there is no one 'perfect model' of supervision. There are advantages and limitations with each model that should be recognized and acknowledged before any decision is reached.

Fourth, it is important that supervision should have a clearly identified place alongside other staff-related activities such as performance review and appraisal; and the relationship between these activities should be made explicit to all in the organization. There is plenty of opportunity for confusion if these relationships are not clarified at an early stage.

Finally, organizations should recognize and value the informal support mechanisms that youth support workers identify and develop for themselves. That said, it is not enough simply to rely upon these, neither is it enough to offer staff 'personal', or 'stress' counselling. Counselling may well have a role to play in the support of staff, but it is not the same as supervision and it does not replicate its functions and purpose. Organizations that rely exclusively on informal support and/or counselling services for staff, will risk at best, unhappy and under-performing youth support workers, and at worst, negligence in their duty of care to provide adequate support to the workforce.

Bibliography

Bimrose, J. and Wilden, S. (1994) 'Supervision in careers guidance: empowerment or control?' *British Journal of Guidance and Counselling*, 22 (3): 373–383.

British Association of Counselling (1987) *How Much Supervision Should You Have?* Rugby: BAC.

Brown, A. and Bourne, I. (1996) *The Social Work Supervisor*, Buckingham: Open University Press.

Bucknall, D. (2001) 'Supervision in social work – messages for the Connexions service', in A. Edwards (ed.) *Supporting Personal Advisers in Connexions: Perspectives on Supervision and Mentoring from Allied Professions*, Occasional Papers Canterbury: Canterbury Christ Church University College.

Carroll, M. (1996) *Workplace Counselling*, London: Sage.

Department for Education and Skills (2003) *Requirements and Guidance for the Connexions Service*, www.connexions.gov.uk (accessed 27 August 2003).

Edwards, A. (2001) 'Developing a framework for personal advisers', in A. Edwards (ed.) *Supporting Personal Advisers in Connexions: Perspectives on Supervision and Mentoring from Allied Professions*, Occasional Papers Canterbury: Canterbury Christ Church University College.

Feaviour, K., Trelfa, J. and Watkins, K. (2002) *Defining Supervision: Taking a Holistic and Systemic Approach*, Institute of Career Guidance Training Managers' Conference, Liverpool, November 2002.

Garrod-Mason, R. (2001) *Evaluation of Models of Supervision*, Humberside: The Humberside Partnership (now Connexions Humber).

Hawkins, P. and Shohet, R. (2000) *Supervision in the Helping Professions*, 2nd edn, Maidenhead: Open University Press.

Hughes, L. and Pengelly, P. (1997) *Staff Supervision in a Turbulent Environment – Managing Process and Task in Front Line Services*, London: Jessica Kingsley.

Inskipp, F. and Proctor, B. (1993) *The Art, Craft and Tasks of Counselling Supervision, Part 1. Making the Most of Supervisors*, Twickenham: Cascade Publications.

Institute of Career Guidance (2004) *Support and Supervision for Career Guidance*, ICG Position Statement, Stourbridge: Institute of Career Guidance.

Nixon, J. and Carroll, M. (1994) 'Can a line manager also be a counsellor?' *Employee Counselling Today*, 6 (1): 10–15.

Reynolds, H. (2001) 'Supervision in counselling and psychotherapy: a critical space', in A. Edwards (ed.) *Supporting Personal Advisers in Connexions: Perspectives on Supervision and Mentoring from Allied Professions*, Occasional Papers Canterbury: Canterbury Christ Church University College.

Senge, P. (1990) *The Fifth Discipline: the Art and Practice of Learning Organisations*, London: Random House.

Senge, P., Kleiner, A., Roberts, C., Ross, R. and Smith B. (1994) *The Fifth Discipline Fieldbook: Strategies for Building a Learning Organisation*, London: Nicholas Brealey Publishing.

Woods, J. (2001) 'Supervision from an informal education/youth work perspective', in A. Edwards (ed.) *Supporting Personal Advisers in Connexions: Perspectives on Supervision and Mentoring from Allied Professions,* Occasional Papers Canterbury: Canterbury Christ Church University College.

Youth Board of Connexions Humber (2002) *Young People's Charter*, Humberside: Connexions Humber.

10 Support and supervision

A lifelong learning process

Mary McMahon

Introduction

During the latter part of the twentieth century the profile of career guidance has risen and it has been placed firmly on the agenda of many national governments including those of England and Australia. Essentially, there seems to be a global convergence of interest in how career guidance might be used to improve the efficiency of education systems and the labour market, contribute to social equity, and assist with challenges arising out of lifelong learning and active labour market policies (Organisation for Economic Cooperation and Development 2003). This context augurs well for the future of career guidance.

However, just as the spotlight has fallen on career guidance, a challenge has emerged about how the ongoing professional development, support and learning needs of career guidance practitioners or personal advisers may be met. Traditionally viewed by some as less intense and easier than personal counselling, career counselling has more recently been viewed as a challenging, complex and holistic process that generates a range of support and learning needs for practitioners. Within the UK career guidance has extended its remit into other areas of youth support work that now encompass these wider needs.

To the external observer, career counselling may appear as a relatively smooth-flowing interaction between two people. However, what is not visible to the external observer is the process of reactions, responses, and feelings that occurs within the counsellor. An internal observation process may reveal career counsellors filled with doubts about their ability, knowledge or effectiveness, wracked with concern about the wellbeing of a client, painfully reminded of something in their own past or present, or exhausted from the relentlessness of constant client work, organizational change, and little support. In this context, it is not surprising that workers may become disenchanted, routinized, or experience burnout. Such a scenario is clearly not a desirable situation and unchecked, ultimately disadvantages clients, workers and organizations.

Support and supervision has been suggested as a mechanism that may ameliorate this unfortunate situation or prevent it from occurring in the first place. Indeed, supervision provides a venue for the internal observations of the career counsellor or personal adviser to be expressed and further explored in a supportive and non-judgemental manner. However, there is not a tradition of supervision in career counselling as there is in other helping professions such as social work, counselling and psychology. Thus, a further challenge is to conceptualize supervision in the context of career guidance work and for the new role of the personal adviser in England. A conceptualization that has previously been proposed is to embed supervision into a broader discussion of lifelong learning where supervision is viewed as a possible lifelong learning mechanism (McMahon 2003, 2004; McMahon and Patton 2000, 2002). In essence, lifelong learning is personal and results in the development of the individual. Such development may be personal, planned, accidental or experience-based (Holmes 2002), elements that clearly relate to the internal observer and supervision.

To date, supervision has not featured significantly as a professional practice in career counselling. Even in settings such as the Connexions service in England, where supervision is deemed necessary because of the intensive nature of the work of personal advisers, implementation is variable. McMahon (2004) suggested that in Australia this situation may be accounted for by the diverse backgrounds of those who enter the profession and a corresponding diversity or lack of understanding about supervision. For example, practitioners frequently have backgrounds in professions such as social work, psychology, education and human resource management and little or no career guidance specific training (OECD 2003). This situation may be further compounded by a lack of understanding about supervision by managers and administrators who, also, may have no background in consultative or clinical supervision.

A consequence of the varied professional backgrounds of career practitioners, is that in recent years the career guidance profession has been focused on a more fundamental challenge, that of its professional standing and the qualifications and standards of its members. This challenge corresponds with recognition that career guidance has an important role to play in the knowledge economy towards the achievement of policy goals related to lifelong learning, employment and social equity (OECD 2003). Thus, in recent years, most endeavour in the career guidance profession has gone into defining the profession and its standards and demonstrating its ability to meet the needs of clients. In light of the urgency for career guidance to redefine itself and guarantee its standards in order to maintain relevance in the knowledge economy, it is perhaps not surprising that supervision has received little attention. Indeed, McMahon (2004) claimed that until these issues are adequately addressed, supervision is likely to remain a peripheral issue to the career guidance profession.

Similar thoughts were also expressed a decade ago when Bimrose and Wilden (1994) suggested that elevating the place of supervision in the priorities of the career guidance profession would be a major challenge. In light of the more pressing issues now facing the profession, this seems to remain an accurate prediction.

The emergence of the knowledge economy has seen the concept of lifelong learning promoted as essential to life/career management. Without exception, everyone is required to engage in lifelong learning in the knowledge economy. While career practitioners are familiar with this as a concept to promote and foster in their clients, it is also a concept with direct relevance to the practitioners themselves. Lifelong learning will position career practitioners well to thrive and adapt in a world of rapid change. Further, a lifelong learning culture in the career guidance profession will assist it to remain relevant and responsive to societal needs (McMahon 2004). However, it has been claimed that in career guidance 'we still have much to learn about the role of learning in different forms for our practice' (Bimrose 2004: 3).

Essentially, this chapter will advance the conceptualization of support and supervision as a lifelong learning process for career counsellors and youth support workers. Where appropriate in this chapter, the generic term 'youth support worker' will be used to encompass terms such as career practitioner, career counsellor, and personal adviser. Throughout the chapter, parallels will be drawn between self-reflection, self-supervision, self-monitoring, supervision, learner-driven learning, and lifelong learning. First, the relationship between lifelong learning and supervision will be discussed. Second, learner-driven learning will then be explored in relation to self-supervision and self-monitoring. Following this, the relationship between self-supervision and supervision will be examined. A brief discussion on the supervisory learning environment will then be presented. In essence, the chapter will examine supervision's possible location under the umbrella of lifelong learning.

The relationship between lifelong learning and supervision

The concept of lifelong learning is seen as pivotal to successful life/career management in the twenty-first century (Commission of the European Communities 2000). Thus it is as critical for youth support workers to engage in lifelong learning as it is for their clients. Described by the Commission of the European Communities as ongoing purposeful learning activity that enhances knowledge, skills and competence, lifelong learning is viewed as a learner-driven process (Ellyard 1998), primarily focused on 'maintaining longevity within one's working life' (Holmes 2002: 9). Learning is the process of individuals constructing and transforming experience into knowledge, skills, attitudes, values, beliefs and emotions (Holmes

2002), all of which are also desirable outcomes of supervision, and all of which may be translated into practice.

Parallels between lifelong learning and supervision may be further examined by a definitional comparison. For example, Longworth and Davies (1996) define lifelong learning as: the development of human potential through a continuously supportive process which stimulates and empowers individuals to acquire all the knowledge, values, skills and understanding they will require throughout their lifetimes, and to apply them with confidence, creativity and enjoyment in all roles, circumstances and environments.

In order that the outcomes of lifelong learning processes are achieved, Longworth and Davies suggest that the supportive process they describe as lifelong learning is best facilitated by specially trained professionals with a welcoming attitude to learners. In addition they recommend that a learning infrastructure be developed whereby the individual needs of each learner are catered for in a personal and success-oriented manner, and where there is a non-threatening assessment and qualification system.

Such a learning infrastructure may be provided through supervision. For example, Inskipp and Proctor describe supervision as

> a working alliance between a supervisor and a counsellor (or counsellors) in which the counsellor can offer an account or recording of her work, reflect on it, receive feedback and where appropriate guidance. The object of the alliance is to enable the counsellor to gain in ethical competence, confidence and creativity so as to give her best possible service to clients.
>
> (1993: 313)

This definition is clearly reflective of that proffered by Longworth and Davies (1996) to describe lifelong learning. Further, it concurs with Holmes' (2002) notion of lifelong learning as a process whereby individuals construct and transform experience into knowledge, skills, attitudes, values, beliefs and emotions. Specifically, counsellors bring to supervision an account of their experience, and through supervision transform it in such a way that it is meaningful and able to be transferred into their work and personal learning.

Learning and development have been widely viewed as lifelong processes (Hawkins and Shohet 2000), and increasingly supervision has been regarded as a learning process that continues across counsellors' professional lifespan (Borders 1989). In this regard, supervisors have been described as 'facilitators of learning' (Patton and McMahon 1999: 245) and as facilitators and designers of environments that support learning (Scaife 2001). Further, supervisees have been described as 'self-managed learners' (Proctor 1994: 314) who must be committed to the process of exploring and learning (Scaife 2001). Thus, youth support workers who engage in supervision have responsibility for identifying their own learning needs: a reflection of Ellyard's (1998) claim that lifelong learning must be learner-driven. Thus, in terms of process and conceptualization, supervision may be located comfortably as a learning process that may facilitate lifelong learning.

Learner-driven learning

In relation to lifelong learning, Amundson *et al.* (2002: 27) describe a process whereby people are viewed as active agents who 'make sense of the world of work through subjective interpretation of their own career experience. In living through the complexity of economic life, they draw new insights and formulate new strategies that make sense of this complexity'. Further these authors suggest that there is 'a continuing tension between leveraging past experience and positioning for future opportunity' (ibid.). Individuals increasingly need to focus on learning the skills that will assist them in taking responsibility for the direction and evolution of their own careers.

While the process described by Amundson *et al.* (2002) may be familiar to career practitioners and personal advisers in relation to their client work, it may be less familiar to them in its application to their own work and learning. However, the process also describes supervision that may be viewed as an environment where learners are seen as actively exploring and trying to make sense of their experiences (Scaife 2001). Developing skills, knowledge and attitudes that enhance current performance and equip youth support workers for their future work, is an important outcome of the learning process of supervision.

The notion of individuals as active agents, striving to make sense of their experience in order to better position themselves for their future work, is compatible with that of learner-driven learning (Ellyard 1998). Learner-driven learning may be conceptualized under the broad guiding philosophy of constructivism and specifically through a learning model such as that of Kolb's (1984) experiential learning cycle. Essentially, learning is viewed as an active process that involves interaction, experience and relationships in all facets of life including work. Specifically, learning needs emerge out of the experience of individuals in their day-to-day work as youth support workers, and supervision provides a space in which they may further reflect on their experience. In supervision, learning and meaning are constructed through language in relation to what individuals already know. Through this process youth support workers may conceptualize new ideas, approaches or strategies which they in due course apply in their day-to-day work. Hawkins and Shohet (2000: 177) describe this learning process as one that moves from 'action, to reflection, to new thinking, to planning and then back to action'.

Learner-driven learning, self-supervision and self-monitoring

The learning process facilitated in supervision is grounded in the concrete work-experience of youth support workers, and is predicated on them reflecting on their own work. In this regard, Littrell *et al.* advocate that counsellors become the 'principal designers' (1979: 134) of their learning through the use of reflective processes. Borders and Leddick (1987) suggest that counsellors observe and reflect on their own thoughts, feelings and actions in relation to client behaviours, and also on clients' responses to them and their work. The use of reflection in this way raises practitioners' levels of awareness or consciousness about practice (Shapiro and Reiff 1993). It also illustrates Dewey's (1933) notion that the purpose of reflection is to 'transform' a state of affairs where confusion, doubt and conflict, disturb and unsettle and turn it into a situation that becomes coherent and 'harmonious': a purpose that may be realized in supervision.

In this way, youth support workers may act as their own internal observers, observing the process within them, the process between them and their clients, and the process between them and their clients within the context of work and society. Observations occur at a subjective level through feelings, reactions and emotions and at a cognitive level through thoughts and observations. Such observations provide an impetus for self-reflection through which practitioners actively attempt to make sense of, understand or create meaning around their experiences.

This process of self-reflection has been variously referred to in the literature as self-supervision and self-monitoring, terms that have been used interchangeably (Morrissette 2001). Self-supervision, Morrissette suggests, is best understood as an underlying philosophy rather than as a set of techniques or strategies. Morrissette claims that reflectivity is the essence of self-supervision while Shepard and Morrow (2003) assert that self-reflection and self-monitoring may also be used interchangeably. They define self-monitoring as 'a process of self-scrutiny where therapists reflect honestly and realistically on their values, limitations, cultural competence, countertransference issues, life stressors, or any other aspects of their personal and professional lives that inevitably bear on their clinical work' (Shepard and Morrow 2003: 30). It is through reflective practices such as self-supervision or self-monitoring that practitioners may develop their clinical wisdom and professional judgement (Morrissette 2001).

Career guidance has increasingly been recognized as complex and multifaceted work. Consequently self-supervision or self-monitoring requires practitioners to engage all of their senses to process both cognitive and subjective input. Shepard and Morrow (2003) claim that self-monitoring may be precipitated by behavioural, affective or cognitive cues. Practitioners' internal observers may alert them to behavioural cues such as an inability to respect a client, affective cues such as anxiety or boredom, and cognitive cues such as ethical dilemmas: all of which may serve as a stimulus for self-monitoring or self-supervision. In a similar way, Holmes (2002) suggested that individuals position themselves for lifelong learning by being sensitive and open-minded to the opportunities around them, a suggestion that fits comfortably with the antecedents of self-supervision previously described.

McMahon and Patton (2002) urge practitioners to monitor the content of their client work as well as the process. Possible components of career counselling supervision have been proposed (e.g. Bronson 2000; Crozier and Lalande 2000) that could also be a focus for self-supervision. For example, Bronson proposes that career counselling supervision should attend to:

a   the supervisory relationship
b   counselling skills
c   case conceptualisation
d   assessment skills
e   resources and information
f   the interconnection between personal issues and career issues
g   promoting supervisee interest in career counselling
h   addressing career issues in age appropriate ways
i   multicultural issues
j   ethics.

(2000: 224–225)

In addition McMahon and Patton (2002) suggest that career practitioners also need to reflect on their own career development process. These authors claim that it is not uncommon for career practitioners to deal with client issues with which they too have had some personal experience such as choosing jobs, thinking about changing jobs, juggling work and study, redundancy or downsizing in their workplace. Thus a possibility exists for career practitioners to operate from within their own frame of reference rather than from the frame of reference of the client. For that reason, career counsellors need self-awareness of their own career development and understanding of its possible influence in their work.

In this regard, Peavy (1998: 162) proposed that counsellors 'observe their own processes of emotional, cognitive, embodied experiencing of self and other' in the counselling interaction. This is reflected by Kottler and Jones (2003) who suggested that to facilitate self-monitoring, practitioners need to develop the capacity to:

1   Identify skills and knowledge deficits.
2   Recognise difficulties as they are occurring in sessions.
3   Notice recurrent themes and unresolved issues in real time.
4   Become aware of the blocks interfering with progress.

5 Rekindle passion and curiosity.
6 Access intuition and creativity.

(269)

The development of such capacities is also recognizable as possible goals or purposes of supervision.

Self-supervision, supervision and lifelong learning

Carroll (1996) suggests that there may be some disadvantages to an exclusive focus on self-supervision, and Yager and Park (1986) claim that self-awareness is probably the major obstacle to effective self-supervision. For example, practitioners may be unaware of or in denial about elements of their own process, or of that between them and their clients. While Kottler and Jones (2003) propose that practitioners reflect on a range of issues, these same issues may not be visible to practitioners until they are made explicit in supervision. Further, self-supervision, inherently, allows for only one perspective, that of the practitioner, which may result in a lack of challenge. A further obstacle to self-reflection and self-supervision is that the pressure of day-to-day client work generally does not permit time for adequate reflection (Reid 2003). Thus it is to be hoped that youth support workers use self-monitoring and self-reflection in conjunction with supervision. For example, through self-supervision, practitioners may become aware of difficulties in their client work, and through supervision develop an understanding of the difficulties and devise strategies to address them. Indeed self-monitoring prepares practitioners well for supervision and may broaden and deepen the reflection process.

Lowe (2002) advocates that self-supervision be integrated into the process of supervision as a central organizing principle. Essentially, Lowe suggests that self-supervision emanates from counselling practice and is then followed up in supervision. Following a supervision session, the practitioner engages in a further process of self-supervision before re-engaging in practice. Such a process is able to accommodate Dewey's (1933) concept of reflection whereby the issues surrounding uncertainty in counselling practice are identified, processed during supervision, and the outcomes of the process applied in practice. In this way Lowe claims that practitioners 'assume primary responsibility for monitoring their own professional development' (2002: 77). Thus practitioners may be regarded as being actively engaged in a learner-driven lifelong learning process. Importantly, Lowe suggests that through supervision the self-reflective skills of the practitioner may be further developed. Essentially supervision may be seen to have a dual focus, the development of practitioners' skills, knowledge and attitudes in regard to their client work, and the development of their self-supervision skills. In this way, practitioners' capacity for self-reflection and self-supervision is enhanced as is the potential for their learning to be self-driven. Thus supervision also provides a mechanism to facilitate and promote lifelong learning through a personal process that results in the development of the practitioner.

Support and supervision

The previous discussion illustrates how lifelong learning may be facilitated through self-supervision and supervision. However, consideration also needs to be given to the learning environment of supervision. Internal observation may leave youth support workers filled with doubts about their ability, knowledge or effectiveness, wracked with concern about the wellbeing of a client, painfully reminded of something in their own past or present, or exhausted from the relentlessness of constant client work, organizational change, and little support. In this context, it is not surprising that workers may become disenchanted, routinized, or experience burnout. Such situations prompted Inskipp and Proctor (1993) to stress the importance of the support function of supervision in relation to the personal wellbeing of the counsellor, which they view as pivotal to counsellors' capacity to be competent, confident and creative in their work.

It is against this background that Scaife emphasizes the creation of a learning environment in supervision where the 'emotional tone' is safe and supportive and 'encourages learners to value their own experience and to trust themselves to draw conclusions from it' (2001: 29). The 'emotional tone' of supervision should not be understated. In addition, learning may be challenging as it may disturb and unsettle practitioners' existing beliefs and views (Reid 2003). Equally, challenge from a supervisor may be needed to stimulate learning. Blocher (1983) proposed that supervision requires a learning environment in which challenge and support are balanced. Where the balance swings too much in the direction of support, Feltham and Dryden (1994) suggest that supervisory relationships may become too 'cosy' for honest feedback to occur. On the other hand, supervisory relationships that provide challenge and little support may also inhibit learning. Thus the role of supervisors may be viewed as providing both support and challenge in order that supervisees' learning needs are met. The learning environment described here is also consistent with that viewed as desirable for facilitating lifelong learning (Longworth and Davies 1996).

Conclusion

Throughout this chapter, a number of parallels have been drawn. First, parallels were drawn between lifelong learning and supervision. Second, parallels were drawn between one of the tenets of lifelong learning, learner-driven learning, and self-reflection, self-supervision and self-monitoring. Finally, the relationship between self-supervision and supervision was then discussed and the conditions of a learning environment for supervision were outlined. Clearly, support and supervision may be viewed as a mechanism for lifelong learning.

To date, supervision has remained peripheral to career guidance practice. Indeed, it is likely to remain so in light of the pressing need for the career guidance profession to attend to issues such as its professional identity and its potential to remain relevant in the knowledge economy. Unlike supervision, lifelong learning is a concept that has been embraced in the knowledge economy and is already becoming embedded in the client work of career practitioners and personal advisers. Lifelong learning positions individuals well to thrive and adapt in a world of rapid change, and increasingly there is an expectation that everyone will engage in lifelong learning.

In this regard, career practitioners and personal advisers are no different. Indeed, it is highly desirable that a lifelong learning culture be fostered in the career guidance profession in order that it remains relevant and responsive to societal needs (McMahon 2004). It is also highly desirable that personal advisers in the Connexions service, and holistic youth support services elsewhere, engage in support and supervision because of the intensity of their work. Unlike supervision, lifelong learning is a concept that is familiar to career practitioners. To conceptualize supervision as a lifelong learning mechanism locates it within a contemporary issue facing workers in the knowledge economy. It is hoped that such a conceptualization will foster greater understanding of the possibilities of supervision, and provide a rationale for its conduct and an incentive for its more widespread adoption.

Bibliography

Amundson, N.E., Parker, P. and Arthur, M.B. (2002) 'Merging two worlds: linking occupational and organisational career counselling', *Australian Journal of Career Development*, 11: 26–35.

Bimrose, J. (2004) 'Reflection on practice: lifelong learning for guidance', in H. L. Reid and J. Bimrose (eds) *Constructing the Future: Reflection on Practice*, Stourbridge: Institute of Career Guidance.

—— and Wilden, S. (1994) 'Supervision in careers guidance: empowerment or control', *British Journal of Guidance and Counselling*, 22: 373–383.

Blocher, D. (1983) 'Toward a cognitive developmental approach to counseling supervision', *The Counseling Psychologist*, 11: 27–34.

Borders, L.D. (1989) 'Facilitating supervisee growth: implications of the developmental models of counseling supervision', *Michigan Journal of Counseling and Development*, 1: 9–14.

—— and Leddick, G.R. (1987) *Handbook of Counseling Supervision*, Alexandria, VA: Association for Counselor Education and Supervision.

Bronson, M.K. (2000) 'Supervision of career counseling', in L.J. Bradley and N. Ladany (eds) *Counselor Supervision – Principles, Process, and Practice*, Philadelphia, PA: Brunner-Routledge.

Carroll, M. (1996) *Counselling Supervision: Theory, Skills and Practice*, London: Cassell.

Commission of the European Communities (2000) *Commission Staff Working Paper: a Memorandum on Lifelong Learning*, Brussels: http://europa.eu.int/comm/education/life/memoen.pdf (accessed 14 February 2003).

Crozier, S. and Lalande, V. (2000) 'Critical issues in the supervision of career counselling professionals', *International Career Conference*, Perth, Western Australia.

Dewey, J. (1933) *How we Think*, Chicago, IL: Regnery.

Ellyard, P. (1998) *Ideas for the New Millennium*, Melbourne, Australia: Melbourne University Press.

Feltham, C. and Dryden, W. (1994) *Developing Counsellor Supervision*, London: Sage.

Hawkins, P. and Shohet, R. (2000) *Supervision in the Helping Professions*, 2nd edn, Buckingham: Open University Press.

Holmes, A. (2002) *Lifelong Learning*, Oxford: Capstone Publishing.

Inskipp, F. and Proctor, B. (1993) *The Art, Craft and Tasks of Counselling Supervision. Part 1. Making the Most of Supervision*, Twickenham: Cascade.

Kolb, D.A. (1984) *Experiential Learning*, Englewood Cliffs, NJ: Prentice Hall.

Kottler, J.E. and Jones, W.P. (2003) 'Final thoughts', in J. E. Kottler and W.P. Jones (eds) *Doing Better: Improving Clinical Skills and Professional Competence*, New York: Brunner-Routledge.

Littrell, J.M., Lee-Bordin, N. and Lorenz, J.A. (1979) 'A developmental framework for counselling supervision', *Counselor Education and Supervision*, 19: 119–126.

Longworth, N. and Davies, W.K. (1996) *Lifelong Learning: New Vision, New Implications, New Roles for People, Organisations and Communities in the 21st Century*, London: Kogan Page.

Lowe, R. (2002) 'Self-supervision: from developmental goal to systematic practice', in M. McMahon, and W. Patton (eds) *Supervision in the Helping Professions: A Practical Approach*, Frenchs Forest, Australia: Pearson Education.

McMahon, M (2002) 'Supervision: Lifelong learning for career counsellors', in M. McMahon, and W. Patton (eds) *Supervision in the Helping Professions: a Practical Approach*, Frenchs Forest, Australia: Pearson Education.

—— (2003) 'Supervision and career counsellors: a little explored practice with an uncertain future', *British Journal of Guidance and Counselling*, 31 (2): 177–189.

—— (2004) 'Career counsellors as reflective practitioners and lifelong learners: what is the place of supervision?' in H.L. Reid, and J. Bimrose (eds) *Constructing the Future: Reflection on Practice*, Stourbridge: Institute of Career Guidance.

—— and Patton, W. (2000) 'Career counsellors, support and lifelong learning: a case for clinical supervision', *International Journal for the Advancement of Counselling*, 22: 157–169.

Morrissette, P.J. (2001) *Self-supervision: a Primer for Counsellors and Helping Professionals*, New York: Brunner-Routledge.

Organisation for Economic Cooperation and Development (2003) *Career Guidance and Public Policy: Bridging the Gap*, www.oecd.org (accessed 10 January 2004).

Patton, W. and McMahon, M. (1999) *Career Development and Systems Theory: A New Relationship*, Pacific Grove, CA: Brooks/Cole.

Peavy, V. (1998) *Sociodynamic Counselling: a Constructivist Perspective*, Victoria, Canada: Trafford.

Proctor, B. (1994) 'Supervision: competence, confidence, accountability', *British Journal of Guidance and Counselling*, 22: 309–318.

Reid, H.L. (2003) 'Space for reflection: reasserting a professional identity', *Career Guidance Today*, 11 (2), Stourbridge: Institute of Career Guidance.

Scaife, J. (2001) *Supervision in the Mental Health Professions*, Hove: Brunner-Routledge.

Shapiro, S. and Reiff, J. (1993) 'A framework for reflective inquiry on practice: beyond intuition and experience', *Psychological Reports*, 73: 1379–1394.

Shepard, D. and Morrow, G. (2003) 'Critical self-monitoring', in J.E. Kottler and W.P. Jones (eds) *Doing Better: Improving Clinical Skills and Professional Competence*, New York: Brunner-Routledge.

Yager, G. and Park, W. (1986) 'Counselor self-supervision', *Journal of Counseling and Human Services Professions*, 1: 6–17.

11 Evaluation in supervision across a continuum of practice

Andrew Edwards

This chapter begins with an attempt to define what is meant by evaluation in supervision. It does so by contrasting perspectives on evaluation, which are evident within professions with established traditions of supervision. It then ventures to describe a fledgling systemic model of evaluative analysis, which is related to case-study material arising from the author's own experiences of providing facilitative support for practising supervisors. The chapter also offers a short summary of the methods of evaluation found within the current literature, but endeavours to see where else the debate can be taken. In this discussion the concern is more with gaining a broader view of evaluation in supervision, rather than focusing on the more usual one-dimensional orientation, with its concern for the supervisee's therapeutic relationships and skills.

Current perspectives

Even the established approaches towards the role and function of evaluation in supervision vary. Perspectives are influenced by different historical and professional contexts, by different traditions, working cultures and practices. Out of this mix a range of paradigms has emerged that offer similar but distinct forms of explanation and analysis. For this reason, it is probably easier to articulate a coherent pattern of debate about the role of evaluation from within bounded professional groups, rather than to attempt to extrapolate across these boundaries in the search for the features of a common approach. That said the search for transtheoretical models, though challenging, might be a worthy aspiration.

The number of professionals and volunteers working with young people in complex and demanding circumstances continues to expand, and many of these practitioners need to use counselling skills as part of their role (Inskipp 1996). Not all of these agencies have 'regulated' approaches to supervision. Indeed, where supervision exists, the arrangements may be relatively underdeveloped and provisional in nature. Although McMahon (2002) has noted that the onward movement towards greater professionalisation in 'helping' services for young people and adults may serve to raise the profile of supervision, this may be a long process. The literature therefore needs to be able to speak to a wide community of practice that extends far beyond the therapeutic, health and social work communities out of which so much of the history of supervision has evolved. It needs to offer illumination to those agencies, organisations and practitioners who may be new to the process.

Evaluation in current practice

On the basis of what follows, it may soon be evident why we may struggle to achieve a definition of evaluation and its role in supervision, which would enlist widespread support and endorsement. Different elements of evaluative practice have been chosen for comment, since it is some-times easier to define the characteristics of practice rather than the terms themselves.

There is a clear emphasis in the literature on the role that *assessment* plays as part of the evaluation process in supervision (Kadushin 1985; Clarkson and Gilbert 1991; Pickvance 1997; Hughes and Pengelly 1997; Gould and Bradley 2001). This often relates to counsellors or other help-ing professionals who are undergoing a pre-registration period in which training and assessment form an important part. In this context, the supervisor may undertake a range of roles, which include making judge-ments about the readiness of the supervisee to practise as a qualified and independent practitioner (Scaife 2001). This has been referred to as a 'gatekeeper' role (Carroll 1996). In this context, 'assessment', sometimes described as 'evaluation', is concerned with the supervisee's knowledge and skills, and with their ability to utilise these resources effectively in achieving the 'therapeutic wellbeing' of their clients. One focus of evaluation is therefore on the performance of the individual supervisee.

Assessment may also be linked to the question of *accountability*, as organisations want to be sure that a supervisee's practice is being main-tained at the professional standard expected. The supervisor may play a role in verifying this evidence, on the basis that competence cannot be assumed. But, supervision as a form of quality control raises its own issues. Feltham (2002) for example, argues that there remains a lack of clarity as to whether the focus of evaluation rests on the client, the super-visee or the supervisory relationship. He suggests that most methods of evaluation give marginal attention to how clients benefit from therapeutic practice.

Evaluation is also linked to the concept of *periodic review* (Hawkins and Shohet 1989), which may occur at regular intervals within the super-vision process. A review may or may not include a formal assessment, although it will be concerned with monitoring the quality of the super-visee's work and with their relationship to their supervisor. It is an opportunity for critical and informed dialogue within the supervisory relationship. Houston (1995) suggests that the process of review should be two-way, in the spirit of mutuality, and give space to considering the effectiveness of the supervisor as well as the supervisee. This approach sees evaluation as a shared activity. Similarly, Pickvance (1997) sees such review meetings as providing both parties with an opportunity to air doubts and concerns. Gould and Bradley (2001) suggest that the supervisor who fails to encourage feedback about their supervisory performance is, thereby, losing a valuable source of information for improving their own skills. Gilbert and Sills (1999) add a further perspective by suggesting that a supervisee who is working effectively, reflects on the competence of their supervisor. The supervisor's skills are therefore critical in helping the supervisee to be effective in their work with clients.

Kemshall (1995) has linked supervision with *appraisal*. She regards both functions as integral parts of the same managerial responsibility, concerned with the maintenance and enhancement of performance. This perspective sees supervision as a function of management and more, in that data arising from supervision should be included within the appraisal process. This is an interesting but contentious position. In sharp contrast, Cottrell and Smith (2003) posit a different view and make reference to the UKCC Position Statement (1995), which strongly emphasises that clinical supervision is not to be confused with individual performance review or managerial supervision. This contrast of approaches is yet another illustration of the difficulties involved in reaching shared meanings and definitions concerning supervision, and thereby also reaching a consensus about the role of evaluation.

Evaluation is also linked to the *diagnosis of development and learning needs*. Tash (1967) stresses the importance of evaluation in fostering the supervisee's ability to use the supervisory relationship in order to meet their own needs in learning. Inskipp (1996) similarly emphasises the importance of training supervisees in order that the power imbalance can be addressed. This can be achieved by empowering the supervisee to be clear about what they need from supervision. In addition it can help them to take greater ownership of the working alliance, which sets the boundaries for the work in supervision.

Anxieties about supervision

Supervisees may however experience some ambivalence about supervision. Wheeler and King (2001: 83) acknowledge that formal evaluation can 'give rise to a great deal of negative transference', with the attendant risk that supervisees come to regard their supervisor as yet one more figure in the assessment process. With reference to the lasting impact of school cultures on learner confidence, Gilbert and Sills (1999: 181) speak critically of 'a shame-based educational process', which adversely impacts on training practitioners, in that it leads to any 'critical' feedback having devastating effects on some people. One outcome is that this disempowers trainers and supervisors as a result. The authors state:

> Part of teaching evaluation becomes the healing of wounds that people have incurred in previous learning situations where being assessed has led them to conclude that they are 'stupid', 'ineffectual' or even 'bad'.
>
> (1999: 181)

Supervisees are therefore liable to suffer anxieties in relation to supervision, especially in respect of the process of assessment where they occupy an unequal position of power in the supervisory relationship. The assessment function of supervision is not unproblematic for supervisors either. Inskipp (1996) notes, for example, how the assessment function can be a source of role conflict for the supervisor. She argues that supervision cannot be unconditional since supervisors must evaluate and judge. However, she suggests that many supervisors are unclear about determining when practice is 'good enough' or 'not good enough', and are sometimes reluctant to pass judgement as a result. Scaife (2001: 215) notes that those trained in the core conditions for psychotherapy, such as unconditional positive regard, might perceive these as 'incompatible with giving feedback and making evaluations'. Kadushin (1985) likewise describes the difficulties that new social work supervisors may experience concerning those aspects of their role that they may regard as contrary to the prevailing ethos of social work, in requiring them to assume a position of authority and to make judgements about the workers they now supervise.

That said, Kadushin (1985: 331) also takes a positive stance and argues that 'evaluation relieves supervisees' anxiety since it helps them to know where they stand'. Evaluation, in his terms, helps to 'motivate, direct and integrate learning'. Such outcomes are clearly dependent on the presence of other key facilitative factors within the supervisory relationship, but the emphasis on the positive learning and motivational gains that can be generated through evaluative activities, is a useful counter-balance to seeing just the 'problems'. The issue of positioning the relationship is clearly crucial in this respect. Shohet and Wilmot (1991: 88) advocate the benefits of creating an environment in which both supervisee and supervisor see themselves as on the 'same side', able to 'drop their judgemental attitudes and become co-researchers' as they investigate issues together. Other creative approaches towards managing evaluation may be helpful in establishing more ownership of the process and making it less threatening. Carroll (1996) maintains that feedback should become a regular feature of supervision in order to avoid shocks or surprises that can arise from only dealing with evaluation on a periodic or summative basis. The introduction of alternative approaches can also assist with embedding these tasks, such as the use of reflective self-evaluation and personal development portfolios. Hellman (1999) describes how this approach has been used with supervisors to support their professional development.

Cautionary voices

As noted earlier, supervision is increasingly being introduced and practised in non-therapeutic and non-clinical contexts, where perhaps there is less emphasis on monitoring or regulating performance and more on providing professional support. But there are also shared concerns which cut across culture and context and which go to the heart of any meaningful discussion about evaluation, since evaluation has, among other things, to be concerned with questions such as, 'Why are we doing this?' 'How, if at all, can we measure reliably the impact of supervision in relation to the practitioner's skills and client outcomes?' 'How well do our methods of supervision work and how do we know?' 'What could we do differently that may give us better or alternative approaches to practice?' For evaluation to be effective, we have to be able to ask the difficult questions to which Feltham (2002) alludes. Without this, evaluative practice risks becoming collusive in accepting certain givens that in some cultures may be difficult to challenge.

In addition, approaches to evaluation cannot be divorced from a culture of learning. In fact, it could be argued that if the prevailing culture of learning within an organisation is truly learner-centred, then the place of evaluation is likely to be regarded more positively by everyone involved in the process. A learner-centred culture also aims to ensure that learners – in this case supervisees – receive training in the very skills which will facilitate self-guided learning. It seems essential that at the very least, new practitioners are inducted early on into the skills of reflective practice: these are a precursor to the broader-based evaluative skills that will feature at some point in the supervisory relationship. Properly contextualised, possession of these skills helps to increase practitioners' confidence in examining and valuing their own data, and in recognising the power that such data offers them in deepening their understanding of practice-based evidence. Against this backcloth, the practice of shared evaluation within supervision seems far less threatening.

Organisational factors

If we step beyond the more immediate concerns of evaluating the effectiveness of a supervisee's work with clients, or with the development of their micro-skills, or even with the supervisory relationship itself; we soon see that there is a wide range of other potential influencing factors that can impact on the quality of supervisory practice. Some of these broader factors are of an organisational nature, in that although the influence or 'effect' may impact in some way upon the supervisory relationship, the 'cause' may well arise from elsewhere in the 'system', as Figure 11.1 illustrates. Such influencing factors may not be particularly visible, especially within the narrow parameters of an assessment paradigm that focuses principally on a supervisee's 'performance'. Yet organisational culture(s), staffing levels and structures, policies, resourcing or funding arrangements, contractual requirements and training, do have a bearing on supervisory practice.

As Figure 11.1 indicates, a supervisee's work does not take place within a vacuum, and neither does that of the supervisor. Moreover practitioners working for agencies which have few if any conventions relating to supervision and support, may find themselves *directly* affected by what else happens, or does not happen, within the organisational system. Those professionals for whom supervision is an established adjunct to professional training and accreditation may be afforded some control and protection from the vagaries of the wider environment. A supervisor attuned to a systemic perspective of evaluation will be open to processing and working with this knowledge. Such knowledge has the power to exert considerable influence on their work and that of their supervisee, as the following examples show.

Wheeler and King (2000) note that supervisors frequently report that their supervisee counsellors experience role conflict and boundary problems in their workplace setting. The risk of role conflict in emerging 'helping agencies' may be even more problematic. Supervisors in the Connexions case study reported the same phenomena, which given the relative newness of this service, is not altogether surprising. Here, confusion concerning the boundaries of the personal adviser's role had not been fully resolved. The power to resolve ambiguities of this kind did not lie with the practitioner, or supervisor for that matter, but both needed to take account of the dynamics of their situation. This example also illustrates the extended influence of the 'system' within which practice often operates, since the system in public sector terms extends to the very apex of government policy making.

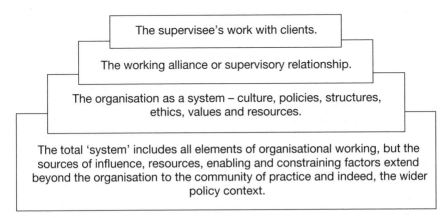

Figure 11.1 Supervision and its system

Butterworth (1997) reports findings from an 18-month, multi-centre study of clinical supervision, which showed that supervision afforded a stabilisation or amelioration of the effects of emotional exhaustion and depersonalisation. The study also indicated that where supervision is withdrawn, there are measurable detrimental effects on the workforce. Similarly, McMahon's (2002) study showed that school counsellors wanted supervision not only for support and skill development, but also to reduce their sense of isolation and to reduce their risk of burnout. Hulbert's (2000) study drew the same conclusion. With reference to the needs of Connexions personal advisers working with 'difficult to help' young people, she pointed to the

> need [for] appropriate support/supervision in order to enhance their competence and to effectively recognise and manage the emotional impact of their work in order to reduce stress and prevent 'burnout'.
> (Hulbert 2000: 15)

Clarkson and Gilbert (1991) likewise stress the importance of counsellors attending to their *self-care* in order to avoid the dangers of burnout, as does Reid (2005) in a study on support and supervision for personal advisers. Inescapably, this is also an organisational matter if employers are to exercise a duty of care towards their employees. But, it also has to figure in the supervisor's evaluation about how environmental conditions may be impacting upon their supervisee's wellbeing.

These few examples illustrate the complex nature of providing supervision in an organisational context. Supervisors have to navigate a series of relationships – supervisee, peers and managers – as well as a series of concerns that include the wellbeing of the supervisee, the quality of the supervisee's work with clients, and organisational priorities and expectations. For reasons such as these, Copeland (1998: 385) stresses the essential importance of supervisors possessing 'a knowledge of culture and organisational change, and the skills to work in multiple relationships whilst still practising ethically'.

Connexions Service case study

The case study that follows is an example of how evaluative skills and methods have been applied to *supervision-in-action* across a continuum (Table 11.1). The material arises from work undertaken with one particular guidance agency, which over a three-year period, had to adjust its working practices and priorities in order to meet the new contractual demands of the evolving Connexions Service. This change was policy-driven by central government. Changes to working practice included, for example, engaging intensively with young people aged 13–19 who 'present' with a wide range of complex needs and issues that often form barriers to their educational participation and inclusion.

Recognising that challenges associated with major role changes were looming, I offered to facilitate several seminars on support and supervision to which senior managers were invited. This provided an opportunity to introduce supervision as a concept and to explore with them how support structures, including supervision, could be embedded as organisational changes were implemented. My colleagues and I published an occasional paper (Edwards 2001) to help with the dissemination of ideas, which also provided insights into the ways in which supervision is practised in the related areas of social work, counselling, teaching, youth work and career guidance. The paper concluded by advocating a systemic approach for embedding supervision within organisational culture and structures. These initial steps enabled the formation of a proactive partnership, involving myself as a teacher from higher education, and a major guidance service for young people. I was able to adopt an advisory role, which enabled us to explore together how a systemic approach to support and supervision could be developed in practice. My role was to extend still further through assistance with an evaluation of a pilot supervision project, and latterly through providing accredited and non-accredited training and facilitative support for groups of supervisors.

Working together at the beginning of the change process was significant. A senior manager within the agency was appointed to lead on the development of support and supervision. She made it her responsibility to begin practising as a supervisor in order to advance her own skills and insights into this role, and in turn, ensured that she too received supervision. Extending the use of reflective practice as a keystone of supervision and its evaluation was also actively promoted. Training programmes, both accredited and non-accredited, introduced practitioners to some of the theories of reflective practice and development planning, through the use of reflective logs or journals; through the use of peer 'mentoring-supervision' during training, and through the use of audio-recordings for personal reflection and analysis.

Emphasis was also given to preparing practitioners for supervision. Those relatively new to the organisation and already practising as an 'intensive personal adviser', were ready and receptive for the new systems of support. Guidance workers who had no real experience or tradition of supervision were initially very mixed in their response. The policy-driven change was not welcome by all, and some were fearful about the dilution of their expertise and reticent to embrace new practices associated with anticipated role changes. Economies of scale meant that group supervision was used as the chief means to support 'universal personal advisers', while those working in the 'intensive' role benefited from one-to-one support. Later evidence (King 2004) appeared to indicate a significant majority of guidance workers had come to appreciate and value their supervision sessions, although not all found the group sessions entirely to their liking. Of the sample (58), just over 50 per cent rated the current system of supervision as good or very good and felt that it had helped them to work more effectively.

The final element of this partnership involved me in providing consultative support (a form of supervision for supervisors) to a group of six experienced and senior practitioners who had undergone accredited basic training in supervision and had, as a result, been appointed to new lead roles as supervision and assessment coordinators (SACs). In addition to coming to terms with a new and demanding role, they also had to brace themselves for organisational change that subsequently led to a transfer of employers. Despite the change, their new employer kept the group intact. Part of our voluntary work together was to identify ways in which we could build a form of collegiality, which would promote shared learning and agency within and by the group.

It was soon evident that although the SAC group shared concerns relating to the micro-skills of supervision, they were equally concerned with understanding system influences and their impact upon their practice. Understanding the organisation as a system began to offer new and important insights into problem-solving and strategies for change. We were able to examine how systems may be highly regulated or relatively unregulated, how they may impose rules and boundaries, how they will allocate resources, whether sufficient or not, and how they will create expectations and demands. We discussed how and why an organisation, through its culture and systems, may be highly committed to supervision and value its contribution to the organisation's goals, or why it may attach a low priority to the activity and adjust its level of support accordingly. We considered, too, how the organisation and its system may articulate a highly evolved policy of supervision, or lack a policy altogether. By exploring these issues in broader, more general terms, we were then able to examine the new organisation and system of which they were a part, as a step in the 'meaning-making' process. These discussions helped the group to explore and examine their own new organisational and cultural context. Their highly developed insights from reflective practice prompted detailed and sensitive analysis, which we were able to extend through the use of basic evaluative questions to develop shared learning and whole group perspectives.

This account resonates strongly with the conclusions drawn by Copeland (1998). If collegial working could be established, fears of isolation could be reduced while the scope for shared learning could be increased. More than this, by utilising some of the skills of action research and reflective action planning, the group's sense of agency could be extended. One outcome of this consultative process is that the group has grown to recognise and value its collective knowledge and emerging expertise; to understand that its 'critical mass' is a resource to the organisation that can be used to help 'manage upwards' on those issues in the new system which are still weak or underdeveloped. The group is now able to set itself goals that reflect either the needs of individual members or shared common concerns. Collegial working has led to shared responsibility for research and data gathering, for setting objectives that can be reviewed together at a following meeting. These have included, for example, offering to support senior managers in drafting new policies and practices for supervision and for improving support structures more widely. It is as if a clearer understanding of the organisation as a system has reduced the sense of powerlessness, and given instead more access to the levers of decision-making. This has had a liberating and motivating effect, as these professionals stop seeing themselves as helpless in the face of uninvited organisational change. Instead, they demonstrate a greater sense of agency and have been active in supporting change by feeding information and problem-solving data into the system (Figure 11.2). A final benefit is that these supervisors are able to model these skills in their own work with supervisees. When we incorporate the 'system' within our evaluation paradigm the context for learning therefore extends still further.

Developing a culture of evaluation for supervision

In the context of supervision, the landscape of evaluation is therefore much wider than might be expected. Knowing what to pay attention to is perhaps the key, for we do not always need to be concerned with evaluating the same things, and we cannot evaluate everything at the same time. The choices of what to include within the process of evaluation should be directed by our knowledge of each given situation. Gilbert and Sills (1999: 166) offer one model for thinking about the different 'lenses for evaluation', which, presented in a pyramidal form, situate 'effective

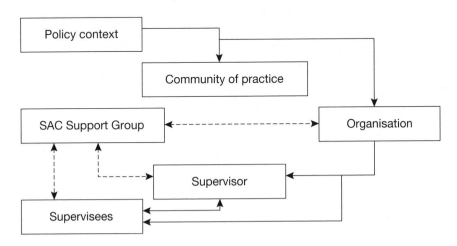

Figure 11.2 Sources of influence from across a system which impact upon all stakeholders

micro-skills' at the apex, with 'effective sessional skills and sessional outcomes' in the middle, and 'satisfactory supervisory development and effective outcomes over time' at the base. On the basis of this discussion, we could offer a model that draws upon, but extends, this thinking still further (Table 11.1).

When we look at the features of this 'systemic' model, we see that accountability for learning and action is not only invested in the supervisee; it also belongs elsewhere in the system. This model offers something of a shared agenda in which each can see more of the whole and hopefully, make more sense of the constituent parts as a result. As noted earlier, this does not suggest that all evaluation 'concerns' are viewed all of the time, but it does suggest that they will all be considered over time.

Conclusion

Evaluation works best when there are no secrets or hidden procedures. If practitioners are to value evaluation rather than fear it, then they must understand it and possess the skills to use the techniques of evaluation within their own practice. By developing their own skills in evaluation supervisees are likely to approach evaluative work with their supervisors with greater confidence. Evaluation must also be robust enough to command commitment from both supervisee and supervisors, and to generate worthwhile data. In the context of supervision, as in any other area of practice, it is therefore best approached as a collaborative enterprise.

Training in evaluation skills and techniques is also relevant to this debate. Poor evaluation serves no one's interests, but done well, it can contribute to learning across the continuum described above. Potentially, good evaluation can even provide robust data in respect to client gains from the service offered, which is frequently missing from discussions in supervision about the outcomes of practice. This is, after all, the most important data we can have. Practitioners can be enabled to become co-researchers into their own and others' practice, particularly where collegial working is encouraged. Collaborative working on action research projects is one such model where the emphasis is placed on problem-solving to improve practice, rather than upon the more instrumental use of evaluation as a vehicle for performance measurement.

Partnerships between organisations, practitioners and the research community also offer rich opportunities to generate new and worthwhile evidence about the effectiveness of practice. Partnerships of this kind may enable some of the broader issues around supervisory practice to be evaluated more freely, since they offer agencies access to a larger repertoire of skills and expertise, as well as an independent voice. As Feltham (2002) has argued, even our foundational assumptions about supervision need to be tested. Evaluation on a macro scale can tackle such issues, and in so doing, also contribute to organisational learning.

Table 11.1 Evaluation across a continuum

Evaluation Focus	Evaluation Focus	Evaluation Focus	Evaluation Focus
The competence and work of the practitioner	The supervisee's engagement with the supervisory relationship	The supervisor's effectiveness in creating a mutually shared and effective learning environment	Organisational and system characteristics which act as enabling or constraining factors
Evaluation concerns	*Evaluation concerns*	*Evaluation concerns*	*Evaluation concerns*
• Supervisee's learning and its application to practice • Micro-skills and their application in work with clients • Assessment of performance • Ethical practice • Personal support and wellbeing	• The engagement of the supervisee with the process and tasks of supervision • The outcomes of supervision in promoting the effectiveness of the supervisee's practice	• The supervisor's ability to create and sustain an effective learning environment which enjoys shared ownership and more equal power relations • The supervisor's ability to model good practice across a range of skills and attitudes • The supervision or support for supervisors	• The supervisor and supervisee's ability to read and understand organisational and professional cultures and assess their bearing as an impediment or resource for practice – both for the supervisee and supervisor • The ability to use the resources within a system, organisational or beyond, to promote learning or resolve problems • The effectiveness of the feedback loop

←————   Evaluation across continuum   ————→

Bibliography

Butterworth, T. (1997) ' "It is good to talk"; an evaluation study in England and Scotland', University of Manchester, Department of Nursing and Midwifery, in S. Cottrell and G. Smith, *The Development of Models of Nursing Supervision in the UK*, www.clinical-supervision.com (accessed 10 April 2003).

Carroll, M. (1996) *Counselling Supervision: Theory, Skills and Practice*, London: Continuum.

Clarkson, P. and Gilbert, M. (1991) 'The training of counsellor trainers and supervisors', in W. Dryden and B. Thorne (eds) *Training and Supervision for Counselling in Action*, London: Sage.

Copeland, S. (1998) 'Counselling supervision in organisational contexts: new challenges and perspectives', *British Journal of Guidance and Counselling*, 26 (3): 385.

Cottrell, S. and Smith, G. (2003) *The Development of Models of Nursing Supervision in the UK*, www.clinical-supervision.com (accessed 10 April 2003).

Edwards, A. (2001) 'Developing a framework for support for personal advisers,' in A. Edwards (ed.) *Supporting Personal Advisers in Connexions: Perspectives on Supervision and Mentoring from Allied Professions*. Occasional Paper, Centre for Career and Personal Development: Canterbury Christ Church University College.

Feltham, C. (2002) 'Supervision: a surveillance culture?' *Counselling and Psychotherapy Journal*, February 2002.

Gilbert, T.M. and Sills, C. (1999) 'Training for supervision evaluation', in E. Holloway and M. Carroll (eds), *Training Counselling Supervisors*, London: Sage.

Gould, L.J. and Bradley, L.J. (2001) 'Evaluation in supervision', in L.J. Bradley and N. Ladany (eds) *Counsellor Supervision: Principles, Processes and Practice*, 3rd edn, Philadelphia, PA: Brunner-Routledge.

Hawkins, P. and Shohet, R. (1989) *Supervision in the Helping Professions*, Milton Keynes: Open University Press.

Hellman, S. (1999) 'The portfolio: a method of reflective development', in E. Holloway and M. Carroll (eds) *Training Counselling Supervisors*, London: Sage.

Houston, G. (1995) *Supervision and Counselling*, rev. edn, London: The Rochester Foundation.

Hughes, L. and Pengelly, P. (1997) *Staff Supervision in a Turbulent Environment: Managing Process and Task in Front-line Services*, London: Jessica Kingsley.

Hulbert, S. (2000) *Working with Socially Excluded and 'At Risk' Young People: Research into the Need for, and Appropriate Form of, Support and Supervision for Personal Advisers Working Within the New Connexions Support Service*, Stourbridge: Institute of Career Guidance.

Inskipp, F. (1996) 'New directions in supervision', in R. Bayne, I. Horton, and J. Bimrose (eds) *New Directions in Counselling*, London: Routledge.

Kadushin, A. (1985) *Supervision in Social Work*, New York: Columbia University Press.

Kemshall, H. (1995) 'Supervision and appraisal in the Probation Service', in J. Pritchard (ed.) *Good Practice in Supervision: Statutory and Voluntary Organisations*, London and Bristol: Jessica Kingsley.

King, M. (2004) *Professional Supervision System – Evaluation*, Maidstone: Careers Management Kent and Medway.

McMahon, M. (2002) 'Career counsellors as reflective practitioners and life-long learners: what is the place of supervision?' in M. McMahon and W. Patton (eds) *Supervision in the Helping Professions: a Practical Approach*, Frenchs Forest, Australia: Pearson Education.

—— and Patton, W. (2000) 'Conversations on clinical supervision: benefits perceived by school counsellors', *British Journal of Guidance and Counselling*, 28 (3): 339–351.

Pickvance, D. (1997) 'Becoming a supervisor', in G. Shipton (ed.) *Supervision of Psychotherapy and Counselling; Making a Place to Think*, Buckingham: Open University Press.

Reid, H.L. (2005) 'What advisers want from support and supervision: "pit-head time to wash off the dust of their labours"', *Career Guidance Today*, 13 (1), Stourbridge: Institute of Career Guidance.

Scaife, J. (2001) *Supervision in the Mental Health Professions: a Practitioner's Guide*, London: Brunner-Routledge.

Shohet, R. and Wilmot, J. (1991) 'Key issues in the supervision of counsellors: the supervisory relationship', in W. Dryden and B. Thorne (eds) *Training and Supervision for Counselling in Action*, London: Sage.

Tash, M.J. (1967) *Supervision in Youth Work*, London: YMCA George Williams College.

United Kingdom Central Council for Nursing, Midwifery and Health Visiting (1995) *Position Statement on Clinical Supervision for Nursing and Health Visiting*, Registrar's letter, 1 May, 11/96, London.

Wheeler, S. and King, D. (2000) 'Do counselling supervisors want or need to have their supervision supervised? An exploratory study', *British Journal of Guidance and Counselling*, 28, (2): 279–290.

—— and —— (eds) (2001) *Supervising Counsellors: Issues of Responsibility*, London: Sage.

12 Support work with children
Ethical dilemmas, confidentiality and the law

Debbie Daniels

Introduction

This chapter sets out to address and clarify some of the complex questions regarding ethics and the law when working with children in a supportive role. Youth support workers and supervisors will at times encounter ethical dilemmas in working with children and may experience confusion, often through misinformation, in relation to the law. Ethical codes may add to the confusion, as guidelines can appear to be vague or contradictory and render support workers and supervisors uncertain of their remit. In some instances the ethical guidelines of an organisation may conflict with personal beliefs, while some may not seem to correspond with legal perspectives. Yet it is of vital importance that youth support workers and supervisors work within an ethical framework and within the boundaries of the law.

The anxiety for the support worker who is presented with a serious ethical dilemma, or who is uncertain about their legal responsibilities can sometimes feel overwhelming. There seem to be two basic issues that cause support workers anxiety in working with children, which are frequently presented in supervision. The first involves issues around parental consent and parental involvement within the context of support work. The second concerns issues of disclosure from child clients, sometimes involving risk of abuse or neglect. These issues are of concern as parental involvement and disclosure by the support worker of client material can conflict with the ethical principle of confidentiality.

Throughout this chapter some of the scenarios that support workers often encounter in relation to these issues will be explored, together with some analysis of the ethical and legal implications. Supervision from a well-informed supervisor, who can clarify the ethical and legal requirements in working with children, may go a long way to diminish the anxiety that support workers encounter. It would seem that a number of myths and assumptions have been generated regarding the law and working with children; the chapter will clarify relevant pieces of legislation in order to dispel some of these myths.

It should be noted that for convenience, support workers, including counsellors, psychotherapists, youth workers, advice workers, careers advisers and mentors will be referred to as 'practitioners'. The term 'children' will refer to those under eighteen years of age, in accordance with the definition in the Children Act 1989, as those under the age of majority. It should also be noted that a far more extensive exploration of all of the areas covered in this chapter can be found in this author's previous book *Therapy with Children: Children's Rights, Confidentiality and the Law* (Daniels and Jenkins 2000).

Ethical perspectives

The psychoanalytic tradition is the basis for the thoughts and ideas in this chapter (as in Chapter 3). The rationale for this is that all of the talking therapies, including counselling, psychotherapy and youth support work, pastoral care and supervision, evolved from psychoanalysis. All of these processes rely upon 'talking' as the method through which change can take place in the internal world of the client. Freud encouraged his patients to talk about their concerns and anxieties and required 'complete candour' from them (Freud 1938). In this, Freud instructed his patients to say whatever came into their thoughts, without censorship, through the technique that became known as 'free association'. In return he promised the 'strictest discretion' and a pact of confidentiality was formed. Freud understood that patients had a tendency to withhold or censor their thoughts often through feelings of shame or guilt. Confidentiality and trust in the therapist became a crucial aspect of the therapeutic treatment in helping to release these thoughts. Contemporary therapists and counsellors, whether they work from the psychoanalytic, humanistic or behavioural approaches, all accept that confidentiality and trust are at the heart of the therapeutic relationship. Confidentiality has become part of the accepted ethical code of practice and is most usually written into the ethical guidelines of organisations such as the British Association for Counselling and Psychotherapy (BACP 2001).

Daniluk and Haverkamp (1993) and Thompson (1990) have outlined six ethical principles which can be applied as guidelines to inform ethical practice for therapeutic practitioners. Confidentiality is encompassed under the term 'fidelity'. The six principles are as follows:

- autonomy: the promotion of the client's freedom of choice and action;
- fidelity: faithfulness, loyalty, the keeping of trust;
- justice: achieving equity, fairness, avoiding discrimination;
- beneficence: doing good, promoting the client's welfare;
- non-maleficence: avoiding harm or damage to the client;
- self-interest: promoting the self-knowledge, self-protection and self-development of the counsellor.

An exploration of these principles reveals how complex they are to work towards as they often conflict. For instance, a child may access a confidential service in which the practitioner maintains respect for the therapeutic relationship based on the ethical principle of fidelity. The child begins to disclose some difficult material, which suggests that they may be at risk, but nevertheless they request that this material remains confidential. The practitioner may agree to this, not only in respect of the principle of fidelity, but also in respect of the principle of autonomy; that the child should have freedom of choice. It could then be argued that the practitioner is failing to adhere to the principle of beneficence as a child left at risk may be a child whose welfare is being neglected, and it may be suggested that the practitioner is no longer 'doing good'.

However, if the practitioner then involves parents or outside agencies there will have been a breach of the principles of fidelity and autonomy, which may have a detrimental effect on the therapeutic relationship. The end result may be loss of the therapeutic space for the child who no longer trusts the relationship, or an external intervention that may contribute to a worsening of the child's situation. It may then be suggested that the practitioner has not adhered to the principle of non-maleficence and has instead caused the client harm. These are the complex issues that need to form part of discussions in the context of good supervision and training. There are no straightforward answers and each individual practitioner must eventually decide upon which stance they wish to take, using these principles as guidelines. However, it is of vital importance that whatever ethical stance is taken, the practitioner works within the boundaries of the law. The following section explores some of the most important legal issues regarding work with children, supported by examples from the author's own case material.

Parental involvement and the child's right of access to confidential treatment

In establishing support work for children in schools and agencies, the question often arises about whether parental permission should be sought. For many practitioners, a contract of total confidentiality with no parental involvement whatsoever, may not sit comfortably with the ethos of their working environment. In schools for instance, there may be a policy of parental consent for any activity in which their child participates. Parental permission may be sought for events such as school outings or a child being assessed by an educational psychologist, to more personal issues such as the child being seen by a counsellor. If parental permission is sought, then a further question arises on how far parents should be involved in the process. Practitioners wishing to offer children a confidential space often assume that this is not possible as parents always have to be informed, and sometimes they have to be involved either through regular feedback or actual participation. The following section will now address this assumption through an examination of the Gillick ruling.

The most radical piece of legislation that has reshaped the idea of parental rights came about through the Gillick ruling (Gillick v. Norfolk and Wisbech Area Health Authority 1985[1]). Mrs Victoria Gillick requested that her local health authority should not give contraceptive advice or treatment to her daughters who were under sixteen years of age. The health authority then placed this responsibility with the doctor's judgement and Mrs Gillick thus took the issue to court. It was felt that as this issue was of public importance it should be taken to the House of Lords. The Law Lords had to decide whether children under the age of sixteen were competent in making decisions regarding their own medical treatment. The outcome was as follows:

> the parental right to determine whether or not their minor child below the age of 16 will have medical treatment terminates if and when the child achieves a sufficient understanding and intelligence to enable him or her to understand fully what is proposed.
>
> (Gillick v. West Norfolk AHA 1986: 423)

The colloquial term used to describe sufficient understanding became known as 'Gillick competence'. A child was considered to be Gillick competent according to chronological age in conjunction with mental and emotional maturity, intelligence and comprehension. The child's age was therefore not the sole consideration in assessing Gillick competence. The ruling not only gave considerable rights to the child, but Lord Scarman also went on to clarify the position of the parent:

> The common law has never treated (parental) rights as sovereign or beyond review and control. Nor has our law ever treated the child as other than a person with capacities and rights recognised by law. Parental rights are derived from parental duty and exist only so long as they are needed for the protection of the person and property of the child.
>
> (Gillick v. West Norfolk AHA 1985: 420)

Parents were thus seen to have responsibility for, and not rights over their child: 'the parental power to control a child exists not for the benefit of the parent but for the benefit of the child' (Gillick v. West Norfolk AHA 1986: AC 112). The term parental *right*, reframed as parental *responsibility*, was further emphasised in the Children Act (Department of Health, 1989 S. 3(1)). A child's rights are defined further:

> The Gillick ruling highlights the principle of 'sufficient understanding' and enables children to make their own decisions concerning their own welfare, if they are considered to be Gillick competent. The result of the Gillick ruling was clear, children under the age of sixteen could seek confidential treatment from their doctor on matters of

contraception without parental consent or knowledge if the child understood the implications of the advice and treatment.

(Gillick v. West Norfolk AHA 1986: 423)

The Gillick ruling when applied to situations other than the patient/ doctor relationship can broaden the base of confidential relationships for children. Solicitor and social worker, Mitchels and Prince, state:

> The implications of the Gillick judgement are far greater than the specific issue of a child's right to confidentiality when seeking advice on contraception when under the age of 16 ... 'sufficient understanding' means that all children should be as involved as possible in decisions which affect their health or welfare ... not only should the child be consulted but his [sic] views *must* be taken into account.
>
> (1992: 83)

In applying the Gillick ruling to the school situation, children can be seen to have an ethical right to confidential treatment from counsellors, psychotherapists, mentors and youth support workers without the knowledge or consent of parents or outside agencies. Providing that the child is of mature understanding, then, there is a case to argue that the child is entitled to confidential professional support.

Parents need not be excluded unnecessarily from the support their child receives, indeed, involving parents can be of crucial benefit for the child. However, there are instances in which a child might request that parents should not be informed. In my experience of counselling in schools, two situations frequently occurred which were detrimental to the counselling process. Parents either requested that the counselling should be terminated, or intruded upon their child's counselling by asking so many questions about session content that the child felt compelled to terminate the process. There are many complex and understandable psychological reasons for such a response often based on envy and anxiety. Tsiantis *et al.* (1996) summarise this response by saying

> parents can also be intrusive, trying to manipulate the therapist as they manipulated the child in response to the feeling of being threatened by the possibility that their defects and faults will be revealed: they will be narcissistically unable to sustain their own emotional balance.
>
> (23)

In my experience, children seem to have a good awareness and insight into how their parents might respond and I have found that I need to take their requests for confidential counselling very seriously. In schools where consent is automatically sought from parents I have often heard it reported that practitioners are aware that a number of children refuse to work with them on this basis. During my earlier experiences as a counsellor in a school, a situation arose where a parent enforced what was seen to be her right to have her 12-year-old daughter's counselling terminated. The mother's anxiety was understandable as the girl was disclosing instances of emotional neglect and some physical abuse from her mother. The counselling was terminated with the detrimental effect that the girl's behaviour, which had been showing signs of significant improvement, rapidly deteriorated and after attacking the headteacher she was sent to a special school for disruptive pupils.

This scenario raises two questions; did the mother have to be informed of the child's counselling and could she prevent it from taking place? In applying the case law of the Gillick ruling, the mother certainly need not have been informed that the child was in counselling as the child was indeed of mature understanding. In trying to prevent her daughter from having further counselling, the mother would have had to bring a private case under tort law against the school. The mother would then have to demonstrate that damage to her child had been caused through the counselling. It would be extremely unlikely that either this could be shown, or that the case would reach court. It certainly would not be considered a good enough reason to terminate the counselling simply because, as in this situation, the mother disapproved of and felt anxious about the counselling.

It should be noted that the Gillick ruling is sometimes overturned, although this is more in cases where children are not seeking, but rather refusing, treatment, such as medical intervention in life and death situations. However, the ruling is there to be used and children of mature understanding do have a right to access confidential services. Therefore support workers and their schools need to proceed with caution. To state that there is an automatic policy in a school to inform parents is in breach of the Gillick ruling. In addition, the child's right to privacy under Article 8 of the Human Rights Act 1998 could be seen to be denied.

Assumptions about mandatory reporting

An area of confusion that I have encountered among practitioners is where they stand in relation to mandatory reporting. Practitioners often tell me that generally they would like to offer a contract of confidentiality for the children they work with. They report some moving examples of situations in which they feel they have betrayed a child's trust in reporting information that the child told them in confidence. The reason they often give for this is that they felt they had to report, as it is the law to do so, when it is deemed that a child might be at risk. The Children Act is often cited as the document where this piece of legislation is set out. In this section I would like to outline what are the legal and contractual requirements when working with children. While this is not entirely a straightforward matter, the intention is to dispel some of the myths and assumptions whereby practitioners may make a more informed decision in either reporting or maintaining confidentiality.

Lord Mackay, the author of The Children Act 1989, described it as 'the most comprehensive and far-reaching reform of child care law which has come before Parliament in living memory' (Hansard 1989: col. 488). The Act is long and complex, much of it was the subject of debate for some six years, and clearly it would be beyond the scope of this chapter to cover the many aspects of this lengthy document here. In brief, the Act set out to promote the care and welfare of children, stating that 'the child's welfare shall be the paramount consideration' (DoH 1989: S.1). Another significant aspect was that parents no longer have *rights* over, but rather a *responsibility* for their child. The Act brought together private law concerning issues such as divorce and custody, and public law concerning the duties of local authorities in looking after children. In all areas the views of the child were to be considered; for example, in public law a statement was made that, 'Before making any decision with respect to a child whom they are looking after, or proposing to look after, a local authority shall, so far as is reasonably practicable, ascertain the wishes and feelings of . . . the child' (DoH 1989: S. 22).

There is often a myth among practitioners working with children that the Children Act also introduced mandatory reporting. This is indeed a misapprehension, as so far there are no mandatory reporting laws in the United Kingdom. A proposal to enforce mandatory reporting laws was made in 1985, but this was rejected in no uncertain terms by the Review of Child Care Law. It was stated that it might

> be counter-productive and increase the risks to children overall, first by weakening the individual professional's sense of personal responsibility and secondly, in casting the shadow of near automatic reporting over their work, by raising barriers between clients and their professional adviser and even between professionals concerned in the same case.
>
> (Department of Health and Social Security 1985: para.12.4)

Therefore, no individual citizen or professional has a duty to report under the law. It appears that the myth on the duty to report may have evolved first from a misinterpretation of section 47 of the Children Act 1989 (Department of Health 1989). There it is stated that the local authority is required to investigate cases where it is suspected that a child is suffering or is likely to suffer significant harm. Therefore, if an individual practitioner chose to report a case of abuse then the local authority would have to investigate. The local authority would then ask the education authorities or health authorities to assist with the enquiries. However, this part of the Act 'does not oblige any person to assist a local authority where doing so would be unreasonable in all the circumstances of the case' (DoH 1989: S. 47).

A greater misconception is more likely to arise from practitioners confusing the Children Act with a set of guidelines from the policy document 'Working Together' (Department of Health/Home Office 1991). This document sets out guidelines for child protection procedures for multi-disciplinary teams compiled from education, health, police, social services and voluntary agencies. Therefore, under education, the guidelines may be in place and form part of a teacher's contract. The teacher would then have an obligation to report should they suspect that a child has been abused or is at risk of abuse. If the teacher failed to report, then they could be disciplined for a breach of contract, which could involve dismissal. However, again it must be stressed that neither the Children Act nor the law requires mandatory reporting; therefore, for practitioners working with children a conflict occurs. The conflict lies between the practitioner's contract of employment that may require mandatory reporting, and the common legal requirement that does not demand mandatory reporting. In addition the practitioner has a fiduciary duty to maintain a client's trust through confidentiality. This is somewhat different to the right of 'privilege', which is a right of total confidentiality that only applies to lawyers in England and Wales. A fiduciary duty implies that it is accepted in law that certain professionals such as doctors, priests, and counsellors may operate from a contract of confidentiality and that they have a certain obligation of trust to their clients. Practitioners therefore have to consider, seriously, the following legal and ethical questions:

- What contract of employment am I working under? Does it involve mandatory reporting?
- What are the ethical codes of the organisation I belong to?
- What is my fiduciary duty of trust and confidentiality to my clients?
- What do my clients request in relation to confidentiality? Are my clients Gillick competent?

Supervision with a well-informed and open- minded supervisor can offer an opportunity for thorough discussion of the points raised above. The supervisor and practitioner may not always agree on which course of action to take, and right and wrong answers are not necessarily available in the area of ethics. What is important is that the practitioner can present a sound ethical argument and a factual legal basis for any decision that is reached. It is possible that the practitioner may be held to account for the decision they have reached through a court of law. They may be asked to explain how and why they reached certain decisions regarding their work. The practitioner may then need to offer explanations about the importance of confidentiality and trust to the supportive relationship. While it is unlikely that such a scenario would occur, it is more probable that the practitioner will experience ongoing ethical dilemmas during the course of their work. It is then that an informed supervisor can offer a containing space in which these issues can be explored.

Legal responsibility and litigation

Practitioners usually attempt to do everything they can to help the children they are working with, and do hold that the child's welfare is of paramount consideration. Sometimes, difficult professional decisions have to be made and practitioners and supervisors often feel overwhelmed and frightened by what can appear to be enormous responsibilities. In my role as a supervisor and author on this subject, I am often presented with worried practitioners who fear litigation and are concerned that they could be sued should something go wrong in their client's life. Numerous examples from the USA seem to have filtered into the UK media; but here I would like to explore some of the myths around the likelihood of practitioners being called to court, held responsible and even sued.

There is no doubt that keeping a child's confidence can be extremely anxiety provoking, especially if the practitioner feels that the child might be at risk of harm. This is not an easy situation and the aim to protect the child has to be balanced against the possible alternative outcomes. One major concern of reporting could be that the child experiences an acute feeling of betrayal and refuses any further assistance from the practitioner. The child may then have to deal with the backlash of reporting with no support from the practitioner. In some circumstances the external situation for the child may be made worse if intervention is provided without great care being taken. Children often acknowledge that they experience the intervention following disclosure as equally traumatic as the original abusive situation. A practitioner may instead decide that it might be in the child's greatest interest to work with the child's internal world, for example through therapeutic intervention, rather than making an attempt at altering the child's external circumstances. It may be that a parent or another adult concerned with the child's welfare, such as a relation, teacher or neighbour, would object to this stance claiming that the practitioner had not acted professionally.

If in the unlikely event that, for instance, the family of a child took a practitioner to court, then the court would have to assess the situation. Fortunately, the extensive litigation and cases of suing that appear all too often in the USA have not yet invaded the UK legal system. Courts in England and Wales are not generally very sympathetic to those who bring this type of legal action against a practitioner. However, in the event that it might occur, evidence would have to be produced to show that there was a breach of 'duty of care' on behalf of the practitioner. This goes back to the ethical principles outlined at the beginning of this chapter of maleficence, to not cause harm, and beneficence, to do good. There are two different situations that could amount to a breach of duty of care. The first occurs when a particular action is taken by the practitioner leading to harm: this in effect is malpractice. The second occurs when an action is not taken, leading to harm: this is negligence. The court would have to assess whether something was done that should not have been done, or not done, that should have been done, under a duty of care.

One important question to be considered in examining the details in a case of negligence is whether the practitioner could *foresee* that harm would come to the client as a consequence of the practitioner not taking action. This is clearly very difficult to assess. There are numerous scenarios in which we as practitioners are not entirely sure what a client's 'reality' is. An extreme scenario, but nevertheless one which practitioners often bring to mind when debating risk to clients, is that of suicide by a client. In my own experience of 16 years of clinical work with both children and adults I have never lost a client to suicide. However, I have sat through literally thousands of clinical sessions in which clients have talked about suicidal fantasies and many sessions in which they have threatened suicide. One particular client threatened suicide for over three years and there were some anxious times for myself between sessions. This anxiety increased whenever the client followed a threat by arriving late to the next session or missing the session entirely. Through supervision I was able to discuss, from a psychoanalytic perspective, the possible interpretations concerning these threats of suicide and the client's acting out behaviour. I was encouraged to explore with the client his fantasies around the suicidal thoughts and such exploration led to some interesting revelations. For example, the client revealed fantasies that displayed a punitive theme about how he imagined I might react to news of the suicide. There was an understanding between my supervisor and I that adhering to psychoanalytic technique, in this particular case, would serve a far greater purpose than intervention by external agencies. The client never did attempt suicide and through interpretation we worked through his fantasies until they diminished.

In cases of a different outcome then it would be for the court to decide whether the practitioner could have *foreseen* that the client would commit suicide and whether the practitioner could have taken action to prevent it. Expert witnesses (such as a psychiatrist, psychoanalyst or psychotherapist) would then be called to perhaps discuss issues such as fantasies and transference and how one might, or indeed might not, be able to foresee that this was a real threat of the client's and not a fantasy. The practitioner's qualifications and skills would also come under examination, taking into consideration their ability to work with children with emotional difficulties. In addition there could be an examination of the practitioner's employment contract. The practitioner may actually be in breach of contract if it was stated that there was a duty to report. The latter in isolation, however, would be more of a disciplinary than legal matter.

Another difficult scenario presented itself when I was working with a highly intelligent, but borderline psychotic adolescent boy. The boy insisted he did not want his parents to know he was attending therapy, as he felt sure they would prevent it continuing. My supervisor, a very experienced child psychoanalyst, was concerned that the boy might have a psychotic breakdown and would have to be institutionalised. The supervisor asked how the boy's parents had reacted to their son's illness and therapeutic treatment. I informed my supervisor that I usually worked from a contract of total confidentiality, which I wished to maintain with this client. My client had insisted that his parents should not be informed and in spite of his illness, the boy was perfectly able to provide sensible reasons for this request. Should he not expect the same confidential treatment that my other clients expected and were granted? My supervisor, who was employed by a family therapy service and familiar with working with parents and children, considered the different implications of working with a child in isolation. While initially surprised by my contract, my supervisor observed this work unfolding with respectful interest. Further opportunities were available to discuss this client and my approach (Daniels and Jenkins 2000: 121). I maintained confidentiality throughout this case and after two years of treatment the boy greatly improved and some years later went on to university. Had the outcome been different, the parents may have wanted a court case where it would have to be proved that there was negligence through inaction in the form of not reporting the boy's illness. It would also have to be proven that I could have foreseen that the boy would have a psychotic breakdown and should have taken action to prevent it, probably through medical intervention. As evidenced from the actual outcome, this is not easy to predict, as there was no action, and there was no breakdown.

In summary, it may be very difficult for a court to prove that a practitioner could foresee the consequences of their inaction. Perhaps because of this, courts do not usually encourage individuals to sue practitioners. Again, it is unlikely that such a scenario would occur, and certainly the courtroom is not the place to begin thinking about such issues. Instead, it is vital to discuss ethical dilemmas as and when they arise in the context of supervision, and for both practitioner and supervisor to continually update themselves on legal issues. It is the responsibility of every supervisor and practitioner to adhere to ethical codes of practice, to be well trained, informed and qualified in their field, and to abide by their contract of employment.

Conclusion

The law in England and Wales does allow for those working with children to provide a confidential support service. The Gillick ruling may seem to be losing some of the initial impact it had, particularly in life and death situations, but it still prevails. Following the Laming Inquiry (Department of Health 2003), into the death of Victoria Climbie, the issue of mandatory reporting for child abuse has been discussed, but at present there is still no legal compulsion for mandatory reporting. The practitioner therefore has the freedom, but also the enormous responsibility, to decide how to offer a child a confidential therapeutic service, while taking into consideration the child's safety and welfare. This is not an easy task but it is one that can be best discussed within the context of supervision. There is no doubt that these issues raise numerous questions and anxieties for the support worker. A skilled supervisor may be able to contain these anxieties by fully discussing the ethics of each case, carefully balancing child protection issues with the framework of the counselling process. Questions may arise such as, how urgent is the need for external intervention? Is external intervention needed at all? Will there be a negative impact on the therapeutic relationship if there is seen to be a breach of trust? However, it is not sufficient to explore such dilemmas only from an ethical perspective. Skilled supervision in working with children also involves the supervisor becoming aware and informed about legislation in England and Wales as it relates to children. The supervisor might then be better equipped to guide and support the supervisee through the complexities of ethical, legal and contractual obligations.

Bibliography

British Association for Counselling and Psychotherapy (2001) *Ethical Framework for Good Practice in Counselling and Psychotherapy*, Rugby: BACP.

Daniels, D. and Jenkins, P. (2000) *Therapy with Children: Children's Rights, Confidentiality and the Law*, London: Sage.

Daniluk, J. and Haverkamp, B. (1993) 'Ethical Issues in Counselling Adult Survivors of Incest', *Journal of Counseling and Development*, 72: 16–22.

Department of Health (1989) *Children Act*, S.3[1], S.1, S.22, S.47, London: HMSO.

Department of Health (2003) *The Victoria Climbie Inquiry*, Lord Laming, London: HMSO.

Department of Health/Home Office (1991) *Children Act 1989. Guidance and Regulations*, vol. 2, 'Working Together', London: HMSO.

Department of Health and Social Security (1985) *Review of Child Care Law*, London: HMSO.

Freud, S. (1938) *An Outline of Psychoanalysis*, New York: Norton.

Gillick v. West Norfolk Area Health Authority (1986) at 423, (1985) at 420, (1986) AC 112, (1986) at 423, London: HMSO.

Hansard (1989) *House of Lords Debates*, vol. 502, No. 7 Col. 488, London: Hansard.

Mitchels, B. and Prince, A. (1992) *The Children Act and Medical Practice*, Bristol: Jordan and Sons.

Thompson, A. (1990) *Guide to Ethical Practice in Psychotherapy*, New York: Wiley.

Tsiantis, J., Sandler, A.M., Anastasopulos, D. and Markindale, B. (1996) *Countertransference in Psychoanalytic Psychotherapy with Children and Adolescents*, London: Karnac.

Note

1   Gillick v. West Norfolk AHA references are taken from documents dated 1985 and 1986.

13 A cautionary note on support and supervision

Hazel L. Reid

Introduction

The preceding chapters suggest that the purpose of support and supervision is, at times, contested. However, there is an overall view in all of the chapters in this book that support and supervision is needed for personal advisers and youth support workers. That said, it is important to question a taken-for-granted belief that support and supervision is 'a good thing' beyond initial professional training. This final chapter adds a cautionary note by questioning our common sense view of the importance of the practice.

The chapter begins by exploring the assumption that supervised and experienced practitioners perform better than unsupervised experienced practitioners. It draws on criticisms in the literature and considers the implications of a practice that can lead to the 'infantilisation' of practitioners within a time-costly bureaucracy (Feltham 2002a). It links this to insights that can be gained from a Transactional Analysis approach to support and supervision. It then explores how supervision can be viewed as an aspect of the prevailing discourse of self-governance located in many critical perspectives around individualised lifelong learning. In so doing it discusses the issue of surveillance, where power is exercised through the disciplining practices of self-regulation, self-improvement and self-development.

However, debates about issues in practice are rarely solved if presented as dichotomous. Having taken a cautionary view, the chapter moves on to consider alternative approaches to established thinking about methods for support and supervision. It reasserts the importance of acknowledging a range of 'meaning' given to the practice and the need for open, flexible approaches. The chapter concludes by giving voice to practitioners' need for 'care of self' in order to support their professional ability to take 'care of others'.

Supervision is 'a good thing'

Writing from a counselling perspective, Feltham (2002a) suggests that supervision is not universally understood, accepted or viewed as a 'good thing' by all therapists. While arguing that supervision is a necessary activity for trainees, he claims there is no clear evidence to support the view that supervised and experienced practitioners perform better than unsupervised experienced practitioners. There can be an assumption that supervised practice overcomes complacency, arrogance and potentially dangerous behaviour. This assumption ignores the possibility of unwitting collusion where supervisees (and supervisors) play the game within a professional, resource-intensive process. Feltham refers to anecdotal evidence of supervisees, 'feeling cowed, deskilled and wary in relation to supervision, however skilled and ethically competent the supervisor' (2002a: 27).

The writers in this book emphasise the importance of a shared process for support and supervision. They discuss what can often 'go wrong' with the practice from a number of perspectives. In particular, issues related to transference and counter-transference have been explored. Space restricts a comprehensive discussion here, but insights from Transactional Analysis can also help to investigate the issues related to power at the level of individual and organisational communication within supervision practice. For example, Hughes and Pengelly (1997) invoke the use of the drama triangle to describe the dynamics of a supervisory relationship when difficulties occur. The drama triangle comprises the roles of *persecutor*, *rescuer* and *victim*, and these roles can be defensive positions when problems arise. The tale of the Pied Piper is given as a good example of the persecutor–rescuer–victim triangle and demonstrates how the roles are not fixed, but can switch rapidly.

To relate this to supervision, the practitioner may have a difficult 'case' where they are aware that they are trying to 'rescue' a young person who appears to be a 'victim', 'persecuted' by another individual. However, in acting on this belief the practitioner may report the situation, which can then place them in the role of persecutor. The practitioner then turns to their supervisor to be rescued. When the supervisor moves on from empathy and begins to explore the action, the practitioner may then view the supervisor as a persecutor and try to hide the issue and withdraw. The supervisee feels persecuted and a victim, the supervisor feels left out and may revert to a rescuing role.

If this, or something similar, happens, it takes care and some struggle for both parties to think about what is going on and how to address the problem. Youth support workers and their supervisors will find it difficult to conceive of themselves as 'persecutors' and it is likely that they will react to avoid taking this position – both in their work and in their supervision of colleagues. If the supervisor takes the rescuer position, prompted by an anxiety of being a persecutor, then issues that do need addressing are likely to be hidden as too troubling to explore, even in supervision. To ignore an issue in supervision, for fear of being unfair or too challenging, leads to the adoption of what transactional analysis refers to as the ego state of Nurturing Parent, which in turn may infantilise the supervisee: evoking a Child ego-state response.

Feltham regards supervision as an institution that can lead to 'infantilisa-tion' and states, 'We might have learned from Foucault and others the dangers of a surveillance culture' (2002a: 27). This reminds us of the need to examine the assumptions inherent in our thinking about the 'virtue' of support and supervision. And, the need to question how supervision could itself be viewed as an aspect of Foucault's notion of power and the products of power, as exercised through the governing practices of self-regulation, self-improvement and self-development (Edwards 1997). Before moving on, it may be useful to offer, however tentative, a definition of discourse and power, as used in this chapter.

Discourse theory proposes that the spoken word arises not purely from the knowledge of a language, but from the impact of experience that gives meaning to an individual's use of the language. It is viewed as above language. Thus, language for the individual is not neutral, but resonates with meaning interpreted via their position within society. Our perspectives, background, beliefs and language, then, shape the way the world is viewed. In turn, the way we read the world shapes the meaning we bring to the written word. Further, discourse is located in a historical context, in so far as a particular view becomes valid over other possible viewpoints at any one time. This suggests that words and their meanings are not fixed, but shift, and will alter according to the particular context and who is speaking. In other words, 'Discourse structures our comprehension to the point where action is defined by our concept of what is possible' (Reid 2002: 53). So, what is both included and excluded from our system of meanings – what is meaningful – leads to competing discourses, based on a different view of what is valid. These different discourses can stand, therefore, in antagonistic positions. Discourse theory would suggest that the governing influence of a dominant discourse is, of course, subtle not overt or coercive. This 'governmentality' works through educating people to govern themselves rather than through coercion (Edwards 1997).

Edwards explores the concept of power and discourse while looking at reflective practice and the decline in professional autonomy. This is particularly important when considering support and supervision as an arena for identifying strategies for client intervention and for the self-development of the practitioner. As discussed elsewhere in this book, support and supervision could be viewed as a key site for the development of effective practice, where lifelong learning can take place. This may lead to what Edwards defines in the statement, 'Knowledgeable practice requires more than practical knowledge' (1997: 155).

What is suggested in the above statement is more than a mechanistic understanding of 'what works' in practice: it suggests a need for deeper reflection and development. One of the Connexions service key principles is, 'Evidence based practice – ensuring that new interventions are based on rigorous research and evaluation into "what works"' (DfEE 2000: 33). The meaning of the statement is not entirely clear. It could indicate a distrust of academic research that is not seen as directly 'useful', and/or it could indicate a more important role for research. It could suggest the need for continuous reflective development and dissemination of good practice, i.e. 'knowledgeable practice'. I return to the 'what works' agenda later in the chapter.

Moving on, Feltham (2002a) claims there is no clear evidence to support the view that supervised and experienced practitioners perform better with, rather than without, supervision. As he acknowledges, within counselling in the UK, all practitioners operating within the British Association of Counselling's code (BAC 1988) must undertake supervision, therefore a comparative evaluation is not possible. McMahon and Patton (2000) would contest the view that supervision is not needed after initial training and state that supervision should continue throughout practice. Writing about school counsellors in Australia, the evidence from their research suggested that without ongoing supervision the skill level of practitioners was seen to decrease. In the light of increased concerns over child protection and inquiries into child deaths, there is real anxiety about placing practitioners, however experienced, in positions where their practice is unsupervised or under-supervised. There are some very real tensions here between supporting a worker on the one hand, and undermining their autonomy, integrity and professionalism on the other. While discipline and accountability are important, we need to be mindful that support and supervision can add to the development of a low-trust, surveillance culture for youth support workers. Such ideas can be related to the work of Foucault and are discussed in the next section.

Foucault, discourse and support and supervision

Foucault's use of discourse is always linked to social institutions, such as education, law and the family, and to disciplinary practices, such as psychology, medicine, science, psychotherapy and pedagogy. The latter practices *discipline* the conduct of those who come within the influence of the social institutions that sustain these practices (MacLure 2003). Institutionalised languages and related practices highlight certain aspects of the 'real' world as part of our attempts to control and change that world. The work of youth support workers traverses a number of the social institutions listed above. For example, the work is related to education, social work, youth justice and counselling. The above definition would suggest that the practices associated with these institutions *discipline* personal advisers and their clients. In a similar vein, Besley (2002: xvii) discusses how school counsellors need to consider such power-knowledge relationships for their work with clients, in order to 'develop a more self reflexive form of counselling' and to question humanistic assumptions about identity. Put another way, to question the 'modern' and Western view of the centrality of the individual: a view of identity formation that is contested by other worldviews or discourses (as discussed by Bimrose in Chapter 6 of this book).

Power is central to the notion of discourse. However, the view of power is relational, not one that sees power as located only in the hands of a powerful elite. For Foucault, power was not a substance that could be handed from one to another, as power can only exist in relations between individuals. Power is diffuse, fragmented and operates in networks through institutions, which is not the same as saying that power does not become concentrated in the hands of the more powerful, who are more powerful due to social class, gender, ethnicity and the like. In the context of supervision, this discussion must also acknowledge the impact of a power imbalance that exists in line-management supervision, but it would be a mistake to assume that other forms of supervision are immune from the influence of less obvious power relations. Then again, even though power dominates and subjects, through its circulation and operation in localities it always leaves open the possibility for resistance (Besley 2002).

For instance, in relation to the mandatory practice of supervision within counselling, Feltham (2002b) argues that the 'must' imperative is likely to lead to some practitioners taking a negative view of supervision. This can lead to a form of resistance where the practitioner postpones appointments for supervision, or attends, because they 'must', but engages in withdrawal activities. In this way the resistance is constrained by the imperative to attend, but undermines the *purpose* of supervision, particularly where this is imposed 'from above' and not negotiated with the individual practitioner. Power, then, is not just repressive it is also productive. It produces disciplined subjects, some of who may have more *agency* than others; that is, they are more able to exercise freedom of choice to act as they wish.

Knowledge is required of subjects (for example, via government statistical surveys, medical notes, educational reports and so on) in order for power to be exercised. In this sense power governs through knowledge of the population, but is internalised by individuals who are socialised within cultural institutions. This socialisation leads to mechanisms of self-surveillance where practitioners consent to the operations of governmentality. Atkinson, considering how this functions in education, calls this 'the collusion in our own oppression' (2003: 9). In relation to the study of support and supervision this returns us to questioning the 'need' for the practice. Is support and supervision a form of governmentality and a self-disciplining practice? Personal advisers in the author's study (Reid 2005, as outlined in Chapter 2 of this book) were unenthusiastic about imposing support and supervision for personal adviser work, but felt that the need for a structured process overcame their doubts about 'oppression', or loss of autonomy.

The view of power-knowledge described above is not static, as each epoch or each society has its *regimes of truth*; in other words, types of discourses that are accepted and function as true rather than false (Foucault 1980). A 'regime of truth' in the author's study would be that the central purpose of support and supervision is to benefit work with clients. Albeit that ways of speaking about the purpose of support and supervision (discourse positioning) in the study were not fixed, the data suggests that this is not the central purpose from the practitioner viewpoint. It is important to emphasise that these views about 'purpose' are developing and that an interpretive approach in research provides illustrative insights, but any results are always provisional. If not claiming truth, we can say that discourses define what can be said and who can say it, but, by definition, they also define what cannot be said, as they 'rule out other ways of thinking and acting' (MacLure 2003: 178). This suggests that the practitioner viewpoint, where it differs from the common sense *regime of truth*, may be 'ruled out' and not 'heard'.

Powerful discourses at work in personal adviser and youth support work

There are a number of powerful discourses in the field of guidance and youth support work in the UK that shaped what was said about support and supervision in the study. One of these is an instrumental discourse that implies that theoretical knowledge and reflecting on the work are of limited value. Closs (2001: 37/38) suggests that, 'Advisers should concentrate on getting on with the job, which can be increasingly difficult these days'. This is a pervasive view where theory and research is seen as irrelevant to day-to-day practice (Edwards and Usher 1994), and one enhanced by a governmental distrust of what are viewed as self-protecting professional bodies.

Such a view suggests that all that is needed for competent performance is that knowledge which is immediately useful (Edwards 1998a). While this may be acceptable for information-giving interviews, it is unlikely to meet the challenging demands that guidance interventions, or work with the 'harder-to-help' brings. Professional bodies and individual professionals may oppose this view, but resistance at a macro level is dependent on having a powerful voice. In order to survive, many agencies find they must comply with, rather than resist policy.

'Getting on with the job', and complying with government policy demands, is a dominant discourse for managers in public services in the UK and elsewhere. Resistance may be possible 'at the edges', but resistance is most likely where subjects are positioned within more powerful discourses. The effect of this 'getting on with the job' discourse can be seen in the study where time constraints determine what is received for support and supervision. This also affects what is viewed as appropriate or likely to happen by the groups involved: as ultimately 'getting on with the job' refers to the job with clients, and not support for practitioners.

If 'getting on with the job' is a management-led discourse, 'working for the benefit of clients' is a management, professional and practitioner discourse that is closely related. It is enshrined in standards and ethical codes of practice for counselling, guidance and youth support work, and for support and supervision. Ethical codes place 'benefit to the client' as the prime purpose of support and supervision (BAC 1988: 1). This is a discourse that fits with practitioners' concerns about impartiality and client-centredness.

These principles are challenged when getting on with the job in a target-driven environment leads to short, pragmatic interviews if 'low risk', realistic decision-making is the desired outcome (Stacey and Mignot 2000). This target-driven environment leads to the gathering of more and more information about the group seen as outside the 'norm' (DfES 2004). Youth support workers in this context become the implementers of disciplinary strategies aimed at 'normalising' those seen as different. In so doing, practitioners, when trained to value the principles of impartiality and client-centredness, are themselves disciplined in the disciplinary action taken towards their clients. The adviser becomes, in Foucault's terms (1979), the normalised subject that also normalises others.

Within a context which views inclusion in economic terms, the measurement of success in the Connexions service in England has been closely related to 'realistic' decision-making and meeting NEET (not in education, employment or training) targets (ICG 2002; DfES 2004). Consequently the amount of time spent with individual clients is coming under increasing scrutiny. In this pressurised environment, while giving practitioners 'permission to take time out to reflect' is viewed as 'essential' (ICG 2004: 5), this 'time out' remains constrained in a public service where funding regimes are under constant scrutiny. Whatever changes are made to youth support services in England, beyond Connexions, it seems likely that an outcome focused approach to accountability will continue.

A focus on realistic decision-making and working towards measurable outcomes, is linked to another powerful discourse in education and youth support work: that of 'what works'. It is not unreasonable to suggest that this discourse may pervade views about the purpose of support and supervision and the methods employed to 'deliver' it. Simple truths about 'what works' linked to 'common sense' are hard to challenge because they make asking opposing questions difficult. The hardest thing to 'see' and question in any policy statement is that which claims authority based on common sense, with its appeal as natural and unquestionable. In postmodernist thinking the discourse of 'what works', 'shuts down the trouble' (Britzman and Dippo 2000: 32). It also assumes that what works in one context can be generalised and applied to another.

These powerful discourses, which are difficult to challenge, constitute what was described earlier as a society's 'regime of truth': 'the types of discourses which it accepts and makes function as true' (Barker 1998: 93). Although there may be opposing voices, in the end it is the group that can command the greater power whose version of truth becomes dominant. This is nicely summed up by Mehan, 'All people define situations as real: but when powerful people define situations as real, then they are real *for everybody involved* in their consequences' (1999: 573) (emphasis in the original).

If the powerful discourses of 'getting on with the job', 'working for the benefit of the client' and 'evidence-based practice into what works' prevail and dominate the development of support and supervision systems, where is the voice of practitioners? In the study, their central story around the purpose of support and supervision was sited in their need for support 'to manage stress and avoid burnout': the 'restorative' function of support and supervision (Inskipp and Proctor 1993).

Nevertheless, as argued earlier, if pastoral rather than coercive or disciplinary power operates at a distance (Usher and Edwards 1998), this creates a space where individual judgement and action is possible. This space can open up opportunities at the local level for youth support workers to adopt their own strategies. In the Foucauldian view, power is not monolithic but operates through a network of productive relationships: it is in the local spaces that practitioners may be able to resist and negotiate their own needs from a system of support and supervision (there is some evidence of this in Chapter 11, by Edwards). This view of power and resistance helps to avoid overly structured views that ignore the 'agency' negotiated by individuals who struggle with policy at the local level.

If alternative discourses can be heard, it may help to balance the potential for support and supervision to become a 'technology of the self': the term used by Foucault to describe the social process of producing citizens with the right attitudes (1994: 87). In other words, procedures, such as support and supervision and reflective practice, shape identity through processes of 'self-mastery and self-knowledge' (ibid.). In this way subjects are disciplined through the 'normalising' processes of institutions whose practitioners 'police' themselves (Edwards 1998b). From this viewpoint support and supervision can be seen as operating as a practice of surveillance, as practitioners are disciplined into reflecting on their practice in order to understand themselves and their work better (Edwards and Usher 1994).

Self-surveillance and a 'know thyself' discourse are closely associated in guidance to the humanistic work of Carl Rogers (1961). In a postmodern and secular age, guidance and counselling are described as confessional practices (Usher and Edwards 1998) and part of the self-governing process where individuals 'bear public or private witness against oneself' (Foucault 1994: 242). In a similar process, support and supervision can be viewed as a disciplinary form of governmentality, particularly if the 'formative' and 'normative' functions predominate (Inskipp and Proctor 1993). And yet the 'restorative' function, through its confessionary nature, is perhaps a more powerful form of self-regulation: empowering on the one hand but potentially invasive and self-perpetuating on the other.

Much counselling and guidance work is dominated by humanistic assumptions of self-improvement and by theories related to 'finding self' (O'Doherty and Roberts 2000). Similarly, support and supervision can be seen to mirror this approach, and, similarly, the power–knowledge relationship needs to be problematised by questioning whose discourse the practice serves. How vulnerable do practitioners make themselves by engaging in self-regulatory and confessional practices?

Exposing the power of dominant discourses and how support and supervision can be a 'technology of the self' can provide a space to think differently and to negotiate alternative views about its purpose. There is a notion here that the naming of 'regimes of truth' has liberating possibilities: 'Naming a discourse can challenge unconscious acceptance of it, and enable resistance to its disciplinary function' (Colley 2003: 98). And, where there is power there is resistance, which opens up spaces for negotiation. So, what are the alternative methods for a practice that is not yet embedded in all personal adviser and youth support work?

Alternative methods for support and supervision practice

To avoid 'collegial cosiness' (Feltham 2002b: 333) and to take seriously the capacity for experienced practitioners to engage in creative reflection on their work, Feltham (2002a: 27) suggests a number of possible alternatives. For example, first, changing supervisor after a maximum of two years and using a mix of methods is thought advisable. Second, as well as individual, facilitated group and peer group supervision, including in this mix periods of intermittent supervision (which may include an agreed break from supervision). Third, use of other forms of professional training and retraining. Fourth, employing distance supervision: using the telephone or video-conferencing as an alternative to face-to-face. Fifth, adopting meaningful forms of self-supervision (Morrissette 2002). Sixth, specifically targeted supervision or consultation with an expert in a particular field of knowledge, for example, on eating disorders or specific phobias. We can add to the list by a) recognising the potential of electronic means for support and supervision, and b) advocating the use of creative methods employing art or drama.

In the mix of methods Feltham (2002a) also suggests taking the risk that some practitioners may practice best without supervision, or can develop their practice if left to their own resources. And, most radically of all, he suggests stopping the requirement for supervision altogether after a period of five to ten years. The latter point would need serious consideration for the reasons already outlined, however, it does alert us to the view that some practitioners may be resistant to continuous supervision. The message seems to be that we should not assume that all practitioners share views about the ongoing value of support and supervision.

In terms of the author's study none of the participants spoke against support and supervision: all viewed it as essential despite the variance as to purpose and process. However, the costs of implementing support and supervision cannot be ignored and some of the alternatives above merit consideration. Then again, there is a risk that alternatives on the grounds of cost may lead to processes that do not meet the needs of youth support workers. In the study there was a clear need for 'taking care of yourself' and, before concluding, the next section will discuss this further.

Taking care of self: an ethical position

For personal advisers in the study, 'taking care of yourself' was thought necessary in order to equip them to 'take care of clients'. In a criticism of humanism and the moral principles of the Western world, Rabinov notes that for Foucault 'know yourself' has obscured 'take care of your self' (Rabinov 1997: 228).

To varying degrees the personal advisers in the study viewed support and supervision as a 'bit of a luxury', not really believing in some cases that time would be made available, or feeling that where they took this time it was rather self-indulgent. However, being client-centred is a deeply held construct linked to the powerful discourses within the helping professions: as such it is an ontological view where practitioners working as 'intensive' personal advisers or youth support workers, view meeting the needs of young people as the core focus of their working lives. Foucault would view 'care of self' as an ethical position (Rabinov 1997). Giving due priority to 'care of self' over 'care of others', could be a mechanism for countering any negative effects of a power imbalance, discussed earlier, in relation to the disciplinary forces of self-regulation. In turn, it may enhance a practitioner's ability to take care of their clients.

What we can learn from Foucault, Feltham and others is the lesson of not adopting whole scale models from other professions where support and supervision is already an established practice. There is a need to negotiate 'best fit' with the personnel involved and avoid the oppressive 'one-size-fits-all' approach. Also, it is important to recognise the competence and skill of youth support workers, and the possibility that they can self-regulate much of their work via their professional common sense. At the same time cautionary tales should not lead to an either/or situation that ignores practitioners' need for a restorative space. How that space is used however, should be part of the negotiated process that is not static but develops over time.

Conclusion

If the practice of support and supervision is to be effective it needs to be acknowledged that there are different views about its purpose. There also needs to be space for those involved in the process to negotiate a range of methods that they view as appropriate. Flexibility extends to the ongoing practice of support and supervision in order to recognise that needs and discourses about purpose will change over time. It would seem essential to ensure time for the restorative function of support and supervision and to avoid the narrow doorway to 'what works'.

It seems important also to avoid a therapeutic approach that either 'pathologises' or makes 'victims' of practitioners. In enhancing the nature of a collaborative approach, clarity is needed about the aims and process for the practice. There needs to be a recognition that imposing support and supervision can be counter-productive in some cases and can lead to participation without engagement. Managers, supervisors and supervisees will need to be sensitive to the ways in which power is used, abused or hidden in the practice and to the ways in which support and supervision can de-skill and 'infantilise' practitioners. It needs to be seen that support and supervision can extend the low-trust, surveillance culture that professionals have to navigate. It also needs to be recognised that many will resist an approach that pushes them to expose feelings that may make them feel vulnerable.

The key story for the personal advisers in the author's study appeared to be the need for a restorative space to manage stress and avoid burnout. Although practitioners struggled with ideas about what was more important, this discourse on the purpose of support and supervision was positioned above the function of benefiting work with clients. This needs to be heard and valued. Providing time for restorative conversations, alongside the formative and normative dialogue in supervision, requires a change in ethos where 'care of self' is given a higher priority. In the study, one personal adviser responded to the question about the need for supervision by saying:

PA: I'm *desperate* for supervision and I've been *desperate* for some time!

Hazel: Desperate is a very strong word.

PA: I know, and I used it deliberately.

Since that interview, support and supervision has been introduced into her work role. But, understanding about the purpose and provision of support and supervision across careers/Connexions partnerships in England, has varied considerably (ICG 2003; Ofsted 2003). In many cases what is offered is focused on standards, or feels like remedial help in a crisis. The latter does not address the 'challenging' context of the work or the need for ongoing support to prevent 'burnout'. In discussing work with clients and the importance of understanding the social context of such work, Egan and Cowan (1979: 3) use the metaphor of upstream versus downstream helping:

> The story goes that a person walking alongside a river sees someone drowning. This person jumps in, pulls the victim out, and begins artificial respiration. While this is going on, another person calls for help; the rescuer jumps into the water again and pulls the new victim out. This process repeats itself several times until the rescuer gets up and walks away from the scene. A bystander approaches and asks in surprise where s/he is going, to which the rescuer replies, 'I'm going upstream to find out who's pushing all these people in and see if I can stop it!'

Connexions, as one example, in one country, of a 'holistic' youth support service, has moved to upstream helping for 'harder-to-help' young people who face multiple problems, or who are 'in danger' of entering this group. It has sought to change the conditions that create circumstances that require remedial help, in order to meet a 'duty of care' for vulnerable young people. That said, the service is being reviewed and the framework for delivering youth support is changing, albeit that the role of youth support worker will remain.

Although starting with a cautionary note, this final chapter ends by emphasising the requirement for support and supervision for personal advisers and youth support workers, wherever that work is located. In order to meet their support and supervision needs in this challenging area of intensive work, what they are asking for is some structured, but negotiated, 'upstream helping'. It seems essential to intervene before they risk drowning or need artificial respiration: after all, 'desperate' is a very strong word.

Bibliography

Atkinson, E. (2003) 'Education, postmodernism and the organisation of consent', in J. Satterthwaite, E. Atkinson and K. Gale (eds) *Discourse, Power, Resistance: Challenging the Rhetoric of Contemporary Education*, Stoke on Trent: Trentham Books.

Barker, P. (1998) *Michel Foucault: an Introduction*, Edinburgh: Edinburgh Press.

Besley, A.C. (Tina) (2002) *Counselling Youth: Foucault, Power and the Ethics Of Subjectivity*, Westport, CT: Praeger.

British Association of Counselling (1988) *Code of Ethics and Practice for the Supervision of Counsellors*, Rugby: BAC.

Britzman, D. and Dippo, D. (2000) 'On the future of awful thoughts in teacher education', *Teaching Education*, 11 (1): 31–37.

Closs, J. (2001) 'Theory in practice', *Career Guidance Today*, 9 (3), Stourbridge: Institute of Career Guidance.

Colley, H. (2003) 'The myth of mentor as a double regime of truth: producing docility and devotion in engagement mentoring with "disaffected" youth', in J. Satterthwaite, E. Atkinson and K. Gale (eds) *Discourse, Power, Resistance: Challenging the Rhetoric of Contemporary Education*, Stoke on Trent: Trentham Books.

Department for Education and Employment (2000) *Connexions: The Best Start in Life for Every Young Person*, London: DfEE.

Department for Education and Skills (2004) *Connexions Service Advice and Guidance for all Young People*, Report by the Comptroller and Auditor General, 31 March 2004, www.nao.org.uk/publications/naoreports/03-04.030448es.pdf (accessed 19 April 2004).

Edwards, R. (1997) *Changing Places? Flexibility, Lifelong Learning and a Learning Society*, London: Routledge.

—— (1998a) 'Mapping, locating and translating: a discursive approach to professional development', *Studies in Continuing Education*, 20 (1): 23–38.

—— (1998b) 'Flexibility, reflexivity and reflection in the contemporary workplace', *International Journal of Lifelong Education*, 17 (6): 377–388.

—— and Usher, R. (1994) 'Disciplining the subject: the power of competence', *Studies in the Education of Adults*, 26 (1): 1–13.

Egan, G. and Cowan, R.M. (1979) *People and Systems: an Integrative Approach to Human Development*, California: Brooks/Cole.

Feltham, C. (2002a) 'Supervision: a surveillance culture?' *Counselling and Psychotherapy Journal*, February 2002: 26–27.

—— (2002b) 'Supervision: critical issues to be faced from the beginning', in M. McMahon and W. Patton (eds) *Supervision in the Helping Professions, a Practical Approach*, Frenchs Forest, Australia: Pearson Education.

Foucault, M. (1979) *Discipline and Punish: the Birth of the Prison*, (trans) A. Sheridan, London: Tavistock.

—— (1980) *Power/Knowledge: Selected Interviews and other Writings 1972–1977*, London: Harvester Press.

—— (1994) *Essential Works of Foucault 1954–1984*, P. Rabinov, (ed.) London: Penguin.

Hughes, L. and Pengelly, P. (1997) *Staff Supervision in a Turbulent Environment, Managing Process and Task in Front-line Services*, London: Jessica Kingsley.

Inskipp, F. and Proctor, B. (1993) *The Art, Craft and Tasks of Counselling Supervision, Part 1. Making the Most of Supervisors*, Twickenham: Cascade Publications.

Institute of Career Guidance (2002) *Career Guidance: One Aim, Three Routes*, ICG Briefing Paper, December, Stourbridge: Institute of Career Guidance.

—— (2003) *Support And Supervision,* an ICG Briefing Paper, May, Stourbridge: Institute of Career Guidance.

—— (2004) *Support and Supervision for Career Guidance*, ICG Position Statement, Stourbridge: Institute of Career Guidance.

MacLure, M. (2003) *Discourses in Educational and Social Research*, Buckingham: Open University Press.

McMahon, M. and Patton, W. (2000) 'Conversations on clinical supervision: benefits perceived by school counsellors', *British Journal of Guidance and Counselling*, 28 (3): 339–351.

Mehan, H. (1999) 'Oracular reasoning in a psychiatric exam', in A. Jaworski and N. Coupland (eds) *The Discourse Reader*, London: Routledge.

Morrissette, P.J. (2002) *Self-supervision: a Primer for Counselors and Helping Professionals*, New York: Brunner-Routledge.

O'Doherty, D. and Roberts, I. (2000) 'Career or slide? Managing on the threshold of sense', in A. Collin and R.A. Young (eds) *The Future of Career*, Cambridge: Cambridge University Press.

Ofsted (2003) *Connexions Inspection Report, Devon And Cornwall*, www.ofsted.gov.uk/reports/servicereports, published 8 October, (accessed 1 January 2004).

Rabinov, P. (1997) *Michel Foucault: Essential Works of Foucault 1954–1984*, New York/London: New Press and Penguin.

Reid, H.L. (2002) 'Are you sitting comfortably? Story telling and the usefulness of narrative approaches for work with the "difficult-to-help"', in K. Roberts (ed.) *Constructing the Future: Social Inclusion, Policy and Practice*, Stourbridge: Institute of Career Guidance.

—— (2005) 'What advisers want from support and supervision: "pit-head time to wash off the dust of their labours"', *Career Guidance Today*, 13 (1), Stourbridge: Institute of Career Guidance.

Rogers, C. (1961) *On Becoming a Person*, Boston, MA: Houghton Mifflin.

Stacey, L. and Mignot, P. (2000) 'The discourse of the careers guidance interview: from public policy to private practice', *Youth and Policy*, winter 2000/01, 70: 25–39.

Usher, R. and Edwards, R. (1998) 'Confessing all? A "postmodern guide" to the guidance and counselling of adult learners', in R. Edwards, R. Harrison and A. Tait (eds) *Telling Tales: Perspectives on Guidance and Counselling in Learning*, London: Routledge/Open University.

Index

Page numbers in *italic* refer to tables or figures

eBooks – at www.eBookstore.tandf.co.uk

A library at your fingertips!

eBooks are electronic versions of printed books. You can store them on your PC/laptop or browse them online.

They have advantages for anyone needing rapid access to a wide variety of published, copyright information.

eBooks can help your research by enabling you to bookmark chapters, annotate text and use instant searches to find specific words or phrases. Several eBook files would fit on even a small laptop or PDA.

NEW: Save money by eSubscribing: cheap, online access to any eBook for as long as you need it.

Annual subscription packages

We now offer special low-cost bulk subscriptions to packages of eBooks in certain subject areas. These are available to libraries or to individuals.

For more information please contact webmaster.ebooks@tandf.co.uk

We're continually developing the eBook concept, so keep up to date by visiting the website.

www.eBookstore.tandf.co.uk

DATE DUE

	MAY 0 4 2007		
MAY 0 8 REC'D			

GAYLORD   PRINTED IN U.S.A.

LB 1027.5 .P68 2006

Providing support and
 supervision